The Pleasures of Cooking with Wine

Other Books by Emily Chase

SUNSET SALAD BOOK (*Editor*)

SUNSET COOK BOOK OF FAVORITE RECIPES (*Editor*)

The Pleasures
of Cooking
with Wine

by Emily Chase

Prentice-Hall, Inc.,
Englewood Cliffs, N.J.

FOR MY HUSBAND,
GEORGE LEISTNER
AND OUR DAUGHTER,
EMMY LOU

Copyright under International and
Pan-American Copyright Conventions

Library of Congress Catalog Card Number 60-13892
Printed in the United States of America

10 9 8 7 6 5 4 3 2 1

68458-T
0-13-684480-4 pbk.

A Special Toast to Emily Chase

DEAR READER:

Lucky you to have this delicious reading and eating book! And I should know, for I both read and cooked from it even before the manuscript went to the publisher. The price of this flavor-full privilege? A mere bagatelle, really. In fact, the cost of the preview was another privilege—that of introducing the author of this book, Emily Chase, my friend of lo these 20 years.

To retrogress a bit, we first met when Emily was home economics editor of *Sunset Magazine* and I was laying the cornerstone of the Home Advisory Service of the Wine Institute. For six years, she developed and tested recipes highlighting western foods. Naturally, "the magic ingredient," California wine enhanced a goodly number of them. Emily, as with everything she attempts, did an outstanding job as a food editor. In addition to the monthly food pages, she edited *Sunset Salad Book* and *Sunset Cook Book of Favorite Recipes*.

Our close association began several years after she became Mrs. George Leistner and moved to Stockton. From occasional visits, I recall that she was keeping herself fairly well occupied with (1) managing a home, (2) caring for their daughter, Emily Louise, then about 4, and a Bassett puppy, Sherlock Holmes (since joined by a brother, Dr. Watson, no less); (3) assisting her husband in their attractive book store; and (4) engaging in civic and charitable activities.

Knowing her extraordinary abilities and her rich background and interest in wine cookery, we of the Wine Institute decided that Emily should do something with her "spare" time. So, we asked her to become the Home Advisory Service's first foods consultant. Much to our surprise and delight, she accepted. Six happy, busy years ensued. Our files bulged with highly delectable recipes, all developed and tested in the Leistner kitchen. Many of them, I'm happy to say, are within these covers.

There are many reasons for this being such an unusually good cookbook. And most of them are directly due to the author. One thing that always tickles me is that her first academic degree was from Stanford —and in Classical Literature. This may account for her considered and precise way with words. Too, Emily Chase is a home economist, with degrees from Simmons College and the University of Washington. But, she is a home economist whose creative dishes are marked by flair and flavor. In the wish-I'd-said-that-but-didn't department, is this remark (made by the food editor of one of the country's leading women's magazines) about the author's ways with foods: "Emily's ideas are unusual, and, as one would expect from knowing her, they are also sound." You will find that the recipes in this book are different without being esoteric. The characteristic they all have in common is good taste.

Now, tossing verbal bouquets to those who deserve them is easy for me. I'm the flowery type with pen in hand. But the writer of this cookbook definitely isn't. With or without pen, she's the modest type. That is why I have had to watch my words and not sound like the president of the Emily Chase fan club—which I am. Anyway, I hope both you and she will take kindly to this introduction. Most important is that you begin cooking à la Emily. You'll grow to know and appreciate her in a hurry.

Cordially yours,

JESSICA C. MCLACHLIN, Director
The Home Advisory Service
Wine Institute

Contents

vii

Cook's Note

Cooking is my vocation and my hobby. I enjoy it the way other people enjoy bridge or golf. Whether I'm creating my own recipe or preparing a dish dreamed up by someone else, there's no place I'd rather be than among the pots and skillets.

As a result, I've spent lots of time in the kitchen, and many of the pleasantest hours have been devoted to the pursuit of wine cookery. This book is the result of those efforts—a selection of wine recipes that I hope home cooks (and Sunday chefs) everywhere will enjoy.

This is by no means an all-inclusive collection. Most of the classic European wine specialties have been left to such other cook books as are more concerned with *la haute cuisine*. You will not find yourself transported to the realm of "fancy" cookery with myriad steps to master before you place the dish on the table. This is a book of wine recipes that are usable, practical, and (most important of all) guaranteed to result in good eating!

I have had help from many sources in preparation of this book. Friends have been most generous with ideas for new dishes and have always been cooperative when it came time to taste-test. My sincere thanks to Dorothy Canet for sharing with me some of her excellent recipes for venison, game birds, and fish.

ix

A special word of appreciation is in order for Jessica McLachlin, director of the Home Advisory Service of the Wine Institute in San Francisco, with whom I worked for six busy years as the Institute's recipe consultant. Without her wonderful help and enthusiasm this book never would have come to print.

Emily Chase

Wine In
The Kitchen

If you cook, you can cook with wine. It's as simple as that. And the pleasures to be gained from adventures in wine cookery are out of all proportion compared to the small effort involved. No other ingredient in your kitchen will reward you with more experiences in good eating, for wine rounds out the flavor of many a dish to perfection.

Before we go into the kitchen, let's take a look at the wines you will meet most often in the recipes to come.

This very brief chart covers only the essentials as far as wine is concerned, and is designed to give someone who's new at wine cookery a nodding acquaintance with the star of our show. A much more complete wine list will be found in Chapter XII, "Here's to You!," where we meet wine as a beverage.

The what-with-what suggestions given above are merely generalizations, not hard and fast rules. (You'll find lots of exceptions in this book!) As in all matters where flavor is involved, palates differ and it's a matter of what you *like*. The cook who enjoys experimenting will find wine cookery a rewarding field.

Wines Used in Recipes

WHAT WINE?

APPETIZER WINES	Sherry
	    Cocktail (dry)
	    Pale Dry (dry)
	    Medium (not dry, not sweet)
	    Sweet (see DESSERT WINES below)
		Dry and medium Sherry are very versatile. May be found in many soups, sauces, main dishes, etc.

	Vermouth
	    Dry
	    Sweet
		Dry Vermouth is used quite often in a sauce or in a meat or fish dish, sweet Vermouth occasionally.

RED TABLE WINES	Burgundy Claret Rosé	Burgundy and Claret are usually paired with red meats and game, often with poultry. Also good in spaghetti sauces and in many other "robust" dishes. Rosé is used in some punches, occasionally in a main dish or dessert.
WHITE TABLE WINES	Sauterne Rhine Wine Chablis	Featured in recipes with "light" meats, poultry, fish.

DESSERT WINES	Port
	    Red
	    Tawny
	    White
	Muscatel
	Tokay
	Sweet (Cream) Sherry
		Mostly found in desserts, occasionally in a sauce for meat or game.

SPARKLING WINES	Champagne Sparkling Burgundy	At home in the punch bowl, and a de luxe touch for fruit desserts.

THE WHEN AND HOW

In cooked dishes such as stews and sautés, wine is usually added early in the proceedings and simmered along with the other ingredients for a happy blend of flavors. Just before serving it's sometimes added to soups and sauces in order to give the final touch of goodness. With dishes that require no cooking—salad dressings, fruit desserts, and so on—you add wine as you would any other liquid. There's no trick to it, and in every case you'll find it's the wine that adds that "How delicious!" note of flavor.

HOW MUCH

Like the kind of wine that is best in a dish, the amount of wine to use is a matter of taste. The important thing to remember is that the wine should blend into the flavor picture and improve the overall effect without being too obvious. "If a little is good, more is better" doesn't necessarily apply! True, you may taste a good dish and say, "This has wine in it," but the wine shouldn't be the dominant flavor factor. Rather, it should be a subtle part of the delicious whole.

If you have some favorite recipes that you'd like to enhance with wine, you may find this chart helpful:

HOW TO GIVE RECIPES THE WINE TOUCH

FOODS	AMOUNT OF WINE	KIND OF WINE	WHEN TO ADD
SOUPS: *Cream Soups*	1 to 2 tbs. per serving	Dry or medium Sherry, dry Vermouth, or dry white table wine	With other liquid or before serving
Meat & Vegetable Soups	1 to 2 tbs. per serving	Dry or medium Sherry, or dry red table wine	With other liquid or before serving

How to Give Recipes the Wine Touch (Cont.)

Sauces:			
Cream Sauce & Variations	1 to 2 tbs. per cup	Dry or medium Sherry, dry Vermouth, or dry white table wine	With other liquid or before serving
Brown Sauce & Variations	1 to 2 tbs. per cup	Dry or medium Sherry, or dry red table wine	With other liquid or before serving
Tomato Sauce	1 to 2 tbs. per cup	Dry or medium Sherry, or dry red table wine	With other liquid or before serving
Cheese Sauce	1 to 2 tbs. per cup	Dry or medium Sherry, dry Vermouth, or dry white table wine	With other liquid or before serving
Meats:			
Pot Roast, Stew, Braised Meats—			
Beef	Approx. ½ of the liquid	Dry red table wine	After browning
Lamb	Approx. ½ of the liquid	Dry red or white table wine	After browning
Veal	Approx. ½ of the liquid	Dry white table wine or dry Vermouth	After browning
Gravy for Roasts—			
Beef	2 tbs. per cup	Dry red table wine or dry Sherry	With other liquid or before serving
Lamb	2 tbs. per cup	Dry red or white table wine or dry Sherry	With other liquid or before serving
Veal or Pork	2 tbs. per cup	Dry white table wine, dry Vermouth or dry Sherry	With other liquid or before serving
Baked Ham	1 to 2 cups for basting	Any dessert wine or red table wine	At beginning of glazing period

How to Give Recipes the Wine Touch (Cont.)

Poultry & Game: *Chicken—*			
Sauté	½ cup per chicken	Dry red or white table wine, dry Vermouth or Sherry	After browning
Broiled	½ & ½ with oil or melted butter for basting	Dry red or white table wine, dry Sherry or Vermouth	During broiling
Fricassee	Approx. ⅓ of the liquid	Dry white table wine	At beginning or after browning
Gravy for Roast or Fried Chicken	2 tbs. per cup	Dry white table wine, or dry Sherry or dry Vermouth	With other liquid or before serving
Gravy for Roast Turkey	2 tbs. per cup	Dry red table wine or dry Sherry	With other liquid or before serving
Roast Duck (Wild or Tame)	½ cup per duck for basting	Dry red table wine	During cooking
Fish: Broiled or "Plain" Baked	½ & ½ with oil or melted butter for basting	Dry white table wine or Vermouth	During cooking
Poached	½ & ½ with water	Dry white table wine or dry Vermouth	At beginning
Fruit: Cups & Compotes	1 to 2 tbs. per serving	Dry red or white table wine, any dessert wine	Before serving

Remember, this chart is merely a guide. Do experiment!

A Word about Marinating Meats with Wine

To give added tenderness and flavor to the less expensive cuts of meat (pot roasts, meat for stews, etc.) marinate them overnight in table wine to cover before cooking. Use whatever wine you plan to use in cooking the meat and add any seasonings you like—salt, whole peppercorns or ground pepper, sliced onions and garlic, bay leaves and other herbs, cloves and other spices, etc. Turn the meat occasionally to distribute the flavors evenly. When you're ready to cook the pot roast or whatever, strain this marinade, if necessary, and use it instead of the plain wine required in the recipe. If the marinade is highly seasoned, you may want to cut down on the seasonings you put in the cooking pot. Taste and see! Incidentally, you can "tame and tender" almost any cut of venison by marinating it in dry red table wine before cooking.

Keeping Wines for Cookery

The appetizer and dessert wines, well corked or capped, will last a long time. The table wines, once opened and exposed to the air, are fragile, flavorwise. If you plan to serve and cook with the same table wine at a meal, there's no problem, of course. If you are buying wine for cooking only, half bottles may be your answer.

I have found that a partly used bottle of table wine can sometimes be kept successfully for cookery use a few days later if it is tightly corked or capped and stored in the refrigerator. I can't say exactly *how long* it can be kept, and I hesitate to give this system unqualified approval lest a good dish be spoiled by a wine that has started down the vinegar trail. Let your palate—and experience—be your guides.

Thoughts While Stirring

If a recipe calls for chicken or beef stock and you have no homemade stock on hand, use canned chicken or beef broth or make it with bouillon cubes or chicken or beef stock base.

When you're making a flour-thickened cream sauce and add the wine right along with the milk or cream, you may be startled to see the mixture curdle. Don't worry! As soon as the sauce boils and thickens it will smooth out nicely.

When wine and eggs are in the pot together, keep the heat *low*. Don't let the mixture boil! Too high a heat may cause disastrous curdling.

Instant minced onion, dried onion and parsley flakes, and frozen chopped chives and parsley are wonderful to have on hand for those moments when you have neither time nor inclination to chop, chop, chop. . . .

So, then, let's start cooking.

II

Tempting
Bits

Hors d'oeuvres and canapés can be all things to all menus. If you've invited guests for dinner and exerted all your efforts in preparing a memorable meal, you'll do well to settle for something light and crisp in the appetizer line. Crackers and chips with a flavorful dip—a platter of crisp, raw vegetables with a savory dunking mixture—these will titillate the palate without dimming the interest in what is to follow.

On the other hand, if a light supper is on the agenda, or if no meal is involved and your guests have joined you for a sip and a snack, toothsome morsels, both hot and cold, will be well received and happily savored.

As a good cheese mix fits nicely into almost any appetizer picture, be it plain or fancy, let's start with some delectable wine-cheese spreads and dips. Wine and cheese are such perfect partners, flavorwise, that good combinations are legion and I had a difficult time choosing my favorites.

In preparing any of these cheese spreads or dips remember:

Have the cheese or cheeses at room temperature for easy blending of ingredients.

For a delightfully smooth, creamy mixture use an electric blender or an electric mixer. If you prefer to beat by hand, with a fork or spoon, the result will still taste delicious!

Make the mix at least several hours before you plan to use it so that the flavors will have a chance to mingle and mellow. Store, covered, in the refrigerator, then bring to room temperature before serving or spreading.

In addition to being useful as spreads and dips, most of these cheese mixtures are fine for stuffing celery or bite-size cream puff shells, and many of them are equally good with crackers as a salad accompaniment or as a dessert cheese. They make excellent fillings for tea sandwiches (and I've been known to enjoy them on my breakfast toast).

Little jars of a wine-cheese spread, perhaps with the recipe attached, make fine gifts for your cheese-loving friends.

Now for the recipes. If you're a Cheddar fan, try one of these:

KAY'S CHEDDAR AND PIMIENTO SPREAD

Blend cheese and Sherry. Beat in mayonnaise. Add remaining ingredients; beat until well mixed. Makes about 3 cups. Delicious with crisp crackers or melba toast.

1 pound Cheddar cheese, grated
¼ cup dry or medium Sherry
¼ cup mayonnaise
½ cup finely chopped pimiento
2 tablespoons chopped parsley
1 teaspoon grated onion
1 tablespoon catsup
1 teaspoon Worcestershire sauce
½ teaspoon each: salt and celery salt

PORT AND CHEDDAR MIX

Blend cheese and Port; add cream and seasonings; beat until smooth. Makes about one and one-half cups. Serve with thin slices of rye or pumpernickel bread or with crackers, or use to stuff tender stalks of celery.

½ pound Cheddar cheese, grated
¼ cup Port
2 tablespoons cream
¼ teaspoon paprika
Dash of onion salt

Probably there's no cheese appetizer more attractive than a bright red Edam or Gouda that has been hollowed out and refilled with a mixture of the cheese and seasonings. But for me, hollowing out that ball neatly is hard work! My husband agrees, and he speaks from experience. One Christmas he gave me a beautifully wrapped Edam cheese. When I lifted the "lid" that had been cut from the top, I found a Danish porcelain mouse nestling inside.

If hollowing out cheeses is child's play for you, that's fine. If not, you can avoid the issue by removing the red jacket, shredding or grinding the cheese, and serving the finished mix in your prettiest bowl.

EDAM APPETIZER CHEESE

Cut and remove a three-inch circle from the top of an Edam cheese and scoop out the inside. Or forget about scooping and simply remove the red wax coating. In either case, grind or shred the cheese; for each cupful add ingredients listed. Blend cheese and wine; add remaining ingredients. Pack mixture into cheese shell, or heap in a serving bowl. Serve with an assortment of your favorite crackers.

¼ cup dry or medium Sherry, or dry Vermouth
½ teaspoon prepared mustard
1 teaspoon Worcestershire sauce
Salt, onion salt, and garlic salt to taste
Dash of cayenne

Lots of good cheese mixtures combine two or more varieties for a happy blend of flavors. For example:

CREAMY BLUE CHEESE SPREAD

Blend cheeses in a bowl; beat in wine and mayonnaise; add seasonings. Makes about one and one-quarter cups. Use as a spread or as a dip for chips or raw vegetables.

⅓ pound Blue cheese, crumbled
2 (3 oz.) packages cream cheese
¼ cup dry red or white table wine
1 tablespoon mayonnaise
½ teaspoon Worcestershire sauce
¼ teaspoon paprika
Dash each of garlic powder and cayenne
Salt to taste

THREE-IN-ONE CHEESE MIX

Place cheeses in a bowl; blend well with a fork. Gradually beat in Sherry; add seasonings. Beat until smooth and creamy. Makes about two and one-half cups. Wonderful flavor for canapés or sandwiches. An excellent "keeper."

½ pound Cheddar cheese, grated
¼ pound Blue cheese, crumbled
1 (3 oz.) package cream cheese
½ cup dry or medium Sherry
½ teaspoon Worcestershire sauce
½ teaspoon paprika
Salt and onion salt to taste
Dash each of garlic powder and cayenne

Since the eye feasts before the palate, an hors d'oeuvre that *looks* appealing is doubly delicious.

FESTIVE CHEESE BALL

Blend cheeses; beat in wine. Add olives and seasonings; mix well. Shape into a ball; chill overnight. Shortly before serving, roll ball in chopped parsley. Serve on a platter with crisp crackers.

1 pound Cheddar cheese, grated
1 (3 oz.) package cream cheese
⅓ cup dry or medium Sherry
⅓ cup chopped ripe olives
1 teaspoon Worcestershire sauce
Dash of cayenne
Plenty of onion salt, garlic salt, and celery salt
¼ cup chopped parsley

This cheese spread differs from most in that the ingredients are melted and blended in a double boiler.

SAVORY CHEESE SPREAD

Combine all ingredients in the top of a double boiler. Heat over boiling water, stirring frequently with a fork just until cheeses melt and ingredients are smoothly blended. Pour mixture into one or more containers. Let cool thoroughly before serving. Excellent with crisp crackers as an appetizer or as a dessert cheese. Makes about three cups spread. Truly a luscious mixture!

2 (5 oz.) jars process Cheddar cheese spread
1 (4 oz.) package Liederkranz cheese
2 (3 oz.) packages cream cheese
¼ pound Blue cheese
½ cup dry white table wine
½ teaspoon Worcestershire sauce
Dash of cayenne

A well-dressed assortment of dips and spreads should include at least one specialty from the sea such as:

TUNA LOUIS DIP

Mash cheese with a fork. Gradually blend in wine. Beat in remaining ingredients. Chill several hours. Makes about three cups. Serve with chips, crackers, or melba toast.

1 (8 oz.) package cream cheese
¼ cup dry or medium Sherry
¼ cup mayonnaise
3 tablespoons chili sauce
2 (6½ oz.) cans chunk-style tuna
2 tablespoons chopped parsley
1 teaspoon grated onion
1 teaspoon Worcestershire sauce
Dash of Tabasco sauce
Salt and pepper to taste

CLAM DIP

Mash cheese with a fork. Blend in remaining ingredients. Heap in a serving bowl and chill before using. Makes about one and one-half cups. Serve with crisp crackers or chips.

3 (3 oz.) packages cream cheese
1 (7 oz.) can minced clams, well drained (½ cup clams)
2 tablespoons clam liquid
¼ cup dry white table wine
¼ teaspoon each: onion salt and garlic salt
½ teaspoon paprika

P.S. For a delicious hot canapé, fold one stiffly beaten egg white into the clam mixture. Heap on toast rounds or crackers and broil until delicately browned. Serve at once.

Here's a quick and easy mix that pâté devotees enjoy.

LIVERWURST PÂTÉ

Remove casing from liverwurst. Blend liverwurst and cheese; beat in remaining ingredients. Makes one and one-half cups. Serve with crisp crackers or melba toast.

½ pound liverwurst
1 (3 oz.) package cream cheese
1 tablespoon mayonnaise
¼ cup dry or medium Sherry
1 teaspoon lemon juice
Dash each of onion salt and cayenne

When you want something a little fancier, pâté-wise, this is your dish.

PARTY PÂTÉ RING

2 envelopes (2 tablespoons) un-
  flavored gelatin
½ cup dry white table wine
1 (10½ oz.) can condensed consommé
½ pound liverwurst
1 (3 oz.) package cream cheese
2 tablespoons Brandy

Soften gelatin in the wine. Heat about half the consommé to simmering; pour over gelatin; stir until gelatin is dissolved. Stir in remaining cold consommé. Pour a one-half-inch layer of this mixture into a well-oiled, one-quart (eight and one-half-inch) ring mold; chill until very firm. Meantime, keep remaining gelatin mixture at room temperature. Remove casing from liverwurst; blend liverwurst, cream cheese, and Brandy. Spoon liverwurst mixture on top of firm gelatin layer in mold. With a butter spreader or a small spatula, shape mixture into a ring, leaving about one-half-inch space all around between it and the sides of the mold. Now (and no earlier) chill remaining gelatin mixture *just* until slightly *syrupy*. (This won't take long. Watch carefully lest it get too firm!) Spoon this slightly thickened mixture into the mold so it surrounds the liverwurst. Chill several hours or overnight. At party time, unmold ring on a plate and fill center with sprigs of watercress or parsley. Surround ring with crisp crackers or melba toast. To serve, cut ring in thin slices with a *very* sharp knife. Plenty for twelve people.

The saltiness of ham and the nut-like flavor of Sherry contribute good flavor to:

PLANTATION HAM SPREAD

Mash cheese with a fork; add ham and mix well; add remaining ingredients. Makes about one and one-half cups. A delicious spread or dip. For a good canapé, spread mixture on bread rounds and top each with a pecan half.

2 (3 oz.) packages cream cheese
1 cup ground boiled ham (or two small cans deviled ham)
¼ cup dry or medium Sherry
½ teaspoon Worcestershire sauce
   Bit of chopped or pressed garlic
   Salt to taste

If you are the sort of hostess who likes to serve something a little different and doesn't mind spending a few extra minutes preparing it, try these delectable molded canapés:

MOLDED CRAB CANAPÉS

Soften gelatin in wine five minutes; dissolve over hot water; cool. Blend mayonnaise, chili sauce, lemon juice, parsley, and onion; stir in cooled gelatin mixture; fold in whipped cream; add salt and pepper. Chill until mixture begins to thicken, then fold in crabmeat. Spoon mixture into four straight-sided, five-ounce tumblers (or six-ounce frozen juice cans) that have been lightly coated with salad oil. Chill several hours or overnight. Just before serving, carefully unmold and slice each mold (with a *very* sharp knife) into nine or ten thin slices. Place each slice on a crisp round cracker, or on a round of bread or toast. Makes 36 to 40 canapés.

2 envelopes (2 tablespoons) unflavored gelatin
½ cup dry white table wine
1 cup mayonnaise
2 tablespoons chili sauce
1 teaspoon lemon juice
2 tablespoons chopped parsley
1 teaspoon grated onion
½ cup heavy cream, whipped
   Salt and peper to taste
1 (6½ oz.) can crabmeat, flaked, or 1 cup fresh crabmeat

BEEF AND CHEESE ROLL-UPS

Lay pieces of beef out flat and pat together, with edges overlapping slightly to make three rectangles, each about five inches wide and seven inches long. Mix cheese spread and Blue cheese; beat in wine. Spread some of the cheese mixture evenly over each rectangle of beef. Roll up each one, jelly-roll fashion, from one long side to the other. Wrap in waxed paper. Chill 24 hours or longer. At serving time, cut each roll in one-half-inch slices with a very sharp knife. Place on a serving plate and spear each roll-up with a toothpick. Makes approximately three to three and one-half dozen roll-ups.

¼ pound (4 ounces) dried beef
1 (5 oz.) jar process Cheddar cheese spread
¼ pound Blue cheese
¼ cup dry white table wine

I have found that there is no hors d'oeuvre more popular than large, plump shrimp served in some savory fashion. It does take a bit of time to shell and clean them, but the enthusiasm with which they're eaten makes the effort worth while. Here are two good ideas:

SHRIMP SNACK BALBOA

Place shrimp in a serving bowl. Chop the slices of onion, the garlic, and the parsley together until *very, very* fine. Combine this mixture with all remaining ingredients. Mix well, then pour over shrimp. Cover and chill 24 hours, stirring occasionally. Serve accompanied by toothpicks for spearing the shrimp. Serves ten to twelve.

3½ to 4 dozen large shrimp, cooked and cleaned
1 small onion, thinly sliced
1 clove garlic, halved
Several sprigs parsley
½ cup salad oil (preferably olive oil)
½ cup dry Vermouth
2 tablespoons tarragon wine vinegar
2 tablespoons drained capers
½ teaspoon sugar
1 teaspoon salt
Dash of cayenne

P.S. For a marvelous supper or late-evening snack, serve these shrimp with buttered, thinly sliced rye or French bread and mayonnaise for make-your-own shrimp sandwiches.

HELEN'S SHRIMP DIP

Mix all ingredients and chill thoroughly. At serving time, spear large cooked shrimp with toothpicks and arrange on a serving plate. Place dip in a bowl in the center.

1 cup mayonnaise
⅓ cup chili sauce
¼ cup dry or medium Sherry
2 tablespoons chopped parsley
1 teaspoon grated onion
½ teaspoon Worcestershire sauce
Salt to taste

P.S. Crab legs, lobster cubes, avocado balls, raw cauliflowerets, and tiny red or yellow tomatoes are also good with this dip.

Hot hors d'oeuvres and canapés may present a little last-minute cookery problem for the hostess, but when they can be managed they are usually the hit of the appetizer tray.

Here are some good canapés that can be prepared ahead of time and then popped under the broiler just before serving.

CHEDDAR-BACON CANAPÉS

Blend cheese and Sherry; beat in egg yolks and seasonings. Cut each slice of bacon lengthwise in halves, then cut each half crosswise into six to eight small pieces. (There should be 48 small pieces of bacon.) Cook these bacon snippets until almost crisp. Toast slices of bread on one side; spread untoasted side with cheese mixture. Cut each slice in quarters and top each square with a piece of bacon. Broil slowly until cheese mixture puffs up and bacon is crisp. Serve at once. Makes 48 canapés.

½ pound Cheddar cheese, grated
¼ cup dry or medium Sherry
2 egg yolks, slightly beaten
½ teaspoon Worcestershire sauce
Salt to taste
Dash of cayenne
3 or 4 slices bacon
12 slices bread, crusts removed

P.S. For a delicious supper sandwich, follow the recipe for *Cheddar-Bacon Canapés*, but leave slices of bread whole. Allow one slice bacon per sandwich and cut slices crosswise in halves. Cook bacon until almost done and arrange on top of sandwich before broiling.

CRABMEAT CANAPÉS AU GRATIN

Melt butter and stir in flour; add cream and chicken stock; cook, stirring constantly, until mixture is thickened and smooth. Remove from heat and add wine, parsley, onion, crabmeat, salt, garlic salt, and pepper. Chill mixture thoroughly. Toast rounds of bread on one side; spread untoasted side with the crabmeat mixture; sprinkle with Parmesan cheese and paprika. Broil until delicately browned. Serve at once. Makes 60 canapés.

3   tablespoons butter
3   tablespoons flour
½   cup cream
¼   cup chicken stock
¼   cup dry white table wine
2   tablespoons minced parsley
1   teaspoon minced onion
1   cup flaked fresh or canned crabmeat
    Salt, garlic salt, and pepper to taste
60 (1½-inch) rounds of white bread
    Grated Parmesan cheese
    Paprika

P.S. Shrimp, lobster, tuna, and chicken are also good in this recipe. For *Clam Canapés au Gratin,* substitute two (7 oz.) cans minced clams for the crabmeat. Drain clams well and use one-quarter cup clam liquid in place of the chicken stock called for above. A main-dish thought: This canapé mixture makes delicious open-faced supper sandwiches. Simply substitute four or five slices of bread for the little bread rounds.

TOASTED CHEDDAR PICK-UPS

Blend cheese with butter and wine; add seasonings. Toast slices of bread on one side; spread cheese mixture on untoasted side; cut each slice in quarters. Broil slowly until cheese melts. Makes 20 to 24 canapés.

1   cup grated Cheddar cheese
1   tablespoon soft butter
2   tablespoons dry red table wine
½   teaspoon Worcestershire sauce
½   teaspoon prepared mustard
    Salt and cayenne to taste
5   or 6 slices bread, crusts removed

If you have a chafing dish, or one of those candle "warmers" on which you can set a casserole, or any other way of keeping an hors d'oeuvre mixture hot while guests serve themselves, try one of these delicious ideas:

SWISS BEEF DIP

Melt cheese in double boiler. Blend in Vermouth, chili sauce, and Worcestershire sauce. Grind beef and garlic; add to cheese mixture. Serve hot (in chafing dish or in casserole set over candle warmer) with crackers or melba toast. Makes about one and one-half cups.

½ pound process Swiss cheese, sliced
⅓ cup dry Vermouth
2 tablespoons chili sauce
½ teaspoon Worcestershire sauce
¼ pound (4 ounces) dried beef
1 clove garlic

CHEESE-DIPPED VIENNAS

Cut Vienna sausages crosswise in halves; heat thoroughly in their juices and drain well. Spear each piece with a toothpick. Serve this cheese dip in a chafing dish or in a pottery casserole set over a candle warmer. Let your guests dip Viennas in it.

Melt cheese in double boiler. Blend in wine and seasonings. Enough dip for at least three cans of sausages (about 48 halves).

CHEESE DIP
½ pound process Cheddar cheese, sliced
¼ cup dry white table wine
1 teaspoon prepared mustard
1 teaspoon Worcestershire sauce

P.S. Little cocktail frankfurters or chunks of regular-sized ones can be used in place of the Viennas.

Last (but certainly not least) in the hot hors d'oeuvre line are two recipes for cocktail-sized meat balls. I guarantee they will disappear like magic.

Tempting Bits — 19

LILLIPUT MEAT BALLS

Mix beef, bread crumbs, milk, onion, and one teaspoon salt. Shape mixture into tiny balls, using one level teaspoon per ball. Melt butter in a large, heavy skillet; brown balls nicely on all sides. Pour off most of fat from pan. Mix wine, catsup, and oregano; pour over balls; add salt to taste. Cover and simmer gently about 20 minutes, shaking pan gently from time to time to cook balls evenly. Serve in a chafing dish or in a casserole set over a candle warmer, and provide toothpicks for spearing the balls. Makes about 60 tiny balls.

1 pound ground beef
½ cup grated soft bread crumbs
¼ cup milk
1 tablespoon grated onion
  Salt
2 tablespoons butter
½ cup dry or medium Sherry
½ cup catsup
¼ teaspoon oregano (optional)

P.S. Try this same Sherry-catsup sauce with Vienna sausages or cocktail frankfurters. Heat the Viennas or frankfurters in the sauce and serve accompanied by toothpicks.

CURRIED COCKTAIL MEAT BALLS

Prepare the meat balls as directed above in the recipe for *Lilliput Meat Balls*. Brown on all sides in two tablespoons of butter. Pour off most of fat from pan. Mix ingredients and:

Pour over balls. Mix gently and heat thoroughly before serving. Toothpicks are in order, of course.

1 (10½ oz.) can condensed cream of mushroom soup
¼ cup dry or medium Sherry
½ teaspoon curry powder (or to taste)

The appetizers have been enjoyed right down to the last morsel and now it's time for dinner. Assuming it's to be a three-course affair, what shall the "starter" be? Personally, I would choose a shellfish cocktail prepared with this sauce, subtly wine-flavored.

MIMI'S COCKTAIL SAUCE

Mix all ingredients and chill thoroughly. Use with any shellfish. Enough for about six servings.

½ cup catsup
½ cup chili sauce
3 tablespoons dry Vermouth
1 tablespoon lemon or lime juice
1 teaspoon grated onion
2 teaspoons prepared horse-radish
½ teaspoon Worcestershire sauce
Dash of Tabasco sauce
Salt to taste

Two shellfish specialties that make excellent first courses are these:

SHRIMP MOLDS, RUSSIAN HILL

Soften gelatin in the cold water five minutes. Dissolve in the hot consommé. Add cold consommé, wine, lemon juice, Worcestershire sauce, salt, and pepper. Chill until mixture begins to thicken, then fold in shrimp and celery. Turn into six individual molds that have been rinsed with cold water. Chill until firm. Unmold on crisp salad greens and serve with *Russian Hill Dressing* (below). Serves six.

1 envelope (1 tablespoon) un-flavored gelatin
¼ cup cold water
½ cup hot canned consommé
¾ cup cold canned consommé
⅓ cup dry or medium Sherry
1 teaspoon lemon juice
¼ teaspoon Worcestershire sauce
Salt and pepper to taste
1½ cups cooked or canned shrimp (whole if small, cut up if large)
½ cup finely cut celery

RUSSIAN HILL DRESSING

Mix three-quarters cup mayonnaise, one-quarter cup chili sauce, one teaspoon lemon juice, one-quarter teaspoon paprika, and salt to taste. Add one tablespoon *each:* chopped drained capers, green pepper, and pimiento. Cover and chill for an hour or more before serving.

CRABMEAT RAVIGOTE

Combine crabmeat and wine in a bowl; cover and let stand in refrigerator from one to two hours, stirring occasionally. Meantime, grate egg yolks and whites, or force through sieve or ricer. Drain crabmeat in a strainer; press between paper towels to dry *thoroughly*. Combine crabmeat, grated egg whites, catsup, pickle relish, parsley, lemon juice, and Worcestershire sauce; mix lightly but well. Add just enough mayonnaise to moisten mixture nicely; season with salt and pepper. Cover and chill thoroughly. Just before serving, line each of six little baking shells with a leaf of lettuce. Stir crabmeat mixture and spoon into shells. Sprinkle with grated egg yolks and dust with paprika. Serves six.

2 cups flaked cooked or canned crabmeat
1 cup dry white table wine
2 hard-cooked eggs, yolks and whites separated
1 tablespoon catsup
1 tablespoon well-drained sweet pickle relish
1 tablespoon chopped parsley
1 teaspoon lemon juice
½ teaspoon Worcestershire sauce
½ cup mayonnaise (approximately)
Salt and pepper to taste
Lettuce leaves
Paprika

P.S. Lacking little baking shells, you may use lettuce-lined butter plates or sherbet or champagne glasses. Cooked or canned shrimp, cut up if large, are also good here in place of the crabmeat.

———◆———

Quite different from any of these is a first course my parents have often served at company dinners. It is a delicious four-decker affair that starts with a round of toast, ends with a luscious dressing, and has several good things in between. As far as I know it never has had any name except:

THAT CANAPÉ

To prepare each canapé: Brush a three-inch round of toast with melted butter, then spread thinly with Blue cheese mixed to spreading consistency with a little cream. Place toast round on a small salad or dessert plate. Cover it with a thick slice of peeled tomato, cover the tomato with thin slices of peeled avocado, and cover the avocado with thin crosswise slices of hard-cooked egg. Top with a good-sized crab leg or a few shrimp. Spoon some of the dressing (below) over the canapé. Dust with paprika and garnish with sprigs of watercress or parsley. Serve at once (and you will need a knife and fork to eat it).

CANAPÉ DRESSING

¾ cup mayonnaise
¼ cup catsup
2 tablespoons dry or medium Sherry
1 tablespoon lemon juice
¼ teaspoon paprika
Salt to taste
2 tablespoons chopped chives or parsley

Blend well and chill. Makes enough dressing for about eight canapés.

That perennial favorite, the fruit cocktail, is too often lacking in real personality. Flavor it with wine, chill it to frosty perfection, and the picture looks (I should say "tastes") much brighter. If you want to get your dinner off to a good-eating start, try one of these:

RUBY FRUIT COCKTAIL

½ cup Port
¼ cup grape or currant jelly
1 tablespoon lemon juice
Dash of salt
1 cup pitted canned Royal Anne cherries
1 cup diced fresh or canned pineapple
1 cup diced orange sections (or canned mandarin orange sections)

Heat wine to simmering in a small saucepan; add jelly; stir until dissolved. Remove from heat; add lemon juice and salt. Cool. Combine cherries, pineapple, and orange sections in a bowl. (Be sure fruits are thoroughly drained.) Pour wine mixture over fruit. Cover and chill in the refrigerator for several hours. At serving time, heap fruit in cocktail glasses and pour some of the wine mixture over each serving. Serves six.

MINTED MELON BALLS

Crush mint in the palm of the hand. Place in saucepan with the sugar and orange juice. Bring to a boil, stirring until sugar is dissolved; simmer 5 minutes; strain. Add wine, lemon juice, and salt; chill. At serving time arrange melon balls in sherbet glasses; pour chilled syrup over them. Garnish with additional sprigs of mint, if you like. Serves six. This is very refreshing! Incidentally, the same sauce is also good with grapefruit sections.

3 or 4 sprigs fresh mint (or the equivalent in dried mint)
⅔ cup sugar
½ cup orange juice
⅓ cup Muscatel or sweet Sherry
3 tablespoons lemon juice
Dash of salt
6 servings melon balls (honeydew, cantaloupe, and watermelon are a colorful combination)

P.S. You'll find more fruit-cup ideas in Chapter XI, "Happy Endings." Some of them make excellent appetizers as well as desserts.

III

From The Soup Tureen

Like bread baking, soup making has become something of a lost art in the home kitchen, and it's rather a shame because stirring up a good soup from scratch can be a really rewarding experience for the cook. I can think of nothing I enjoy more on a rainy day than making a big kettle of minestrone. It smells so good as it bubbles along, and when supper time comes, what flavor!

But most days I am happy to let the professional soup makers take over, while I content myself with giving their canned and packaged wares a personal touch, adding a bit of this or that, combining two soups to create a "new" one, or otherwise making the finished dish "mine."

In this chapter, I want to tell you about my favorite recipe for minestrone and a few other "rainy day" soups. And I'll pass along some delicious ways with soups from your grocer's shelf. They all have one thing in common: a little wine for good flavor!

Several years ago in the course of doing an article on soup, I asked several Italian friends of mine how to make minestrone. Their answers were all so different that I soon realized there is no such thing as a "standard" minestrone recipe. In Italy, the ingredient list varies like a dialect from one part of the country to another. You're sure to find vegetables in the pot and usually *pasta*, but just which vegetables and what kind of *pasta* is anybody's guess. One thing, though, there's Parmesan cheese in the picture or it isn't minestrone!

After considerable experimenting (and many minestrone suppers), I came up with this version. My family likes it, and I hope you will, too.

MY MINESTRONE

In a large kettle combine the stock, wine, bacon, beans (with their liquid), cabbage, potato, carrots, celery, onion, garlic, tomatoes, Italian seasoning, salt, and pepper. Bring to a boil, then cover and simmer gently for one and one-half hours, stirring occasionally. Add macaroni; cook one-half hour longer, stirring frequently. Just before serving, stir in parsley and cheese. Pass additional cheese at the table. Serves eight to ten.

6 cups beef stock (make it with bouillon cubes or beef stock base, if you like)
1 cup dry red table wine
¼ pound bacon, cut fine with scissors
1 (1lb.) can red kidney beans (undrained)
2 cups shredded raw cabbage
1 cup diced raw potato
1 cup diced raw carrots
1 cup diced raw celery
1 cup diced onion
1 clove garlic, chopped or put through garlic press
1 (1 lb.) can stewed tomatoes
½ teaspoon mixed Italian seasoning
Salt and pepper to taste
¼ pound elbow macaroni
¼ cup chopped parsley
¼ cup grated Parmesan cheese

P.S. This is even better made in advance and reheated. If it needs thinning at any time, add a little beef stock, but, remember, this is supposed to be a *thick* soup!

My favorite menu for a Minestrone Supper: the soup, a tossed green salad with artichoke hearts and sliced hard-cooked eggs added, and hot garlic-buttered French bread. Leave room for a glass of red table wine and, for dessert, a nice wedge of warm apple pie.

A dash of Sherry does good things for any split pea soup, homemade or otherwise. In this recipe it combines with bacon and sundry other seasonings to produce a soup of excellent flavor.

OLD-FASHIONED SPLIT PEA SOUP

1 cup green split peas
4 slices bacon, diced
1 carrot, thinly sliced
1 large onion, thinly sliced
2 stalks celery, thinly sliced
6 peppercorns
1 bay leaf
1 quart (4 cups) boiling water
¼ cup dry Sherry
¼ cup cream
  Salt, pepper, and thyme to taste

Wash peas. Soak overnight if directions on package say to do so; drain. Place peas in a saucepan; add bacon, carrot, onion, celery, peppercorns, bay leaf, and boiling water. Cover and simmer gently from one to two hours, or until peas are very soft, stirring occasionally. Force soup through a sieve. Add Sherry, cream, salt, pepper, and thyme. Heat piping hot before serving. Serves four.

P.S. If desired, one or two slices of bacon may be fried crisp, crumbled, and used as a garnish for the soup. Or, a few thin slices of frankfurter or Vienna sausage may be floated on top of each serving.

Next comes old-fashioned bean soup made in a new-fashioned way.

LAZY BEAN SOUP

1 medium-sized onion, minced
2 tablespoons bacon drippings or butter
2 (10½ oz.) cans condensed bean with bacon soup
1 (10½ oz.) can condensed consommé
1 cup water
½ cup dry red table wine
1 teaspoon Worcestershire sauce
  Salt and pepper to taste

Sauté onion gently in bacon drippings five minutes. Add bean soup, consommé, water, wine, and Worcestershire sauce. Bring to a boil, then cover and simmer gently for 15 minutes, stirring occasionally. Season to taste with salt and pepper. Serve piping hot in heated soup bowls or cups. Serves four or five. Crumbled crisp bacon makes a good garnish for this soup.

Here's a recipe that's definitely an old-timer, but it's just as delicious as it ever was so it bears repeating.

CRAB SOUP MONGOLE

Heat the soups and the cream to simmering; add remaining ingredients. Serve in heated soup bowls. Serves four generously as a main dish soup.

1 (10½ oz.) can condensed tomato soup
1 (10½ oz.) can condensed pea soup
1½ cups light cream or rich milk
1 cup flaked crabmeat (or more for a heartier soup)
½ cup dry Sherry
2 tablespoons chopped parsley
⅛ teaspoon curry powder, mixed with 1 tablespoon water
Salt and pepper to taste

P.S. If by chance you aren't a curry fancier, omit it and the soup will still be wonderful. And for variety, try cooked or canned lobster or shrimp in place of the crab.

———————◆———————

Here's another good candidate for a Sunday supper specialty:

OYSTER BISQUE

Drain oysters and chop fine; heat oysters in their liquid to simmering. Scald milk and cream with onion, celery, and bay leaf; strain. Melt butter and stir in flour; gradually add strained milk and cream; cook slowly, stirring constantly, until mixture boils and thickens. Add oysters and their liquid; season with mace, salt, garlic salt, and pepper. Strain soup, if desired. Reheat. Add Sherry just before serving. Sprinkle chopped parsley over each bowl or cup of soup. Serves four.

1 pint oysters
2 cups milk
¾ cup cream
1 slice onion
1 stalk celery, diced
1 bay leaf
2 tablespoons butter
2 tablespoons flour
Dash of mace
Salt, garlic salt, and pepper to taste
⅓ cup dry Sherry
1 tablespoon chopped parsley

A distant relative of New England clam chowder is this delightful soup:

CREAM OF CLAM SOUP

Drain clams, saving the liquid. In a saucepan, cook bacon until crisp; remove bacon bits from pan. Sauté onion gently in the bacon drippings for five minutes. Blend in flour; add milk and reserved clam liquid; cook, stirring constantly, until mixture boils. Add clams, wine, parsley, salt, celery salt, and pepper. Just before serving, add cream; season with more salt and pepper, if necessary; heat gently but thoroughly. Pour into heated soup bowls; top each serving with a sprinkling of paprika and some of the bacon bits. Serves four or five.

2 (7 oz.) cans minced clams
3 slices bacon, cut fine with scissors
3 tablespoons finely chopped onion
3 tablespoons flour
2 cups milk
¼ cup dry Sherry
2 tablespoons chopped parsley
  Salt, celery salt, and pepper to taste
½ cup light cream
  Paprika

"Luscious" is the best word I know with which to describe this rich and creamy onion soup:

CREAM OF ONION SOUP

Put wine, water, and bouillon cubes in a saucepan; bring to boil, stirring until bouillon cubes are dissolved. Add onions; cover and simmer for about 30 minutes, or until onions are very soft. Force onions and liquid through a fine sieve. Melt butter and stir in flour; add milk and cream; cook, stirring constantly, until mixture is thickened and smooth. To this sauce add the onion mixture, cheese, parsley, salt, and pepper; blend well and heat thoroughly. Pour into heated soup bowls or cups and sprinkle with paprika. Serves five or six.

1 cup dry white table wine
1 cup water
3 chicken bouillon cubes (or 2 tablespoons chicken stock base)
6 medium-sized onions, peeled and thinly sliced
3 tablespoons butter
3 tablespoons flour
2 cups milk
1 cup cream
2 tablespoons grated Parmesan cheese
2 tablespoons chopped parsley
  Salt and pepper to taste
  Paprika

There are lots of good recipes for French-style onion soup and I think this is one of the best. What's more, most of the work is done for me! I highly recommend the special onion-cheese toast that tops each bowlful.

SHELBY'S ONION SOUP

In a saucepan combine onion soup, bouillon, water, wine, and Worcestershire sauce; heat gently to simmering. Mix mayonnaise, Parmesan cheese, and onion. Spread mayonnaise mixture over one side of toast rounds; dust with paprika. Just before serving the soup, place toast rounds under broiler and broil *slowly* until mayonnaise mixture is bubbly and lightly browned. Pour hot soup into heated bowls or cups; top each serving with a toast round. Serve immediately. Serves five or six. Delicious!

1 (10½ oz.) can condensed onion soup
1 (10½ oz.) can condensed bouillon (beef broth)
1¼ cups water
⅓ cup dry Sherry
1 teaspoon Worcestershire sauce
¼ cup mayonnaise
3 tablespoons grated Parmesan cheese
3 tablespoons finely chopped onion
5 or 6 (3-inch) rounds of toast
   Paprika

If you're a beet enthusiast you'll enjoy this version of borsch:

QUICK-AND-EASY BORSCH

Drain beets, reserving liquid; chop beets very fine. Sauté onion gently in butter until tender but not brown. Add beets, beet liquid, consommé, and water. Simmer, uncovered, for five minutes. Add wine, lemon juice, and seasonings. Pour into heated soup bowls or cups and top each serving with a generous spoonful of sour cream and a sprinkling of chopped dill pickle. Serves five or six.

1 (1 lb.) can diced beets
2 tablespoons finely chopped onion
1 tablespoon butter
1 (10½ oz.) can condensed consommé
½ cup water
½ cup dry red table wine
1 tablespoon lemon juice
   Salt, celery salt, and pepper to taste
   Sour cream and chopped dill pickle for garnish

Here's a good first-course cream soup for a light dinner. Don't omit the croutons as a garnish. They look attractive and add a nice bit of texture contrast.

CREAM OF PEA AND CARROT SOUP

Combine peas and carrots, onion, and boiling water in a saucepan; cook, covered, for about 15 minutes, or until vegetables are very tender. Force vegetables and liquid through a sieve or food mill. Add stock, cream, and wine. Heat gently to simmering; season with salt and pepper. Pour into heated soup bowls or cups; top each serving with a few croutons and a dusting of paprika. Serve at once. Serves four or five.

1   (10 oz.) package frozen peas and carrots
1   small onion, chopped
1   cup boiling water
1   cup chicken stock
1   cup light cream
¼ cup dry Sherry
    Salt and pepper to taste
    Croutons and paprika for garnishing

Now for some clear soups that make excellent dinner "beginners." These are nice to serve in the living room with cheese straws or crackers as the prelude to a company meal.

AVOCADO BOUILLON

Heat bouillon and water to simmering; add Sherry, parsley, salt, and pepper. Put some of the avocado in each of five or six bouillon cups; pour in the hot soup and serve at once. Serves five or six.

2   (10½ oz.) cans condensed bouillon (beef broth)
1⅓ cups water
¼   cup dry Sherry
2   tablespoons chopped parsley
    Salt and pepper to taste
1   medium-sized avocado, peeled and very finely diced

TOMATO AND AVOCADO SOUP

Heat soup and water to simmering; add Sherry, lemon juice, salt, and pepper. Put some of the avocado in each of five or six bouillon cups; pour in the hot soup and serve at once. Serves five or six.

2 (10½ oz.) cans condensed tomato soup
2   cups water
½ cup dry Sherry
1   tablespoon lemon juice
    Salt and pepper to taste
1   medium-sized avocado, peeled and very finely diced

TOMATO BOUILLON

Combine tomato juice, onion, celery, bay leaf, and cloves in a saucepan. Bring to a boil, then cover and simmer for 20 minutes. Strain. Add consommé, wine, salt, and pepper. Serve very hot in bouillon cups and float a thin slice of lemon in each cup. Serves five or six.

3 cups canned tomato juice
1 thick slice onion
1 stalk celery, sliced
1 bay leaf
4 whole cloves
1 (10½ oz.) can condensed consommé
½ cup dry red table wine
Salt and pepper to taste
Thin slices of lemon for garnish

———————

These two jellied soups are fine for perking up appetites on a hot day. Be sure to chill the bouillon cups in which the soup is to be served.

JELLIED SHERRY CONSOMMÉ

Soften gelatin in the cold water. Heat consommé and water to simmering; add gelatin and stir until dissolved; add Sherry, lemon juice, and salt. Chill until firm. At serving time, spoon into chilled bouillon cups. Sprinkle with chopped parsley and serve with lemon wedges. Serves four.

2 teaspoons unflavored gelatin
¼ cup cold water
1 (10½ oz.) can condensed consommé
½ cup water
½ cup dry Sherry
1 tablespoon lemon juice
Salt to taste
Chopped parsley and lemon wedges

JELLIED TOMATO BOUILLON

Soften gelatin in one-quarter cup tomato juice. Heat remaining tomato juice and bouillon to simmering; add gelatin and stir until dissolved; add Sherry, lime juice, Worcestershire sauce, and salt. Chill until firm. At serving time, spoon into chilled bouillon cups. Serve with lime wedges. Serves four.

1 envelope (1 tablespoon) unflavored gelatin
¾ cup canned tomato juice
1 (10½ oz.) can condensed bouillon (beef broth)
¼ cup dry Sherry
1 tablespoon lime juice
½ teaspoon Worcestershire sauce
Salt to taste
Lime wedges

IV

Let's Toss
A Salad

What will the salad be? A bowl of crisp greens with a snappy French dressing, a creamy chicken mixture heaped high in a lettuce cup, a shimmering mold of fruits or vegetables wreathed with tender leaves of romaine? There's a salad to fit every brunch, lunch, and dinner. Deciding what it's to be means selecting the one that mingles best, flavorwise, with the rest of the meal and that's properly light or hearty as the menu requires.

Among the recipes to come you'll find appetizer salads, salads that are meals in themselves, salads to go with the main course, and salads that fit almost anywhere. Whatever your choice—salad first, last, or in the middle—have the greens *crisp,* and the plates *chilled!*

There's no salad I enjoy more than a toss-up of two or three kinds of lettuce (butter and romaine are favorites), deep green sprigs of watercress, and a really well-seasoned French dressing. For variety I sometimes add slices of avocado, thin discs of cucumber or radish, halves of canned artichoke hearts, sliced canned mushrooms, slivers of green pepper, and little rings of green onion. Just one or two of these in the bowl can enhance the flavor deliciously.

Now for the dressing (and here's a subject that could fill pages, because "French" dressing recipes are almost as numerous as cooks). True French dressing, of course, combines oil, vinegar, and seasonings. But who's to say what proportion of oil to vinegar is "right" or what seasonings do or do not "belong?" It's a matter of individual taste.

One of my favorite French dressings is made with four parts of oil to one part of vinegar—red wine vinegar, that is—plus just enough dry red table wine to mellow and smooth the mixture, and spices and herbs to make the salad bowl fairly sing with good flavor.

Here is the basic dressing with some variations:

WINE FRENCH DRESSING

Combine in a pint jar and shake vigorously. Chill several hours so flavors can blend. Shake well before using. Makes about one and one-half cups.

1 cup salad oil (I like part olive oil)
¼ cup red wine vinegar
¼ cup dry red table wine
1½ teaspoons salt
½ teaspoon coarse black pepper
¼ teaspoon each: paprika and dry mustard
½ teaspoon Worcestershire sauce
Garlic, as you like it

Now for the variations . . .

ROQUEFORT WINE DRESSING

Cheese should be at room temperature. If you have an electric blender, use it to blend the cheese and dressing together until smooth. If you are blenderless, mash the cheese with a fork, then gradually blend in the dressing, mixing until smooth. Chill several hours. Makes almost two cups. A perfect dressing for greens and vegetables.

¼ pound Roquefort or Blue cheese
1 recipe *Wine French Dressing* (above)

MUSHROOM DRESSING

Combine mushrooms, onion, parsley, and garlic in a chopping bowl; chop *very, very* fine. Add mixture to dressing and shake well. Chill several hours. Makes about two cups. Wonderful with mixed green and vegetable salads. An *outstanding* dressing.

1 (4 oz.) can mushroom stems and pieces, drained
1 thick slice onion
¼ cup (firmly packed) parsley sprigs
½ clove garlic
1 recipe *Wine French Dressing* (page 33), minus garlic

LORENZO DRESSING

Combine all ingredients and shake well. Chill several hours. Makes about two cups. Excellent with mixed green and vegetable salads. Also an ideal dressing for fruit-and-cottage-cheese combinations, especially when pears are featured.

⅓ cup chili sauce
½ cup finely chopped watercress
1 recipe *Wine French Dressing* (page 33)

And with fruit salads try:

CREAMY FRUIT SALAD DRESSING

Beat eggs in the top of a double boiler. Mix sugar and flour; stir into eggs; add orange and lemon peel, wine, pineapple juice, orange juice, and lemon juice. Cook over hot water, stirring constantly, until mixture thickens. Cool. Add mayonnaise and fold in whipped cream. Add salt. Serve with fruit salads. Makes about two and one-half cups.

2 eggs
⅓ cup sugar
2 tablespoons flour
1 teaspoon each: grated orange peel and lemon peel
½ cup Muscatel or sweet Sherry
½ cup pineapple juice
¼ cup orange juice
2 tablespoons lemon juice
½ cup mayonnaise
½ cup heavy cream, whipped Salt to taste

I love a creamy Roquefort cheese dressing—the richer the better! Spooned over thick slices of ripe red tomatoes, or tossed with crisp greens in the salad bowl, either of these next two dressings is my idea of heavenly fare. Remember them, too, when you want a good dip mixture for raw vegetables on the hors d'oeuvre tray.

SPECIAL ROQUEFORT DRESSING

Have cheese at room temperature. Place cheese in a small mixing bowl; mash well with a fork. Gradually beat in cream, then mayonnaise, oil, vinegar, and wine. Add remaining ingredients, mixing well. Cover and chill several hours to blend flavors. Makes about one and two-thirds cups. *Really "special!"*

¼ pound Roquefort or Blue cheese
⅓ cup heavy cream
½ cup mayonnaise
⅓ cup salad oil
¼ cup red wine vinegar
2 tablespoons dry red table wine
1 clove garlic, chopped or put through garlic press
½ teaspoon Worcestershire sauce
Generous dash of salt
¼ teaspoon coarse black pepper

MONTEREY ROQUEFORT DRESSING

Have cheeses at room temperature. Combine cheeses and sour cream in a bowl; blend well with a fork. Gradually beat in wine and vinegar, then salad oil. Add remaining ingredients; mix well. Store, covered, in the refrigerator for several hours to blend flavors. Makes two cups.

1 (3 oz.) package cream cheese
¼ pound Roquefort or Blue cheese
½ cup dairy sour cream
⅓ cup dry white table wine
2 tablespoons wine vinegar
1 cup salad oil
1 teaspoon lemon juice
1 teaspoon grated onion
1 clove garlic, chopped or put through garlic press
½ teaspoon Worcestershire sauce
¼ teaspoon paprika
Salt and coarse black pepper to taste

One of the most popular salads in the West is Crab Louis—crabmeat, or crabmeat and celery, on a bed of lettuce, with Louis dressing topping it off and ripe olives and slices of tomato and hard-cooked egg for garnish.

I'm not certain when or where Louis dressing originated, but I do know that there are lots of different recipes for it! Here is the one I use, plus some good variations on the main theme. The Sherry really *makes* the flavor here.

LOUIS DRESSING

Combine all ingredients. Chill for an hour or longer so that flavors will have a chance to blend. Makes about one and one-half cups. Perfect for all seafood salads. Also good with vegetable and egg salads.

1 cup mayonnaise
¼ cup chili sauce
¼ cup dry or medium Sherry
2 tablespoons chopped parsley
1 teaspoon grated onion
½ teaspoon Worcestershire sauce
  Salt to taste

If you'd like a different and delectable dressing for hearts of lettuce or a tomato or avocado salad, try one of these combinations. This is truly elegant eating.

TUNA DRESSING

One recipe *Louis Dressing* (above) plus one (6½ oz.) can chunk-style tuna plus one-half cup finely cut celery equals *Tuna Dressing*.

CRABMEAT OR SHRIMP DRESSING

One recipe *Louis Dressing* (above) plus one cup flaked crabmeat or finely cut shrimp plus one-half cup finely cut celery equals *Crabmeat or Shrimp Dressing*.

A creamy avocado salad dressing that is excellent with grapefruit and orange salads, sliced tomatoes, and many fruit and vegetable combinations is:

AVOCADO-SHERRY DRESSING

Blend avocado, wine, lemon juice, and mayonnaise. Add seasonings. Makes about one and one-half cups.

1 cup mashed avocado
¼ cup dry or medium Sherry
2 tablespoons lemon juice
2 tablespoons mayonnaise
½ teaspoon Worcestershire sauce
¼ teaspoon each: onion salt and
  celery salt
  Salt to taste
  Dash of cayenne

Two well-known dressings that I make using *Louis Dressing* as the base are:

THOUSAND ISLAND DRESSING
Mix well and chill to blend flavors.

1 recipe *Louis Dressing*
2 hard-cooked eggs, finely chopped
2 tablespoons each: drained capers, chopped pimiento, chopped pimiento-stuffed olives, and chopped green pepper

RUSSIAN DRESSING
Mix well and chill to blend flavors.

1 recipe *Louis Dressing*
2 tablespoons each: well drained sweet-pickle relish, chopped green pepper, and chopped pimiento

Another West Coast favorite is Green Goddess Salad—mixed greens with a luscious and lively anchovy-and-tarragon-flavored dressing that was originated many years ago at the Palace Hotel. This is no salad to choose when the meal is hearty. It's really *rich*, and when shrimp or crabmeat or chicken is added it's the meal all by itself!

Over the years, recipe creators have delighted in whipping up formulas for Green Goddess Dressing, and I'm no exception. Here's my how-to:

GREEN GODDESS DRESSING

Put the anchovy fillets, onion, garlic, and parsley through the food grinder or chop them all together until very, very fine. Add remaining ingredients and mix well. Cover and chill several hours to blend flavors. Makes about two cups. In addition to being glorious with mixed greens, this dressing is fine in a chicken or seafood salad in place of mayonnaise. Try it, too, over cold poached salmon, sliced tomatoes, or green beans.

1 (2 oz.) can anchovy fillets, drained
1 small onion
1 clove garlic
½ cup (firmly packed) parsley sprigs
1 cup mayonnaise
½ cup dairy sour cream
3 tablespoons dry Vermouth or dry white table wine
2 tablespoons tarragon vinegar
1½ teaspoons lemon juice
Salt and coarse black pepper to taste

Let's leave dressings now and talk about the salads themselves. To start, here's a bouquet of vegetable-salad ideas. The ingredients given in each case are for a single serving. Line your salad plates with the prettiest, crispest greens you can find.

GOOD VEGETABLE SALADS

Vegetable Luncheon Salad: Arrange two or three stalks of cooked broccoli atop a peeled tomato half. Lay two anchovy fillets crisscross over the broccoli. Arrange two deviled egg halves and two or three canned (or cooked frozen) artichoke hearts around the tomato. Pass *Mushroom Dressing* or *Wine French Dressing*. With hot cheese biscuits or wedges of your favorite pizza, this makes a fine main course for a salad luncheon. Incidentally, you can substitute asparagus tips, strips of cooked zucchini, or a bundle of green beans for the broccoli.

Vegetable Salad Louis: Top a peeled tomato half with three or four asparagus tips. Arrange a ring of thin cucumber slices around the tomato. Sprinkle with sieved hard-cooked egg and paprika. Pass *Louis Dressing*. Good as an appetizer salad or as a main-dish accompaniment in place of a hot vegetable.

Tomato Supreme: Cut a peeled tomato lengthwise in quarters or sixths, cutting down to, but not through, the center. Spread sections apart, petal fashion. Top tomato with *Crabmeat, Shrimp,* or *Tuna Dressing*. Sprinkle with sieved hard-cooked egg and dust with paprika. Garnish with ripe and green olives. Another delicious main-dish salad.

Palace Court Salad: Top a thick slice of peeled tomato with a good-sized cooked or canned artichoke bottom. Top artichoke with a generous mound of crabmeat, shrimp, tuna, or chicken salad. Surround tomato with a ring of finely shredded lettuce and cover the lettuce with sieved hard-cooked egg. Pass *Thousand Island Dressing*. Definitely a main-dish salad. This is another specialty of San Francisco's Palace Hotel, and one of my real favorites.

P.S. To prepare the artichoke bottoms, cook large artichokes as usual.

When cool, pull off all leaves from the bottom, scoop out the fuzzy choke, and trim off the stem.

Celery Salad Francisco: Marinate a well-drained canned celery heart (or two hearts, if small) in *Wine French Dressing* for several hours in the refrigerator. Drain celery and place, flat side up, on a bed of watercress. Top with two or three crab legs (or large shrimp) arranged alternately with two or three slices of hard-cooked egg. Sprinkle with paprika and serve with additional *Wine French Dressing* or with *Roquefort Wine Dressing*. This is my simplified and "personalized" version of Celery Victor, a salad for which the St. Francis Hotel in San Francisco is justly famous. As given, it is an excellent appetizer salad. For a delicious luncheon main dish, make the portions really generous and garnish with quarters of tomato. Lots of hot popovers and a "well-caloried" dessert can complete the menu.

I like to serve a help-yourself vegetable platter salad as the main feature of a buffet-luncheon menu, or instead of a hot vegetable at a buffet supper. Here are some congenial combinations of vegetables:

VEGETABLE PLATTER SALADS

1. Center the platter with a whole head of cooked cauliflower. Around the cauliflower arrange (each in a separate group) sliced or julienne beets, slices of avocado, strips of cooked carrot, and cooked or canned lima beans. Sprinkle *Wine French Dressing* sparingly over all and serve one of the creamy Roquefort dressings on the side.

2. Center the platter with a bowl of canned garbanzos (chick peas) or red kidney beans (or a combination of the two) that have been thoroughly drained, dressed with just enough *Wine French Dressing* to moisten them, and chilled for several hours. Around the bowl arrange canned (or cooked frozen) artichoke hearts, slices of tomato, cooked or canned green beans, and canned celery hearts. Sprinkle these last four vegetables sparingly with *Wine French Dressing* and serve *Thousand Island Dressing* or *Russian Dressing* separately.

3. Cook and drain frozen mixed vegetables. When cool mix with just enough *Wine French Dressing* to moisten and chill several hours. Center the platter with a bowl of these marinated vegetables. Around the bowl arrange stalks of cooked broccoli, whole baby beets, sliced cucumbers, and tender stalks of celery stuffed with your favorite cheese mix. Sprinkle the broccoli, beets, and cucumbers with *Wine French Dressing* and on the side serve *Louis Dressing* to which you have added a sieved hard-cooked egg.

Potato salad can be "just potato salad," or it can be something really special. I feel that an interesting ingredient list puts this one in the latter category.

POTATO SALAD PIQUANT

Combine potatoes, celery, cucumber, onion, parsley, and pimiento in a mixing bowl. Add wine. Cover and chill in the refrigerator from one to two hours. Drain thoroughly. Add remaining ingredients, using just enough mayonnaise to moisten the mixture. Mix gently to avoid mashing the potatoes. (A rubber spatula is handy here.) Chill again until time to serve. Serves six to eight. This salad makes a delicious filling for a tomato aspic ring.

4	cups diced, cooked potatoes
1	cup thinly sliced celery
1	cup diced cucumber (or an additional 1 cup celery)
¼	cup chopped onion
¼	cup chopped parsley
2	tablespoons chopped pimiento
1½	cups dry white table wine
3	hard-cooked eggs, chopped
1	tablespoon wine vinegar
2	teaspoons prepared mustard
1	teaspoon celery seed
½	cup mayonnaise (approximately)
	Salt and pepper to taste

———◆———

A good molded salad is the hostess-cook's best friend. It's attractive to the eye, easy to serve, and definitely a prepare-ahead dish. I suspect that the man of the house may not share my enthusiasm. Men seem to prefer their salads *au naturel*, but I'm pretty sure that these next three recipes will appeal to the distaff side, especially for summer luncheons and buffet suppers. First, what is doubtless the most familiar of all molded salads:

TOMATO ASPIC

Soften gelatin in the cold water for five minutes. Heat tomato sauce to simmering; add softened gelatin and sugar; stir until dissolved. Add remaining ingredients. Pour into an oiled one-quart ring mold or into six individual molds; chill until firm. Unmold on crisp salad greens. Serve with *Thousand Island* or *Russian Dressing*, one of the seafood dressings, or mayonnaise. Serves six.

2 envelopes (2 tablespoons) un-flavored gelatin
¾ cup cold water
2 (8 oz.) cans tomato sauce
⅓ cup sugar
⅓ cup dry or medium Sherry
¼ cup wine vinegar
2 tablespoons lemon juice
1 teaspoon grated onion
½ teaspoon Worcestershire sauce
   Salt to taste

P.S. *Crabmeat-Tomato Molds* are delicious. Prepare tomato aspic mixture as directed above; chill until mixture begins to thicken, then fold in one cup flaked crabmeat (or shrimp), one cup finely cut celery, and one-half cup thinly sliced pimiento-stuffed olives. Turn into molds; chill until firm. Unmold and serve with mayonnaise. Serves six to eight.

This is a really exceptional salad with an elegant flavor.

TOMATO CREAM SALAD MOLDS

Heat tomatoes to simmering; add gelatin and stir until dissolved. Remove from heat. Add wine and salt. Cool to lukewarm, then gradually blend in mayonnaise. Chill. When mixture begins to thicken, fold in celery, green pepper, and onion. Taste and add additional salt, if needed. Pour into six individual molds or custard cups. Chill until firm. Unmold on crisp salad greens and serve with French dressing. Serves six.

1 (1 lb.) can stewed tomatoes
1 (3 oz.) package lemon-flavored gelatin
¼ cup dry or medium Sherry
   Salt and pepper to taste
1 cup mayonnaise
1 cup finely cut celery
¼ cup finely chopped green pepper
1 tablespoon finely chopped onion

A colorful, frosty-cold fruit salad with a flavorful dressing makes a fine main dish for luncheon, especially if cheese biscuits, blueberry muffins, toasted English muffins, or some other delectable hot bread goes along with it. Smaller portions of a fruit salad, one that isn't too sweet, fit nicely into many luncheon and dinner menus as a side dish with the main course. These are some fruit combinations I've enjoyed (given in single-serving portions).

GOOD FRUIT SALADS

Pear Salad Lorenzo: Stuff two fresh or well-drained canned pear halves with a mixture of equal parts of crumbled Blue cheese and grated Cheddar cheese. (Moisten cheeses with a few drops of cream, if needed.) Place a ring of canned pineapple on a bed of crisp greens. Put two pear halves together and place on top of pineapple. Serve with *Lorenzo Dressing*.

Stuffed Peach Salad: Place two fresh or well-drained canned peach halves, cut side up, on a bed of watercress. Fill one half with seasoned cottage cheese, the other with a mixture of your favorite berries and seedless grapes. Serve with *Creamy Fruit Salad Dressing*.

Avocado and Fruit Louis: Arrange slices of avocado alternately with grapefruit and orange sections on hearts of romaine. Serve with *Louis Dressing* to which chopped pimiento-stuffed olives have been added.

Fruit-Filled Avocados: Place a peeled avocado half on a bed of lettuce; brush with lemon juice. Fill to heaping with a mixture of pineapple tidbits, seedless grapes, and canned mandarin orange sections. Serve with *Red River Dressing*.

Cantaloupe Ring Salad: Place a thick ring of peeled cantaloupe on crisp greens. In the center heap a mixture of pitted Bing cherries, pineapple chunks, and balls or cubes of avocado. Serve with *Creamy Fruit Salad Dressing*.

Trio Fruit Plate: Stuff three well-drained canned whole apricots with a mixture of cream cheese and finely chopped salted almonds. Place in a lettuce cup. Arrange grapefruit sections in a second lettuce cup; a mixture of diced celery and seedless grapes in a third. Sprinkle chopped parsley and/or paprika over salad for added color. Serve with *Special Roquefort Dressing* or with *Monterey Roquefort Dressing*.

A molded cranberry salad is a "natural" in a menu featuring turkey or chicken. This one is very good.

CRANBERRY-ORANGE RING

Quarter orange and remove seeds; put orange, peel and all, through food grinder. In a saucepan, mix orange, cranberry sauce, and wine; heat to simmering. Remove from heat. Add gelatin and stir until dissolved; add salt. Pour into individua! molds or a large mold and chill until firm. Unmold on crisp salad greens and serve with mayonnaise or any desired dressing. Serves five or six.

1 orange
1 (1 lb.) can whole cranberry sauce
¾ cup dry red table wine
1 (3 oz.) package lemon-flavored gelatin
Dash of salt

As refreshing as its name is this version of the familiar molded pineapple-cucumber salad:

SEA BREEZE SALAD

Drain pineapple, reserving syrup. Measure one cup syrup, adding water if needed to make that amount; heat to simmering; add gelatin, sugar, and salt; stir until dissolved. Remove from heat. Add wine and vinegar. Chill. When mixture begins to thicken, fold in other ingredients and pineapple. Add more salt, if desired. Pour into six individual molds that have been rinsed with cold water; chill until firm. Unmold on crisp salad greens and serve with mayonnaise. Serves six. A good salad to serve with fish.

1 (1 lb. 4 oz.) can crushed pineapple
1 (3 oz.) package lime-flavored gelatin
¼ cup sugar
Generous dash of salt
½ cup dry white table wine
¼ cup white wine tarragon vinegar
1 cup grated, seeded cucumber (1 large cucumber)
2 tablespoons finely chopped pimiento
1 teaspoon grated onion

When baked ham or ham loaf is the main dish, this ring is an excellent choice:

SPICED FRUIT SALAD RING

Drain salad fruits, reserving syrup. Measure one and one-fourth cups of the syrup; add wine and wine vinegar; heat to simmering. Add gelatin, spices, and salt; stir until gelatin is dissolved. Cool thoroughly; strain. Chill until mixture begins to thicken. Arrange salad fruits and grapes in an oiled one and one-half-quart ring mold; spoon slightly thickened gelatin mixture over them. Chill until firm. Unmold on crisp salad greens and serve with mayonnaise or a fruit salad dressing. Serves eight.

1 (1 lb. 13 oz.) can fruits for salad
½ cup Muscatel or sweet Sherry
2 tablespoons wine vinegar
1 (3 oz.) package apple-flavored gelatin
6 whole cloves
6 whole allspice
2 inches stick cinnamon
Dash of salt
1 cup fresh or canned seedless grapes

———————————◆———————————

Rich, luscious, and not for calorie counters is the next salad! It's highly recommended as a summer main dish.

AVOCADO MOUSSE WITH CRABMEAT DRESSING

Soften gelatin in the wine five minutes; dissolve in the hot chicken stock. Add lemon juice. Cool thoroughly. Blend in avocado and mayonnaise; fold in whipped cream; add seasonings. Pour into an oiled one-quart ring mold or six to eight individual molds; chill until firm. Unmold on crisp salad greens. Serve with *Crabmeat Dressing*. Serves six to eight. *Shrimp or Tuna Dressing* may also be used here.

1 envelope (1 tablespoon) unflavored gelatin
½ cup dry white table wine
½ cup hot chicken stock
2 tablespoons lemon juice
1 cup sieved avocado
½ cup mayonnaise
1 cup heavy cream, whipped
1 teaspoon grated onion
Dash of Tabasco sauce
Salt to taste

———————————◆———————————

Chicken salad is a versatile dish. The traditional trio—plump, tender chunks of chicken, crisp cuts of celery, and well-seasoned mayonnaise—

can be the starting point for some delicious and unusual eating adventures.

Seedless grapes are used here for an out-of-the-ordinary touch.

CALIFORNIA CHICKEN SALAD

2 cups diced, cooked chicken
1 cup dry white table wine
1 cup fresh or canned seedless grapes
1 cup finely cut celery
2 tablespoons chopped parsley
1 cup mayonnaise (approximately)
Salt to taste
Watercress or parsley and paprika

Combine chicken and wine in a shallow dish; cover and let stand in the refrigerator for several hours, stirring occasionally. Pour off wine and drain chicken thoroughly between paper towels. Mix chicken, grapes, celery, parsley, enough mayonnaise to moisten the mixture, and salt to taste. Heap in crisp lettuce cups; garnish with sprigs of watercress or parsley and dust lightly with paprika. Serves six.

Some like it hot, some like it cold, and this nut-studded chicken salad is good either way.

TWO-WAY CHICKEN SALAD

2 cups diced, cooked chicken
1 cup dry white table wine
1 cup coarsely chopped walnuts
1 cup finely cut celery
¼ cup chopped pimiento
1 tablespoon grated onion
2 tablespoons chopped parsley
1 cup mayonnaise (approximately)
1 teaspoon lemon juice
½ teaspoon Worcestershire sauce
Salt and pepper to taste

Combine chicken and wine in a shallow dish; cover and let stand several hours, stirring occasionally. Pour off wine and drain chicken thoroughly between paper towels. Mix chicken with all remaining ingredients, using just enough mayonnaise to moisten mixture nicely. Serve in one of the following ways:

1. Chill mixture thoroughly. At serving time, stir well and heap in crisp lettuce cups on a platter or salad plates. Garnish as desired with avocado or tomato slices, ripe olives, celery curls, etc. Or, serve in the center of a tomato aspic ring. Serves six.

2. Spoon mixture into baking shells or little individual casseroles.

Sprinkle with buttered fine bread crumbs and dust with paprika. Bake in a hot oven (425° F) for 15 to 20 minutes, or until piping hot and nicely browned. A good luncheon dish. Serves six.

Avocado and pineapple are excellent flavor-mates for chicken.

AVOCADO AND CHICKEN SALAD WAIKIKI

½ cup mayonnaise
3 tablespoons dry or medium Sherry
1 teaspoon lemon juice
1 cup diced, cooked chicken
½ cup diced canned pineapple
½ cup diced celery
 Salt to taste
3 medium-sized avocados
 Paprika

Mix mayonnaise, wine, and lemon juice. Stir in chicken, pineapple, and celery; add salt to taste. Chill thoroughly. Just before serving, cut avocados in halves lengthwise; remove seeds and peel; place an avocado half on each of six lettuce-lined salad plates. Stir chicken salad mixture well; heap in hollows of avocado halves. Dust with paprika. Serve at once. Serves six.

Now for some seafood salad ideas that I think you'll enjoy.

GOOD SEAFOOD SALADS

Crab Louis: Heap crabmeat (with or without diced heart of celery added) on a bed of shredded lettuce. Garnish with ripe olives, quartered tomatoes, and slices of hard-cooked egg. Pour *Louis Dressing* over the salad or pass dressing separately. *Shrimp Louis* is also delicious.

Special Seafood Plate: In the center of a lettuce-lined salad plate place a little cup of *Louis Dressing* or cocktail sauce. (A Japanese saki cup is perfect for this.) Around the cup arrange small portions of several different kinds of seafood to be dunked in the sauce with a cocktail fork. A good combination: crab legs or flakes, small or large shrimp, slices of lobster meat, flakes of salmon or tuna. With a relish tray of olives, radishes, and celery hearts, and some hot rolls, this makes a fine luncheon or supper dish.

Salmon Salad: Drain and flake a (1 lb.) can of salmon, removing bones and skin. Over it pour one cup dry white table wine and chill for several hours, stirring occasionally. Drain salmon and dry between paper towels. Mix with one cup finely cut celery, two tablespoons *each* drained capers and chopped parsley, and enough mayonnaise to moisten. Season with salt, pepper, and grated onion. Serve on crisp lettuce, garnished with sliced cucumbers and tomatoes, or whatever you like. Serves four.

I like to serve *Shrimp Orleans* for a salad luncheon with quartered tomatoes, deviled eggs, and ripe olives around it on the plate. The combination of flavors here is truly elegant.

SHRIMP ORLEANS

1 cup dry white table wine

2 cups cooked or canned shrimp (whole if small, cut up if large)

1 cup mayonnaise

1 tablespoon prepared mustard (the yellow variety)

1 teaspoon lemon juice

1 tablespoon chopped parsley

1 tablespoon chopped, drained capers

½ clove garlic, chopped or put through garlic press

1 teaspoon grated onion
Salt and pepper to taste

2 cups finely cut celery
Paprika

Pour wine over shrimp. Cover and chill several hours, stirring occasionally. Meantime mix mayonnaise, mustard, lemon juice, parsley, capers, garlic, onion, salt, and pepper. Drain shrimp and dry thoroughly by pressing between paper towels. Add shrimp and celery to mayonnaise mixture. Heap in crisp lettuce cups and dust with paprika. Serves six.

P.S. This may also be used as a filling for hollowed-out tomatoes, or served atop thick slices of tomato or tomato aspic. Lobster or crabmeat may be substituted for the shrimp, if you like.

Here's a recipe that definitely comes under the heading of party fare. It's a perfect main dish for a summer luncheon and it's nice, too, for a wedding luncheon or buffet supper

SEAFOOD MOUSSE LOUISE

Soften gelatin in the wine five minutes; dissolve in the boiling water; cool. Blend mayonnaise, chili sauce, and lemon juice; add cooled gelatin; fold in whipped cream. Add all remaining ingredients; mix lightly but thoroughly. Turn into two (one-quart) molds or ten to twelve individual molds that have been rinsed with cold water; chill until firm. Unmold on crisp salad greens and garnish as desired with slices of tomato and avocado, ripe olives, celery curls, etc. Serve with *Louis Dressing* or French dressing. Serves ten to twelve.

2   envelopes (2 tablespoons) unflavored gelatin
⅓   cup dry or medium Sherry
½   cup boiling water
1¼ cups mayonnaise
1   cup chili sauce
1   tablespoon lemon juice
½   cup heavy cream, whipped
1   cup flaked cooked or canned crabmeat
1   cup finely cut cooked or canned shrimp (use scissors)
6   hard-cooked eggs, grated or finely chopped
1   (4 oz.) can chopped ripe olives, drained
2   tablespoons chopped parsley
2   tablespoons chopped pimiento
1   teaspoon grated onion
1   teaspoon grated lemon peel
1   teaspoon Worcestershire sauce
    Dash of Tabasco sauce
    Salt and pepper to taste

❖ V ❖

Stars At
Lunch And Supper

There are lots of good luncheon and supper specialties that profit from the wine "touch." Egg and cheese dishes, *pasta* served forth in various ways, turnovers and stuffed pancakes, savory sandwiches— over the years my collection of these and other "light" main dishes has grown to sizeable proportions.

Described here are some delicious bits to tempt lady-like appetites at midday that are perfect fare for the bridge club. There are a generous number of good-eating supper ideas, the sort of thing that hits the spot on Sunday night, or any night when dinner's to be on the light side. And, then, there are excellent candidates for the brunch menu here, too.

EGG DISHES

Let's start with some egg dishes. Scrambled eggs with shrimp and a spot of Sherry are tasteworthy, indeed.

SCRAMBLED EGGS WITH SHRIMP

Melt butter in top of double boiler over direct heat; add onion and celery; cook gently for five minutes. Place over simmering water; add shrimp. Beat eggs slightly; add cream, Sherry, parsley, and seasonings. Pour egg mixture into double boiler; cook over simmering water, stirring frequently, until mixture is thick and creamy. Serve at once. Serves four. Good with a tossed green salad and crusty rolls or French bread.

2 tablespoons butter
2 tablespoons finely chopped onion
½ cup finely cut celery
1 cup cooked or canned shrimp (whole if small, cut up if large)
6 eggs
¼ cup cream
¼ cup dry or médium Sherry
1 tablespoon chopped parsley
¼ teaspoon Worcestershire sauce
   Salt and pepper to taste
   Dash of Tabasco sauce or cayenne

P.S. Crabmeat can replace the shrimp, if you like.

———————◆———————

Ham plus eggs, sauce, and cheese equals good eating.

BAKED EGGS ADÉLE

Melt butter and stir in flour; add milk and chicken stock; cook, stirring constantly, until mixture boils and thickens. Add wine, Worcestershire sauce, salt, and pepper. Cover bottom of four shallow individual baking dishes with slivered ham; break two eggs over ham; pour sauce over eggs. Sprinkle with cheese and dust with paprika. Bake in a moderately hot oven (375° *F*) about 15 minutes, or until eggs are as done as desired. Serves four. Excellent for brunch, lunch, or supper.

¼ cup butter
¼ cup flour
1 cup milk
⅔ cup chicken stock
⅓ cup dry white table wine
½ teaspoon Worcestershire sauce
   Salt and pepper to taste
2 cups slivered baked or boiled ham
8 eggs
½ cup grated Cheddar cheese
   Paprika

P.S. For another delectable dish, substitute a layer of canned corned beef hash or roast beef hash for the ham in this recipe.

A sort of "country cousin" of Eggs Benedict is:

EGGS BENBOW

Combine soup, cheese, and Sherry in a saucepan; stir over low heat until cheese melts and sauce is piping hot. Spread each muffin half with some of the deviled ham; top with a poached egg. Pour hot sauce over all; dust with paprika. Serve at once. Serves four. I like this for any meal, from breakfast on up!

1 (10½ oz.) can condensed tomato soup
1 cup shredded process Cheddar cheese
¼ cup dry or medium Sherry
2 English muffins, split, toasted, and buttered (or 4 rounds of bread, toasted and buttered)
1 small can deviled ham
4 poached eggs
Paprika

Curry powder and ginger give the sauce in this recipe its "Indienne" personality. You can serve the mixture with plain rice, but the Chutney-Rice Molds suggested below add a special "something."

EGGS AND CHICKEN INDIENNE

Sauté onion and celery gently in butter five minutes. Blend in flour and curry powder; add stock and white wine; cook, stirring, until mixture boils and thickens; stir in cream, Sherry and seasonings. Add eggs and chicken; heat gently but thoroughly. Serve with *Chutney-Rice Molds* (below). Serves four or five.

¼ cup chopped onion
½ cup finely cut celery
¼ cup butter
¼ cup flour
½ teaspoon (or more) curry powder
1 cup chicken stock
½ cup dry white table wine
½ cup cream
1 tablespoon dry or medium Sherry
½ teaspoon sugar
⅛ teaspoon powdered ginger
Garlic salt, salt, and pepper to taste
4 hard-cooked eggs, cut lengthwise in eighths
1 cup coarsely diced, cooked chicken (or turkey)

Chutney-Rice Molds: Cook one cup rice until tender; drain, if necessary. To the cooked rice add two tablespoons melted butter, one-half cup minced chutney (or orange marmalade), one-half cup flaked coconut, and salt to taste. Mix gently with a fork. Heat thoroughly over boiling water. Mold servings by pressing rice mixture gently into a custard cup; unmold on a serving platter or dinner plates and serve with *Eggs and Chicken Indienne*.

P.S. A cupful of shrimp is good in this recipe in place of the chicken.

———————◄————————

Excellent for luncheon are these delicate, easy-to-prepare timbales. Green beans or peas and canned shoestring potatoes are good accompaniments.

MUSHROOM TIMBALES WITH CRAB SAUCE

3 (10½ oz.) cans condensed cream of mushroom soup
8 eggs, well beaten
2 tablespoons chopped parsley
1 teaspoon grated onion
Salt and pepper to taste
¼ cup dry or medium Sherry
1 pimiento, chopped
1 cup flaked cooked or canned crabmeat (or shrimp, lobster, tuna, or chicken)

Mix two cans of the mushroom soup with the eggs, parsley, onion, salt, and pepper. Pour into six well-greased custard cups. Set cups in a pan of hot water and bake in a moderate oven (350° *F*) for 40 to 50 minutes, or until timbales are firm in the center. Remove from water and let stand five minutes or so before unmolding. While timbales are baking, combine remaining can of mushroom soup, wine, and pimiento in a saucepan; heat gently to simmering. Add crabmeat to sauce; heat a few minutes longer. Unmold timbales on a platter or individual plates; pour sauce over timbales. Serve at once. Serves six.

Cheese Dishes

I've been told that each year in France a marriage is solemnized, complete with clergyman and license, between a bottle of Burgundy and a piece of Roquefort cheese. Be this as it may—straight fact or romantic folklore—wine and cheese *are* perfect partners from the flavor standpoint, and the recipes that follow are but a few of the many good dishes combining them.

Cheese soufflé is such a familiar dish that I suppose practically everybody who cooks has a favorite recipe. I like this one, acquired during my college days. It hasn't failed yet! The Sherry, substituted for one-quarter cup of milk, was a recent and happy inspiration.

CHEESE SOUFFLÉ

3 tablespoons butter
4 tablespoons flour
¾ cup milk
¼ cup dry or medium Sherry
1 cup grated Cheddar cheese
½ teaspoon Worcestershire sauce
½ teaspoon prepared mustard
½ teaspoon salt
3 eggs, separated
¼ teaspoon cream of tartar

Melt butter and stir in flour; add milk and cook, stirring constantly, until mixture is smooth and very thick. Add wine and cheese; stir over low heat until cheese melts. Add seasonings. Remove from heat and cool slightly. Add unbeaten egg yolks, one at a time, beating well after each yolk is added. Beat egg whites until frothy; sprinkle cream of tartar over surface; continue beating until whites are stiff but not dry. Pour cheese mixture over egg whites; blend *gently* just until whites disappear. Pour into an ungreased, straight-sided one and one-half-quart baking dish. Bake in a moderate oven (350° F) about 45 minutes, or until top is a rich golden brown and center is firm to the touch. Serve at once. Serves four. If you want to double this recipe I suggest you use two baking dishes instead of one large one. Also, you can bake the soufflé in individual casseroles if you like. The recipe above is just right for four (one and one-half-cup) casseroles. These little soufflés will require about 30 minutes baking at 350° F.

P.S. For something really elegant, serve creamed mushrooms, chicken, crabmeat, or shrimp over this soufflé. Or serve it with cream sauce to which a spoonful of deviled ham and a bit of prepared mustard have been added. Whatever you do, don't forget to flavor the sauce with a little Sherry!

———————◄►———————

Simpler to make than Cheese Soufflé, and filling more or less the same bill, menuwise, is:

CHEESE CHARLOTTE

Arrange half the bread cubes in the bottom of a greased baking dish (8 x 8 x 2 inches). Sprinkle one-quarter-cup wine over bread. Cover bread with half of the cheese. Repeat layers with remaining bread, wine, and cheese. Beat eggs slightly; stir in milk and seasonings; pour over bread. Sprinkle with paprika. Let stand an hour or so. Bake in a slow oven (325° F) for one hour. Serves four.

8 slices white bread, buttered and cubed
½ cup dry white table wine
½ pound Cheddar cheese, grated
4 eggs
2 cups milk
1 teaspoon Worcestershire sauce
½ teaspoon prepared mustard
  Salt, onion salt, and pepper to taste
  Paprika

P.S. One cup of slivered or ground boiled or baked ham, mixed with the cheese, is a good addition here.

———————◄►———————

Whether you call it "Rabbit" or "Rarebit" it's a dish all cheese lovers enjoy, and this is an especially flavorful version.

WELSH RABBIT SAUTERNE

Melt butter in a chafing dish or double boiler; add cheese and stir until melted. Gradually stir in cream and wine, a spoonful at a time. Blend in seasonings, then eggs. Serve at once on toast or toasted crackers. Serves six to eight.

2 tablespoons butter
1 pound Cheddar cheese, grated
½ cup cream
½ cup dry white table wine
1 teaspoon dry mustard
2 teaspoons Worcestershire sauce
  Salt to taste
2 eggs, slightly beaten

An easy, versatile, and always smooth rabbit is made this way.

QUICK WELSH RABBIT

Melt cheese in a double boiler. Gradually blend in wine and cream. Add seasonings. Serve over toast or toasted crackers. Serves three or four.

½ pound process Cheddar cheese, sliced
¼ cup dry or medium Sherry, or dry white table wine
¼ cup cream or evaporated milk
½ teaspoon Worcestershire sauce
¼ teaspoon prepared mustard

With this recipe as a starting point, you can produce all sorts of good dishes, such as:

Chinese Rabbit: To *Quick Welsh Rabbit* (above) add four sliced, hard-cooked eggs. Serve over oven-heated canned crisp Chinese noodles, and sprinkle with shaved unblanched almonds. Serves four.

Broccoli Luncheonette: Spread four slices of hot, crisp toast with deviled ham. Top each with a serving of hot, cooked broccoli. Pour *Quick Welsh Rabbit* (above) over all. Dust with paprika and serve at once. Serves four. Hot cooked or canned asparagus tips can be used here in place of the broccoli. Slices of tomato are also good. Heat them briefly in the oven before arranging them on the ham-spread toast.

Crab Rabbit: To *Quick Welsh Rabbit* (above) add one cup of flaked fresh or canned crabmeat, one chopped pimiento, and two tablespoons chopped parsley. Serve over crisp toast. Serves four. One cup of shrimp or one (6½ oz.) can of chunk-style tuna may replace the crabmeat.

Frankfurter Special: Split six or eight hot frankfurters lengthwise. Arrange three or four halves on each of four slices of hot toast. Top with hot *Quick Welsh Rabbit* (above). Serves four.

Elegant Cheeseburgers: Prepare and cook four nice thick hamburger patties as usual. Place on toast or toasted hamburger buns. Top with *Quick Welsh Rabbit* (above) and serve at once. Serves four.

———◆———

No collection of wine-and-cheese recipes would be complete without a bow in the direction of Swiss Fondue. However, the recipe merits a word of caution: If you don't follow the directions about keeping the heat *very low* and stirring the mixture *constantly* and *patiently*, you are liable to end up with a stringy and less-than-edible concoction! Take it slow and easy and you'll have something really special in the way of a main dish or an appetizer.

VINTAGE FONDUE

1 pound Swiss cheese, shredded
2 tablespoons flour
½ clove garlic
¾ cup dry white table wine or dry Vermouth
2 tablespoons Kirsch or Brandy
Dash of nutmeg
Salt to taste
French bread, heated and cut in thick slices

You can make the fondue over hot water in a chafing dish or double boiler, or in a heavy casserole or saucepan set on an asbestos mat over very low heat. Toss cheese and flour together until well mixed. Rub the inside of the utensil of your choice with the cut side of the garlic clove. Pour in the wine and heat until air bubbles rise to the surface. Do *not* allow wine to boil! *Slowly* and *gradually* add the cheese-flour mixture, stirring *constantly* until the cheese melts. Don't be in a hurry! When all the cheese is completely melted, stir in the Kirsch or Brandy, then the nutmeg and salt. Serve at once in the chafing dish, or in a pre-heated casserole set over an asbestos mat on a candle warmer or hot plate. Let each person break off a small piece of French bread, put it on a fork, and dip the bread in the fondue. Serves four with a green salad as a main dish, eight or more as an appetizer.

Now if you're pressed for time, or have qualms about attempting the real fondue, the next recipe is for you. Granted it won't produce the traditional dish, but it will give you something exceedingly tasty.

BEGINNER'S FONDUE

Rub the inside of a chafing dish or double boiler with the cut side of the garlic clove. Set pan over hot water. Put butter in the pan; when melted, blend in the flour. Gradually add milk and cook, stirring occasionally, until mixture is thickened and smooth. Add cheese and wine; cook, stirring constantly, until cheese is completely melted. Add remaining ingredients. Serve with hot French bread as directed above in the recipe for *Vintage Fondue*. Serves four as a main dish, eight or more as an appetizer.

½ clove garlic
¼ cup butter
⅓ cup flour
2 cups rich milk
½ pound Swiss cheese, shredded
½ cup dry white table wine, or dry Vermouth
2 tablespoons Kirsch or Brandy
Dash of nutmeg
Salt to taste

PASTA DISHES

I am a *pasta* fan. Spaghetti, macaroni, noodles—I love them all, in all sizes and shapes, in all sorts of sauces. One thing, though, the *pasta* musn't be overcooked! It should be kept on the *al dente* side, tender but still a little firm to the bite.

SPAGHETTI BRAVO

Sauté meat, onion, garlic, and green pepper in bacon drippings until meat is well browned. Add all remaining ingredients except spaghetti and cheese. Cover and simmer gently, stirring occasionally, for two hours, or until meat is very tender. If sauce becomes too thick, add a little more wine. Cook spaghetti in boiling salted water *just* until tender; drain. Arrange spaghetti on a heated platter; pour sauce over spaghetti; sprinkle with grated Parmesan cheese. Serve at once with additional cheese. Serves six to eight.

1 pound beef stew meat, cut in small cubes
1 large onion, minced
1 clove garlic, minced or put through garlic press
1 green pepper, minced
2 tablespoons bacon drippings or olive oil
1 (1 lb.) can tomatoes
2 (8 oz.) cans tomato sauce
1 (6 oz.) can tomato paste
½ cup dry red table wine
1 (4 oz.) can mushroom stems and pieces, drained
1 teaspoon oregano
½ teaspoon sweet basil
1 teaspoon sugar
Salt and pepper to taste
1 pound spaghetti
Grated Parmesan cheese

A recipe for a good casserole dish that serves 12 to 16 can often come in handy. This is really an excellent one, and if you want it for family use you can easily halve the ingredients.

HARVEST SPAGHETTI CASSEROLE

Sauté beef, pork, and onion in oil until meat is no longer red, stirring with a fork so that meat is separated into small bits. Add all remaining ingredients except spaghetti, mushrooms, and cheese. Bring to a boil, then cover and simmer gently for four hours, stirring frequently. Shortly before sauce is done, cook spaghetti in boiling salted water *just* until tender; drain. Drain mushrooms, reserving liquid. When sauce is done, add mushrooms; pour over spaghetti; add one cup grated Parmesan cheese; toss gently and patiently with two forks until ingredients are thoroughly mixed and sauce and cheese are evenly distributed throughout the spaghetti. If extra "juiciness" is desired, add some of the reserved mushroom liquid. Taste and add additional salt, if needed. Turn into one very large or two smaller casseroles; sprinkle generously with additional grated Parmesan cheese. Place in a moderate oven (350° to 375° F) long enough to melt the cheese on top. Serve with additional cheese, if desired. Serves twelve to sixteen.

1½ pounds ground beef
1½ pounds ground fresh pork
1   large onion, minced
¼   cup olive oil
2   (1 lb. 13 oz.) cans tomatoes
2   (8 oz.) cans tomato sauce
1   (6 oz.) can tomato paste
1   cup dry red table wine
½   cup chopped parsley
1   clove garlic, chopped or put through garlic press
2   teaspoons oregano
1   teaspoon marjoram
½   teaspoon allspice
1   bay leaf
2   tablespoons sugar
    Salt and pepper to taste
2   pounds spaghetti
2   (8 oz.) cans mushroom stems and pieces
    Grated Parmesan cheese

A delicious version of a traditional dish is this one:

SPAGHETTI WITH MEAT BALLS

Sauté onion, green pepper, and garlic gently in bacon drippings for five minutes. Blend in flour; add tomatoes, bouillon, and wine; cook, stirring constantly, until mixture boils. Add seasonings. Cover and simmer gently for one hour, stirring occasionally. Meantime, prepare meat balls as follows:

SAUCE

- 1 large onion, chopped
- 1 green pepper, chopped
- 1 clove garlic, chopped or put through garlic press
- 2 tablespoons bacon drippings or olive oil
- 2 tablespoons flour
- 1 (1 lb. 13 oz.) can tomatoes
- 1 (10½ oz.) can bouillon (beef broth)
- ½ cup dry red table wine
- 1 bay leaf, crumbled
  Pinch each of thyme and marjoram
- 1 tablespoon sugar
  Salt and pepper to taste

Combine all ingredients except corn meal, mixing well. Take up mixture by teaspoonfuls and shape into small balls. Roll balls in corn meal.

When sauce has cooked one hour, add meat balls. Cover and continue simmering for 45 minutes, stirring very gently several times to prevent meat balls from sticking to bottom of pan.

Cook one pound spaghetti in boiling salted water *just* until tender; drain. Place spaghetti on a platter; pour meat balls and sauce over it. Sprinkle with grated Parmesan cheese, and serve additional Parmesan cheese separately. Serves six to eight.

MEAT BALLS

- 1 pound ground beef
- ¼ cup fine, dry bread crumbs
- 1 egg, well beaten
- ¼ cup milk
- 1 small onion, finely chopped
- ¼ cup chopped parsley
- ½ teaspoon powdered sage
- 1 teaspoon salt
- ¼ teaspoon pepper
  Corn meal

I wasn't brought up in a "casserole household." My family called them "what-nots" and took a rather dim view of them. I suspect many people do. Perhaps, it's because some casseroles are such conglomerate concoctions that it's hard to know just *what* one's eating. But a *good* casserole often fills the bill better than any other dish. If it's easy to prepare and serve, not too hard on the budget, and has real character, it's worth knowing about.

SEAFOOD CASSEROLE MELBA

½ pound short spaghetti
2 tablespoons chopped onion
¼ cup butter
¼ cup flour
1½ cups chicken stock
1 cup cream
⅓ cup dry or medium Sherry
1 teaspoon lemon juice
½ cup grated Parmesan cheese
1 teaspoon Worcestershire sauce
Salt, celery salt, and pepper to taste
1 cup cooked or canned shrimp (whole if small, cut up if large)
1 cup flaked cooked or canned crabmeat
Paprika

Cook spaghetti in boiling salted water *just* until tender; drain. Sauté onion gently in butter for five minutes. Blend in flour; add chicken stock and cream; cook, stirring, until mixture boils and thickens. Add wine, lemon juice, one-fourth cup of the cheese, and the seasonings; gently stir in shrimp and crabmeat. In a greased casserole arrange alternate layers of spaghetti and seafood mixture, having a layer of seafood mixture on top; sprinkle with remaining cheese; dust with paprika. Bake in a moderately hot oven (375° F) for 30 minutes, or until bubbly and golden brown. Serves five or six.

P.S. Sautéed fresh or canned mushrooms may be added to the seafood mixture if desired. And instead of shrimp and crabmeat, you can use two cups of either one.

◆━━━━━━◆

Plain, old-fashioned macaroni and cheese is a mighty good dish, but a bit of Sherry makes it even better, and for variety, you can add one cup slivered boiled or baked ham to the macaroni and cheese mixture. Or add one cup crabmeat, shrimp, or tuna and one-fourth cup *each* chopped green pepper and pimiento-stuffed olives.

MACARONI AND CHEESE

Cook macaroni in boiling salted water *just* until tender; drain. Melt butter and stir in flour; add milk and cook, stirring constantly, until sauce boils and thickens. Add one and one-half cups of the cheese; stir over low heat until melted. Remove from heat; add Sherry, onion, parsley, Worcestershire sauce, mustard, salt, and pepper. Combine sauce and macaroni, mixing gently but thoroughly. Turn into a greased casserole; sprinkle with paprika. Bake in a moderately hot oven (375° F) for about 25 minutes. Serves six.

½ pound elbow macaroni
¼ cup butter
¼ cup flour
1¾ cups milk
2 cups grated Cheddar cheese
¼ cup dry or medium Sherry
1 tablespoon finely chopped onion
1 tablespoon finely chopped parsley
1 teaspoon Worcestershire sauce
½ teaspoon dry mustard
Salt and pepper to taste
Paprika

Add eggs to macaroni and cheese, bake the mixture in a ring mold, and fill the center with a seafood sauce or creamed chicken.

MACARONI RING WITH SEAFOOD SAUCE

Cook macaroni in boiling salted water *just* until tender; drain. Place milk, bread crumbs, butter, and cheese in a saucepan; stir over very low heat until cheese is melted. Remove from heat; add macaroni, Sherry, eggs, pimiento, green pepper, onion, and seasonings; mix well. Pour into a well-greased ring mold, set in a shallow pan of hot water, and bake in a moderate oven (350° F) about 45 minutes, or until firm. Remove from oven and let stand for five minutes or so before unmolding. Unmold on heated platter and fill center of ring with the following *Seafood Sauce:*

MACARONI RING

1 cup elbow macaroni
1¼ cups milk
1 cup grated soft bread crumbs
4 tablespoons butter
1 cup grated Cheddar cheese
¼ cup dry or medium Sherry
3 eggs, slightly beaten
1 pimiento, chopped
2 tablespoons chopped green pepper
1 teaspoon grated onion
½ teaspoon Worcestershire sauce
Salt and pepper to taste

Melt butter and stir in flour; add milk and stock and cook, stirring constantly, until mixture is thickened and smooth. Add parsley, lemon peel, Sherry, salt, celery salt, and pepper. Add crabmeat and heat gently before serving. Serves five or six.

SEAFOOD SAUCE

¼ cup butter
¼ cup flour
1¼ cups rich milk
½ cup chicken stock (or an additional ½ cup milk)
2 tablespoons chopped parsley
½ teaspoon grated lemon peel
¼ cup dry or medium Sherry
Salt, celery salt, and pepper to taste
1 cup cooked or canned crabmeat or shrimp, or 1 (6½ oz.) can chunk-style tuna

Veal and noodles meet here in a delicious sour-cream mushroom sauce.

VEAL-NOODLE-MUSHROOM CASSEROLE

Heat bacon drippings in a large, heavy skillet; add veal, onion, and garlic; cook, stirring frequently, until meat is no longer pink. Stir in flour; add wine, water, and liquid drained from mushrooms; cook, stirring constantly, until sauce boils and thickens. Add Worcestershire sauce, paprika, salt, and pepper. Cover and simmer for 45 minutes, or until veal is tender, stirring frequently. Cook noodles in boiling salted water *just* until tender; drain. Combine veal and sauce, noodles, drained mushrooms, and sour cream; taste and add salt and pepper if necessary. Turn into a greased casserole; sprinkle liberally with Parmesan cheese. Bake in a moderate oven (350° F) for 30 to 40 minutes. Serves eight generously.

4 tablespoons bacon drippings or butter
2 pounds veal shoulder, cut in small cubes
1 medium onion, minced
½ clove garlic, chopped or put through garlic press
5 tablespoons flour
1 cup dry white table wine
1½ cups water
1 (8 oz.) can mushroom stems and pieces
1 teaspoon Worcestershire sauce
½ teaspoon paprika
Salt and pepper to taste
¾ pound wide noodles
1 cup dairy sour cream
Grated Parmesan cheese

This is definitely one of my favorite casserole dishes. It combines layers of macaroni, a sage-seasoned spinach mixture, and a good, rich-flavored tomato sauce. Wonderful eating guaranteed! The recipe is easily doubled to serve ten or twelve.

ITALIAN SUPPER CASSEROLE

Cook macaroni in boiling salted water *just* until tender; drain. Sauté beef, onion, and garlic in two tablespoons olive oil until meat is no longer red, stirring with a fork so that meat is broken into small pieces. Add tomato sauce, tomato paste, wine, mushrooms, thyme, rosemary, oregano, salt, and pepper. Bring to a boil, then cover and simmer 20 minutes. Mix spinach, parsley, bread crumbs, eggs, remaining two tablespoons olive oil, one-fourth cup Parmesan cheese, sage, salt, and pepper. In a well-greased two-quart casserole spread half the macaroni; cover with half of the spinach mixture; cover spinach with half of the meat sauce. Repeat layers with remaining ingredients. Sprinkle with Parmesan cheese. Bake in a moderate oven (350° F) for 45 minutes. Serves five or six. Best with a green salad and crusty French bread.

½ pound shell or bow-tie macaroni
1 pound ground beef
1 onion, chopped
1 clove garlic, chopped **or** put through garlic press
4 tablespoons olive oil
1 (8 oz.) can tomato sauce
1 (6 oz.) can tomato paste
½ cup dry red table wine
1 (4 oz.) can mushroom stems and pieces, drained
Pinch each of thyme, rosemary, and oregano
Salt and pepper to taste
1 (10 oz.) package frozen chopped spinach, cooked and *thoroughly* drained
¼ cup chopped parsley
½ cup fine, dry bread crumbs
2 eggs, well beaten
Grated Parmesan cheese
½ teaspoon powdered sage

High on the list of my *pasta* favorites is:

LASAGNA

Cook lasagna until tender in boiling salted water to which one tablespoon of the olive oil has been added, stirring occasionally. Drain; rinse with cold water; separate noodles and spread out on a towel to dry. Sauté beef, onion, and garlic in remaining two tablespoons olive oil until meat is browned, stirring with a fork to separate it into bits. Add tomatoes, tomato paste, wine, Italian seasoning, salt, and pepper. Bring to a boil, then cover and simmer very gently for one hour, stirring occasionally. Mix cottage cheese, eggs, Parmesan cheese, parsley, and salt and pepper to taste. Arrange half the lasagna over bottom of a greased 13- x 9- x 2-inch baking dish; cover with half the cottage cheese mixture, half the Mozzarella cheese, then half the meat sauce. Repeat layers. Sprinkle more Parmesan cheese over the top. Bake in a moderate oven (350° *F*) for 45 minutes to one hour. Serves six to eight.

½   pound lasagna noodles
3   tablespoons olive oil
1   pound ground beef
1   medium-sized onion, chopped
1   clove garlic, chopped or put through garlic press
1   (1 lb.) can stewed tomatoes
1   (6 oz.) can tomato paste
½   cup dry red table wine
1   teaspoon mixed Italian seasoning
    Salt and pepper to taste
1½ pints (3 cups) small-curd cottage cheese
3   eggs, slightly beaten
½   cup grated Parmesan cheese
¼   cup chopped parsley
¾   pound Mozzarella cheese, thinly sliced
    Additional grated Parmesan cheese

Corn Meal Dishes

Polenta, the Italian equivalent of our corn meal mush, makes truly elegant eating when it's served with a well-seasoned beef-tomato sauce.

POLENTA

In the top of a double boiler, mix one and one-half cups yellow corn meal with one and one-half cups cold water. Stir in three cups boiling water and one and one-half teaspoons salt. Place over direct heat and cook, stirring constantly, until mixture boils and thickens. Place over boiling water; cover and cook one hour, stirring occasionally. Before serving, add one cup grated Cheddar cheese and three tablespoons butter; stir until melted and blended with the *polenta*.

The *polenta* here is molded, chilled, and sliced, then baked with a savory sauce.

POLENTA RING WITH BEEF SAUCE

Dredge meat with flour. Heat oil in a large, heavy skillet or a Dutch oven; add meat, onion, and garlic; sauté, stirring frequently until meat is nicely browned. Add remaining ingredients (including mushroom liquid); season to taste with salt and pepper. Cover and simmer gently, stirring frequently, about two hours, or until meat is tender. Add a little more wine during cooking if gravy becomes too thick. To serve, spoon *Polenta* in a ring around the edge of a heated platter; pour meat mixture in center. Pass grated Parmesan cheese separately. Serves six.

BEEF SAUCE

2 pounds beef stew meat, cut in small cubes
  Flour
¼ cup olive oil
1 large onion, chopped
1 clove garlic, chopped or pressed through garlic press
1 (1 lb.) can stewed tomatoes
1 (4 oz.) can mushroom stems and pieces (undrained)
½ cup dry red table wine
½ teaspoon oregano
¼ teaspoon each: thyme and rosemary
  Salt and pepper

BEEF AND POLENTA CASSEROLE

Cook corn meal according to directions on package for corn meal mush, adding salt to taste. To the hot mush add one cup of the grated cheese; pour into a loaf pan that has been rinsed with cold water; chill until firm, preferably overnight.

1 cup yellow corn meal
2 cups grated Cheddar cheese
2 tablespoons olive oil
1 large onion, chopped
1 clove garlic, chopped or put through garlic press
1 pound ground beef
1 (1 lb. 13 oz.) can tomatoes
¼ cup tomato paste
½ cup dry red table wine
  Pinch each of oregano, rosemary, and basil
½ teaspoon sugar
  Salt and pepper to taste

Prepare sauce as follows: Heat oil in a heavy skillet with a tight-fitting lid. Add onion, garlic, and beef; cook, stirring with a fork, until meat has lost its red color. Drain off all fat from skillet. Add tomatoes, tomato paste, wine, and seasonings; bring to a boil, then cover and cook gently, stirring frequently, for one hour.

To assemble dish: Unmold chilled mush and cut crosswise in thin slices. Arrange half of these slices in the bottom of a greased shallow casserole (8 x 12 x 2 inches is a good size); cover slices with half of the meat sauce. Repeat layers; sprinkle remaining one cup grated cheese over the top. Bake in a moderate oven (350° F) for one hour. Serves six.

Next comes corn meal in a south-of-the-border dish.

SONORA TAMALE PIE

In the top of a double boiler, mix one cup white corn meal with one cup cold water until smooth. Gradually stir in two cups boiling water; add one teaspoon salt. Stir constantly over direct heat until mixture thickens. Add two tablespoons butter. Cover and cook over boiling water for 20 minutes, stirring occasionally. Line a well-greased two-quart baking dish with the mixture, smoothing it evenly over the surface of the dish with your fingers or the back of a spoon. (This is easier to do when the mixture is slightly cool.) Prepare filling as follows:

Sauté beef, onion, and garlic in oil until meat is no longer red, stirring with a fork so that meat is broken into small bits. Blend in flour; add tomato sauce and wine; cook, stirring constantly, until mixture boils and thickens; simmer five minutes or so. Add seasonings, olives, and corn. Pour filling into corn meal crust; sprinkle with grated cheese. Bake in a moderate oven (350° F) for 45 minutes. Serves five or six.

1 pound ground beef
1 large onion, chopped
1 clove garlic, chopped or put through garlic press
2 tablespoons salad oil
2 tablespoons flour
2 (8 oz.) cans tomato sauce
⅓ cup dry red table wine
2 teaspoons (or more) chili powder
½ teaspoon cumin seed
Salt and pepper to taste
1 cup whole ripe olives (preferably pitted)
1 (1 lb.) can whole-kernel corn, drained
½ cup grated Cheddar cheese

Rice Dishes

If you're feeling extravagant, use wild rice in these first two rice recipes. You'll be rewarded with some marvelous eating!

Creamed crabmeat, shrimp, tuna, or mushrooms can be served in the center of this ring instead of creamed chicken. Excellent for luncheon.

RICE RING WITH CREAMED CHICKEN

Boil or steam rice until tender. Combine cooked rice with remaining ingredients in order given, mixing gently but thoroughly. Turn into a well-greased one and one-half-quart ring mold, set mold in a shallow pan of hot water, and bake in a moderate oven (350° F) about 45 minutes, or until firm. Remove from oven and let stand five minutes before unmolding. Fill center with *Creamed Chicken* prepared as follows:

RICE RING

1 cup uncooked rice (wild or white)
1½ cups grated Cheddar cheese
⅓ cup finely chopped parsley
2 teaspoons grated onion
Bit of chopped or pressed garlic
1¼ cups milk
¼ cup dry or medium Sherry
¼ cup melted butter or salad oil
3 eggs, slightly beaten
½ teaspoon Worcestershire sauce
Salt and pepper to taste

Melt butter and stir in flour; gradually add milk and stock; cook, stirring constantly, until mixture is thickened and smooth. Add wine and seasonings. Add chicken and mushrooms; heat thoroughly before serving. Serves six.

CREAMED CHICKEN

¼ cup butter
¼ cup flour
1 cup rich milk (or ½ cup milk and ½ cup cream)
⅔ cup chicken stock
¼ cup dry or medium Sherry
½ teaspoon Worcestershire sauce
Salt, celery salt, and pepper to taste
2 cups diced, cooked chicken (or turkey)
1 (3 oz.) can chopped broiled mushrooms, drained

Rice, seasoned with curry, is a perfect "background" for flavorful creamed shrimp.

CURRIED RICE MOLDS WITH CREAMED SHRIMP

In a saucepan, dissolve curry powder in a little of the chicken stock; add remaining stock; heat to boiling. Slowly sprinkle in rice, then stir well, cover, and simmer very gently for about 25 minutes, or until rice is tender and stock is absorbed. Sauté celery, onion, and green pepper gently in butter five minutes. Blend in flour; add milk; cook, stirring constantly, until mixture boils and thickens. Add wine, parsley, salt, and pepper; stir in shrimp; heat gently but thoroughly. To serve, mold individual servings of rice by pressing gently in a custard cup; unmold on dinner plates; pour some of the creamed shrimp over each mound of rice. Serves four.

1   teaspoon curry powder
2   cups well-seasoned chicken stock
1   cup uncooked long-grain white rice
½   cup chopped celery
2   tablespoons chopped onion
1   tablespoon chopped green pepper
3   tablespoons butter
3   tablespoons flour
1⅓ cups milk
⅓   cup dry white table wine
2   tablespoons chopped parsley
    Salt and pepper to taste
1½ cups cooked or canned shrimp (whole if small, cut up if large)

P.S. Crabmeat or tuna can be used here in place of shrimp.

Easy to prepare, easy on the budget, and easy to eat is:

RICE VERA CRUZ

Sauté beef, onions, and green pepper in oil until meat is no longer red, stirring frequently with a fork so that meat is separated into small bits. Add tomatoes, consommé, wine, chili powder, salt, and olives. Bring to a boil, then slowly stir in rice. Pour into a two-quart casserole. Cover and bake in a moderately hot oven (375° F) for 30 minutes. Uncover; stir mixture with a fork; sprinkle cheese over the top. Continue baking, uncovered, for 15 minutes. Remove from oven and let stand five to ten minutes before serving. Serves five or six.

1   pound lean ground beef
2   medium-sized onions, chopped
1   green pepper, chopped
2   tablespoons salad oil or bacon drippings
1   (1 lb.) can solid-pack tomatoes
1   (10½ oz.) can condensed consommé
⅓   cup dry or medium Sherry
2   teaspoons chili powder
    Salt to taste
1   cup sliced ripe olives
1   cup uncooked long-grain white rice
1   cup grated Cheddar cheese

Now two recipes for the Italian specialty, *rissotto*. Chicken livers are starred in this first one.

RISSOTTO WITH CHICKEN LIVERS

Melt butter in a large, heavy skillet. Add chicken livers; sauté gently, stirring frequently, for five minutes. Remove livers and set aside. Add rice and onion to butter in skillet; sauté *very* gently, stirring frequently for ten minutes. Dissolve saffron in a little of the wine; add to rice with remaining wine, chicken broth, salt, and pepper; stir well. Cover and simmer slowly for about 25 minutes, or until rice is tender and all liquid is absorbed. With a fork, gently stir in chicken livers and cheese before serving. Serves six.

⅓ cup butter
½ pound chicken livers, cut in small pieces
1½ cups uncooked long-grain white rice
1 medium-sized onion, minced
⅛ teaspoon powdered saffron
½ cup dry white table wine
3 cups boiling chicken stock
Salt and pepper to taste
½ cup grated Parmesan cheese

Here the rissotto is oven-cooked and ham and mushrooms are the featured ingredients.

BAKED HAM AND MUSHROOM RISSOTTO

Sauté onion and ham gently in oil about five minutes. Add rice and cook, stirring, for a minute or so. Dissolve saffron in a little of the chicken stock; add to rice mixture. Add remaining stock, wine, salt, and pepper. Bring to a boil, then pour into a two-quart casserole. Cover and bake in a moderately hot oven (375° F) for 30 minutes. Uncover; with a fork gently stir in mushrooms and parsley. Cover and continue baking ten minutes longer. Serve accompanied by a bowl of grated Parmesan cheese. Serves five or six.

1 medium-sized onion, minced
1½ cups slivered boiled or baked ham
⅓ cup olive oil
1½ cups uncooked long-grain white rice
Pinch of saffron
2½ cups chicken stock
½ cup dry white table wine
Salt and pepper to taste
1 (4 oz.) can mushroom stems and pieces, drained
¼ cup chopped parsley
Grated Parmesan cheese

FILLED PANCAKES, TURNOVERS, SANDWICHES, AND SUCH

I'm a great believer in pancakes for luncheons and buffet suppers. Not just *plain* pancakes, but feather-light pancakes rolled around a delectable meat or chicken filling and covered with a savory sauce. With a tossed salad, relishes, and maybe some French bread or rolls, the main course is complete. Such good eating!

Most of the preparation for these pancake dishes can be done ahead of time. The pancakes, filling, and sauce can all be readied in the morning or even the day before, then covered and put in a refrigerator until time to assemble and heat the dish.

Here are some of my favorites. I hope you'll try them all.

CRÊPES VENETIA

PANCAKES

Follow recipe for pancakes in *Creamed Chicken Pancakes*.

Sauté veal and pork in butter until meats begin to brown. Add mushrooms and onion; sauté gently 15 minutes. Add spinach and seasonings; mix well. Set aside until needed.

FILLING

½ pound ground veal
½ pound ground lean fresh pork
2 tablespoons butter
1 (8 oz.) can mushroom stems and pieces, drained and minced or ground
½ small onion, minced or ground
1 (10 oz.) package frozen chopped spinach, cooked, drained, and chopped even finer
Salt and pepper to taste
Dash of nutmeg or mace

Melt butter and stir in flour; add milk and chicken stock; cook, stirring constantly, until mixture boils and thickens. Add Sherry and one cup of the cheese; stir over low heat until cheese melts. Season with salt and pepper.

SAUCE

½ cup butter
½ cup flour
2½ cups milk
½ cup chicken stock
⅓ cup dry or medium Sherry
1 (8 oz.) package process Swiss cheese, shredded
Salt and pepper to taste

TO ASSEMBLE THE DISH

Spread about one-third cup of the filling on each pancake. Roll up and place side by side in two greased shallow baking dishes (12 x 8 x 2 inches). Pour hot sauce over pancakes; sprinkle with remaining cheese and dust with paprika. Bake in a moderately hot oven (375° F) for 20 to 25 minutes, or until bubbly and piping hot. Serves six.

CREAMED CHICKEN PANCAKES

Mix flour and salt; gradually add combined eggs and milk, stirring until smooth. Add oil. Bake pancakes, one at a time, in a greased skillet measuring six and one-half inches across the bottom. Use about one-fourth cup batter per pancake, and tilt skillet as you pour in batter so that bottom of skillet is completely covered. Turn pancakes once. Stack cooked pancakes on a plate. Makes 12 pancakes.

FANCAKES

1½ cups sifted all-purpose flour
1½ teaspoons salt
3   eggs, well beaten
1½ cups milk
1   tablespoon salad oil

Mix all ingredients.

FILLING

2 cups diced, cooked chicken
1 cup chopped canned or sautéed fresh mushrooms
Salt and pepper to taste

Melt butter and stir in flour; add chicken stock and milk; cook, stirring constantly until mixture boils and thickens. Remove from heat. Add remaining ingredients.

SAUCE

½ cup butter (part chicken fat may be used)
⅔ cup flour
3 cups chicken stock
2 cups rich milk
½ cup dry white table wine
¼ cup grated Parmesan cheese
1 teaspoon Worcestershire sauce
Dash of mace
Salt and pepper to taste

TO ASSEMBLE THE DISH

Put some of the chicken-mushroom mixture in the center of each pancake. Roll up and place side by side in two greased shallow baking dishes (12 x 8 x 2 inches). Pour piping hot sauce over pancakes. Sprinkle one-fourth cup additional grated Parmesan cheese over contents of each baking dish and dust with paprika. Bake in a moderately hot oven (375° F) for about 25 minutes, or until bubbly and delicately browned. Serve right from the baking dishes. Serves six, allowing two pancakes per person.

P.S. Turkey or crabmeat can replace the chicken here very nicely.

MANICOTTI

PANCAKES

Follow recipe for pancakes in *Creamed Chicken Pancakes.*

In large, heavy skillet sauté beef, onion, and garlic until meat is no longer red, stirring with fork to crumble meat into bits. Add remaining ingredients. Cover and simmer one hour, stirring frequently.

SAUCE

1 pound ground beef
1 large onion, finely chopped
1 clove garlic, chopped or put through garlic press
1 (1 lb.) can stewed tomatoes
3 (8 oz.) cans tomato sauce
1 cup dry red table wine
1 teaspoon mixed Italian seasoning
1 teaspoon sugar
Salt and pepper to taste

Blend cottage cheese and cream cheese. Mix with remaining ingredients.

FILLING

1 cup small-curd cottage cheese
1 (3 oz.) package cream cheese
2 cups well drained, chopped, cooked spinach (2 packages frozen)
½ cup grated Parmesan cheese
Nutmeg, salt, and pepper to taste

TO ASSEMBLE THE DISH

Spread a scant one-fourth cup filling on each pancake. Roll loosely and place side by side in two 12 x 8 x 2-inch baking dishes. Pour *simmering* sauce over pancakes; sprinkle one-fourth cup grated Parmesan cheese over each dish. Bake in a moderately hot oven (375° F) for 20 minutes, or until bubbly. Serve with additional Parmesan cheese. Serves six.

First cousin to a turnover is the stuffed roll. The cook who isn't too enthusiastic about making pastry will like these—and so will everybody, for that matter. They're another dish that can be prepared well in advance of serving and then heated at the last minute.

Shrimp and a cheese sauce make these delectable.

BAKED SHRIMP-STUFFED ROLLS

3 tablespoons butter
3 tablespoons flour
¾ cup milk
1 cup grated Cheddar cheese
¼ cup dry or medium Sherry
1 cup cooked or canned shrimp (whole if small, cut up if large)
½ cup chopped celery
2 tablespoons chopped green pepper
2 tablespoons chopped pimiento
1 teaspoon grated onion
½ teaspoon Worcestershire sauce
Salt and pepper to taste
6 large or 8 medium-sized French rolls

Melt butter and stir in flour; add milk and cook, stirring constantly, until mixture boils and thickens. Add cheese and stir over low heat until melted. Remove from heat and add Sherry, shrimp, celery, green pepper, pimiento, onion, Worcestershire sauce, salt, and pepper. Chill thoroughly. About one-half hour before serving time, cut a thin lengthwise slice from the top of each roll; hollow out inside to form a shell. Fill hollowed-out rolls with the chilled shrimp mixture; replace the tops. Wrap each roll securely in aluminum foil. Arrange rolls on a cooky sheet; bake in a hot oven (400° F) for about 20 minutes. Remove foil and serve piping hot. Serves six to eight.

Reminiscent of the oyster loaf, a traditional San Francisco favorite, are these oyster-filled rolls. In a true oyster loaf the oysters are fried. Here they are lightly and flavorfully creamed.

OYSTER ROLLS FERNANDO

Melt butter and stir in flour; add cream and oyster liquid; cook, stirring constantly, until mixture boils and thickens. Add Sherry, lemon juice, parsley, onion, Worcestershire sauce, salt, and pepper. Set sauce aside while preparing the rolls, as follows: cut a thin lengthwise slice from the top of each roll; with fingers, hollow out inside; spread inside with butter. Toast rolls and top slices in a hot oven (450° F) for a few minutes, just until a light golden brown. While rolls are toasting, add oysters to sauce and heat gently. (Do not let mixture boil.) To serve, place toasted roll shells on individual plates; fill with the oyster mixture; put top slices in place. Serve at once. Serves four or six. A combination "fork and finger" dish that is wonderful for Sunday night supper or a late evening snack.

3 tablespoons butter
3 tablespoons flour
½ cup cream
⅓ cup oyster liquid
2 tablespoons dry or medium Sherry, or dry Vermouth
1 teaspoon lemon juice
2 tablespoons chopped parsley
1 teaspoon grated onion
½ teaspoon Worcestershire sauce
Salt and pepper to taste
4 to 6 long French rolls
Additional butter for spreading rolls
2 cups drained fresh or canned oysters (whole if small, cut in bite-sized pieces if large)

The turnover is a sort of sandwich-with-glamour—a savory meat, chicken, or seafood filling encased in flaky pastry and baked to a golden brown. Served warm, with or without a sauce, turnovers are appealing to both eye and palate. What's more, they can be prepared well ahead of time and then baked at the last minute.

The following recipes all make eight six-inch turnovers. At a luncheon, probably one will suffice. At supper time it's a safe guess that the men in the group will want two, so plan accordingly. (There's no trick to doubling these recipes.) In any case, a salad, and perhaps a green vegetable, are the happiest accompaniments.

TURNOVER PASTRY NOTE

To prepare the pastry for these turnovers, use one and one-half (10 oz.) packages of pie crust mix, or make it yourself with two and one-half cups sifted all-purpose flour, one teaspoon salt, three-fourths cup shortening, and five to six tablespoons cold water. Divide dough in half and roll each half out into a 12-inch square. Cut each square into four six-inch squares. (For a larger number of smaller turnovers, simply cut the pastry in smaller squares.)

Now for the recipes. Ground beef is the featured filling ingredient in this first one, and canned beef gravy is used as the base for a delectable sauce.

HAMBURGER POCKETBOOKS

Sauté beef, onion, and celery in bacon drippings until meat is no longer red, stirring with a fork so that meat is separated into small bits. Pour off all but about two tablespoons of the fat. Blend in flour; add one-half cup of the beef gravy and the red wine; cook, stirring, until mixture boils and thickens. Add tomato paste and seasonings. Chill mixture thoroughly. Put some of the filling in the center of each pastry square; fold pastry over to form a triangle; crimp edges with a wet fork and prick tops. Place on baking sheet. Brush tops with milk. Bake in a hot oven (450° F) for 15 to 20 minutes. Heat remaining beef gravy and add Sherry; serve with the Pocketbooks. Makes eight.

1 pound lean ground beef
½ cup chopped onion
½ cup finely cut celery
2 tablespoons bacon drippings or butter
¼ cup flour
2 (10¾ oz.) cans beef gravy
½ cup dry red table wine
1 tablespoon tomato paste
1 teaspoon Worcestershire sauce
 Salt, garlic salt, and pepper to taste
 Pastry (See *Turnover Pastry Note* above)
 Milk (for brushing tops)
1 to 2 tablespoons dry or medium Sherry

———————

Crabmeat in a Sherry- and cheese-flavored cream sauce goes inside these.

CRABMEAT LUNCHEON TURNOVERS

Melt butter and stir in flour; add cream and cook, stirring constantly, until mixture boils and thickens. Remove from heat. Blend in wine; add cheese, salt, and pepper; stir in crabmeat, mushrooms, and parsley. Chill mixture thoroughly. Put some of the chilled crabmeat mixture in the center of each pastry square; fold pastry over to form a triangle; crimp edges with a wet fork and prick tops. Place on a baking sheet. Brush tops with milk. Bake in a hot oven (450° F) for 15 to 20 minutes. Serve hot. Makes eight.

3 tablespoons butter
3 tablespoons flour
¾ cup cream
¼ cup dry or medium Sherry
¼ cup grated Parmesan cheese
  Salt and pepper to taste
½ pound (about 1½ cups) flaked crabmeat
1 (4 oz.) can mushroom stems and pieces, drained and chopped
2 tablespoons chopped parsley
  Pastry (See *Turnover Pastry Note*)
  Milk (for brushing tops)

A little chicken goes a long way here.

CHICKEN TURNOVERS

Melt butter and stir in flour; add milk and stock; cook, stirring constantly, until mixture is thickened and smooth. Add white wine, mace, salt, celery salt, and pepper. To one cup of this sauce add the chicken, eggs, olives, onion, and additional salt and pepper if necessary; chill.

6 tablespoons butter
6 tablespoons flour
1½ cups rich milk
1 cup chicken stock
½ cup dry white table wine
  Dash of mace
  Salt, celery salt, and pepper to taste
1½ cups finely diced, cooked or canned chicken (or turkey)
2 hard-cooked eggs, chopped
⅓ cup chopped ripe olives
1 tablespoon grated onion
  Pastry (See *Turnover Pastry Note*)
  Milk (for brushing tops)
2 tablespoons chopped parsley
2 tablespoons chopped pimiento
1 tablespoon dry or medium Sherry

Place some of the chilled chicken mixture in the center of each pastry square; fold pastry over to form a triangle; crimp edges with a wet fork and prick tops. Place on a baking sheet. Brush tops with milk. Bake in a hot oven (450° F) for 15 to 20 minutes. Add parsley, pimiento, and Sherry to remaining sauce; heat gently and serve with the turnovers. Makes eight.

———————◆———————

These are some of the juiciest and best hamburger sandwiches I know of:

BEST HAMBURGERS

Mix beef, wine, parsley, onion, salt, and pepper. Shape lightly into four nice patties. Broil, or sauté in butter or bacon drippings, until as done as desired. Serve between halves of buttered, toasted hamburger buns, or on toast, with whatever relishes you like. Serves four. Now for some variations on this theme.

1 pound ground beef
¼ cup dry red table wine
2 tablespoons chopped parsley
1 tablespoon grated onion
1 teaspoon salt
⅛ teaspoon pepper
    Hamburger buns or toast

CHEESEBURGERS

If you're broiling your hamburgers, top the cooked patty with a slice of Cheddar cheese and run it back under the broiler long enough to melt the cheese. If you're sautéing them, lay cheese on patties when they are almost, but not quite, cooked, then finish cooking with the cover on the pan so the cheese can melt. Or, melt the cheese on the buns instead of on the patties, or spread the buns with your favorite Roquefort or Cheddar cheese spread. Any way you "cheese it" the result will be flavorful!

CHILIBURGERS

Prepare and cook hamburger patties as directed for *Best Hamburgers* above. While they're cooking, heat two (15 oz.) cans chili con carne (with beans) to simmering; stir in one-half cup dry red table wine. Place patties on toasted buns or toast and pour some of the chili mixture over each one. Serves four amply and deliciously!

SPECIAL BROILED HAMBURGERS

Prepare meat mixture as directed above for *Best Hamburgers*, but do not shape into patties. Toast eight slices of bread on one side; spread meat mixture on the untoasted side, using about one-fourth cup of the mixture per sandwich. (Be *sure* to spread the meat all the way to the edges of the bread!) Dot with butter. Broil *slowly* for about five minutes, or until as done as desired. Serve at once. Makes eight sandwiches. (To make *Special Cheeseburgers*, top each hamburger with a thin slice of cheese when almost done, and let cheese melt under the broiler.) Excellent for a crowd, because they can be prepared ahead and broiled just before serving.

Here the faithful hamburger is served forth in a little different way:

SURPRISE BURGERS

1 pound ground beef
1 large onion, chopped
1 small clove garlic, chopped or put through garlic press
½ green pepper, chopped
2 tablespoons bacon drippings or butter
2 tablespoons flour
⅓ cup dry red table wine
⅓ cup catsup
½ cup grated Cheddar cheese
⅓ cup chopped pimiento-stuffed olives
1 teaspoon Worcestershire sauce
Salt and pepper to taste
6 hamburger buns

Sauté beef, onion, garlic, and green pepper in bacon drippings until meat is no longer red, stirring with a fork so that meat is separated into bits. Sprinkle flour over meat and blend well. Add wine and catsup; cook, stirring constantly, until mixture boils and thickens. Remove from heat. Add cheese, olives, Worcestershire sauce, salt, and pepper. Cut a thin slice from the top of each bun and hollow out insides; fill with meat mixture (about one-half cup per bun); replace tops. Place in a baking pan; cover (with a lid or aluminum foil) and bake in a moderate oven (350° F) for 30 minutes. Serves six. Good with cole slaw and potato chips. These also can be prepared ahead of time.

The name of this next recipe fascinates me. Usually I'm in favor of names that give at least a partial clue to what's in a dish. This one certainly doesn't. But I can't bring myself to change it, so I'll explain that *Snuggle Puppies* are toasted, hollowed-out hamburger buns filled with a chili-flavored meat mixture.

SNUGGLE PUPPIES

Sauté onion in butter until golden. Add meat and cook, stirring with a fork, until meat is no longer red. Sprinkle flour over meat and blend well; add tomato soup and wine; cook, stirring constantly until mixture boils and thickens. Add seasonings. Simmer, uncovered, for about ten minutes, stirring frequently. Cut a thin slice from the top of each hamburger bun; hollow out inside of buns. Brush inside of bun "shells" with butter; toast under broiler to a golden brown, heating bun lids at the same time. Fill shells with the piping hot meat mixture; put lids in place. Serve at once garnished with your favorite relishes. Serves six.

1 medium-sized onion, chopped
1 tablespoon butter
1 pound ground beef
2 tablespoons flour
1 (10½ oz.) can condensed tomato soup
⅓ cup dry red table wine
½ teaspoon Worcestershire sauce
1 teaspoon (or more) chili powder
½ teaspoon cumin seed
Salt and pepper to taste
6 hamburger buns
Additional butter
Ripe olives, pickles, radishes, or other relishes for garnishing

———————◆———————

These are a delectable variation on the chicken-sandwich theme involving chicken, sliced tomatoes, cheese, and mushroom sauce.

CHICKEN SUPPER SANDWICHES

Toast six slices of bread on one side. Cover untoasted sides with thinly sliced, cooked chicken (or turkey); top chicken with thin slices of tomato; cover with thinly sliced process Cheddar cheese. Broil slowly until cheese melts. Serve at once accompanied by the following *Mushroom Sauce:*

Drain mushrooms, reserving the liquid. Melt butter and stir in flour; add cream, mushroom liquid, and bouillon cube; cook, stirring constantly, until sauce boils and thickens and bouillon cube is completely dissolved. Add wine, paprika, salt, and pepper. Stir in mushrooms. Serve piping hot with the sandwiches. Serves six.

MUSHROOM SAUCE

1 (6 oz.) can sliced broiled mushrooms
4 tablespoons butter
4 tablespoons flour
1 cup cream
1 chicken bouillon cube (or 2 teaspoons chicken stock base)
¼ cup dry or medium Sherry
¼ teaspoon paprika
Salt and pepper to taste

———————◆———————

A rich-flavored cheese sauce is the secret of success here.

SWISS CHICKEN AND HAM SANDWICHES

Using the toast, chicken, and ham, make four open-faced chicken and ham sandwiches. Arrange sandwiches in a single layer in a baking pan; cover (with lid or aluminum foil) and place in a slow oven (300° F) to warm while preparing the following sauce. Melt cheese in a double boiler; gradually stir in wine; add mustard and onion; heat piping hot. Place sandwiches on heated plates; pour some of the hot sauce over each one. Dust with paprika and serve at once. Serves four.

4 slices white bread, toasted and buttered
4 servings cooked white meat of chicken (or turkey)
4 thin slices boiled or baked ham
1 (8 oz.) package process Swiss cheese, sliced
⅓ cup dry white table wine
1 tablespoon prepared mustard (the light yellow variety)
1 tablespoon grated onion
Paprika

P.S. A good variation is made with crisp strips of bacon and thick slices of tomato in place of the chicken and ham.

———————◆———————

Deviled ham gives these chicken sandwiches a perky flavor, and the creamy sauce that tops them is delightful.

CHICKEN SANDWICHES MONTE RIO

Spread toast with deviled ham; top with slices of chicken. Place these open-faced sandwiches in a shallow baking pan. Blend soup, mayonnaise, and wine; heat to simmering; spoon mixture over sandwiches. Bake in a moderately hot oven (400° F) about ten minutes, or until sandwiches are piping hot. Dust with paprika and serve at once. Serves four.

4 slices white bread, toasted and buttered
1 small can deviled ham
4 generous servings cooked white meat of chicken (or turkey)
1 (10½ oz.) can condensed cream of mushroom soup
3 tablespoons mayonnaise
¼ cup dry or medium Sherry
Paprika

VEGETABLE MAIN DISHES

A good, lively-flavored bean dish is a happy choice for Sunday supper. All you need to go with it is a salad and some piping hot cheese-topped French bread.

If you're a chili-bean fan, try this recipe:

CHILI MIO

Sauté beef, onion, and garlic in oil until meat is no longer red, stirring with a fork so that meat is separated into small bits. Add consommé, water, wine, and seasonings. Bring to a boil, then cover and simmer, stirring frequently, for about one and one-half hours, or until mixture is still a little moist but no longer "juicy." Add undrained kidney beans; cover and simmer five minutes longer. Serve in heated soup bowls or individual casseroles. Serves five or six.

1½ pounds lean ground beef
1 large onion, chopped
1 clove garlic, chopped or put through garlic press
2 tablespoons salad oil
1 (10½ oz.) can condensed consommé
¾ cup water
½ cup dry red table wine
1 tablespoon cumin seed
1 tablespoon chili powder
2 teaspoons oregano
Salt to taste
2 (1 lb.) can red kidney beans (undrained)

Have you ever baked zucchini in a meat-and-tomato sauce (a spaghetti sauce, really) and served it as a main dish? This is the way I do it, and it's delicious:

BAKED ZUCCHINI, ITALIENNE

Heat oil in a large, heavy skillet or Dutch oven; add onion, garlic, and beef; cook, stirring frequently until meat is nicely browned. Add tomato sauce, wine, and seasonings; cover and simmer very gently for one hour, stirring occasionally. While sauce is cooking, wash zucchini and trim off ends. Parboil whole in salted water for ten minutes. Drain. When cool enough to handle; cut lengthwise in halves and arrange, (cut side up) in a single layer in a greased, shallow baking dish. Pour sauce over zucchini. Bake in a moderate oven (350° F) for 45 minutes. Serve with grated Parmesan cheese. Serves five or six.

3 tablespoons olive oil
1 medium-sized onion, chopped
1 clove garlic, chopped or put through garlic press
1 pound ground beef (or 2 cups ground leftover cooked beef)
3 (8 oz.) cans tomato sauce
1 cup dry red table wine
1 teaspoon mixed Italian seasoning
1 teaspoon sugar
  Salt and pepper to taste
10 or 12 small zucchini (about 2 pounds)
  Grated Parmesan cheese

P.S. You can use this same sauce with spaghetti. It's enough for one-half pound of the *pasta*.

------------------◆------------------

The *torta* in this next recipe is one of my all-time vegetable favorites. No, there's no wine in it. The creamed chicken that's served over it takes care of that.

CREAMED CHICKEN WITH VEGETABLE TORTA

Cook spinach and drain *thoroughly*. Scrub zucchini and trim off ends; slice it crosswise very thin. Heat oil in a heavy saucepan or skillet; add zucchini and stir well; cover and cook gently, stirring frequently, for about ten minutes, or just until tender. Combine spinach and zucchini with all remaining ingredients. Turn into greased 10 x 6 x 2-inch baking dish. Bake in a moderate oven (350° F) for 40 to 45 minutes, or until firm. Cut in squares and serve with *Creamed Chicken*.

VEGETABLE TORTA

2 (10 oz.) packages frozen chopped spinach
1 pound small zucchini
3 tablespoons olive oil
½ cup grated Parmesan cheese
½ cup fine, dry bread crumbs
4 eggs, slightly beaten
2 tablespoons chopped parsley
1 tablespoon grated onion
1 clove garlic, chopped or put through garlic press
  Pinch each of allspice, rosemary, and oregano
  Salt and pepper to taste

Melt butter and stir in flour; add stock and white wine; cook, stirring until mixture boils and thickens. Add cream, Sherry, seasonings, and chicken. Heat gently but thoroughly. Serve over squares of *Vegetable Torta.* Serves six.

CREAMED CHICKEN

¼ cup butter
¼ cup flour
1 cup chicken stock
⅓ cup dry white table wine
⅔ cup cream
1 tablespoon dry or medium Sherry
Dash each of nutmeg and paprika
Salt and pepper to taste
2 cups coarsely diced, cooked chicken (or turkey)

If The Main
Dish Is Meat

Nowhere does wine show off to better advantage as a recipe ingredient than in meat cookery. There isn't a meat dish with liquid involved that doesn't become nobler fare when a bit of wine goes in the kettle.

Take stew, for example. Wine lifts it from humbleness to aristocratic heights of flavor. What's more, wine has a happy way of helping to tenderize the stewing and braising cuts of meat, so a stew made with wine may well be a better stew from the texture standpoint, too.

This first recipe is a sort of American cousin to the French *Boeuf Bourguignon*. The secret of success here, as with all stews, is long, *slow* cooking. A gentle, barely perceptible bubbling is all the action there should be in the pot. Here's an excellent dish-of-honor for a company dinner:

BEEF STEW WITH RED WINE

Heat butter in a Dutch oven or a large, heavy skillet; brown cubes of meat slowly on all sides. Sprinkle flour over meat; stir well. Add all remaining ingredients except whole onions, mushrooms, and Brandy. Bring to a boil, then turn heat very low and simmer, covered, for about two and one-half hours, or until meat is fork-tender. Stir frequently, and if the gravy seems too thick, add a little of the liquid drained from the mushrooms. Shortly before serving, add the whole onions, mushrooms, and Brandy. Taste and correct seasoning, if necessary. Serves six to eight. Buttered macaroni, a green vegetable, and some nice crusty French bread (so there won't be a drop of gravy wasted!) are suggested accompaniments.

3 tablespoons butter or bacon drippings
3 pounds lean beef stew meat, cubed
2 tablespoons flour
2 carrots, diced
1 large onion, diced
1 clove garlic, chopped or put through garlic press
Several sprigs parsley, chopped
Pinch of thyme
1 bay leaf, crushed
4 whole allspice
1 (10½ oz.) can condensed consommé
1½ cups dry red table wine
Salt and pepper to taste
1 (1 lb.) can small whole onions, drained
1 (8 oz.) can mushrooms, drained
2 tablespoons Brandy

PARTY BEEF STEW

Cook salt pork slowly in a Dutch oven or other heavy kettle until crisp and golden brown. Add meat; brown nicely on all sides. Sprinkle flour over meat; stir well. Add wine and beef stock; cook, stirring constantly until gravy is smooth and slightly thickened. Add thyme, marjoram, salt, and pepper. Cover and simmer very, very gently for two hours, stirring frequently. Add vegetables; continue cooking for about 45 minutes, or until vegetables and meat are tender. Before serving, add parsley and correct seasoning as necessary. Serves five or six. Baked potatoes and a tossed salad go well with this dish.

¼ pound salt pork, cut in tiny cubes
2½ pounds lean beef stew meat, cubed
2 tablespoons flour
1 cup dry red table wine
1 cup beef stock or water
Dash each of thyme and marjoram
Salt and pepper to taste
12 small white onions, peeled
1 bunch carrots, scraped and cut crosswise in halves and lengthwise in quarters
½ pound fresh mushrooms, scrubbed and sliced
2 tablespoons chopped parsley

Marinating the meat for 24 hours in red wine and wine vinegar definitely cuts down the cooking time here. And the gingersnap-spiced gravy is delectable.

OLD WORLD BEEF STEW

2	pounds beef stew meat, cubed
1	large onion, sliced
1	carrot, sliced
1	stalk celery, diced
2	bay leaves
5	whole cloves
5	whole peppercorns
1½	cups dry red table wine
½	cup red wine vinegar
	Salt
3	tablespoons butter or bacon drippings
1	(10½ oz.) can condensed consommé
¼	cup flour
¼	cup cold water
⅓	cup fine gingersnap crumbs
2	cups diced carrots, cooked
1	(1 lb.) can small whole onions, drained

Place meat in a deep bowl; add sliced onion, carrot, celery, bay leaves, cloves, peppercorns, wine, vinegar, and one teaspoon salt; mix well. Cover and let stand in the refrigerator for 24 hours, stirring occasionally. Remove meat from marinade and dry with paper towels. Strain and reserve marinade. Heat butter in a Dutch oven or other heavy kettle; brown meat nicely on all sides. Add strained marinade and consommé; cover and simmer gently for about one and one-half hours, or until meat is fork-tender. Remove meat from liquid. Measure liquid and add water to make three cupfuls; return to kettle. Blend flour with the cold water until smooth; gradually blend in some of the meat liquid; stir this mixture into liquid in kettle. Add gingersnap crumbs. Cook, stirring until mixture boils and is smoothly thickened. Taste and add salt, if needed. Return meat to kettle; add cooked carrots and whole onions; heat thoroughly before serving. Serves four to six. Perfect accompaniments are potato pancakes and a beet salad.

For variety, top your stew with a pastry lid and transform it into a meat pie.

EL RANCHO BEEFSTEAK PIE

Trim excess fat from meat. Pound flour into both sides of meat with a meat tenderizer or the edge of a heavy saucer. Cut meat in bite-sized cubes or strips. Heat bacon drippings in a large, heavy skillet or Dutch oven; sauté meat and onion until meat is nicely browned. Add wine, water, soya sauce, thyme, salt, and pepper; bring to a boil, then cover and simmer gently, stirring frequently for 45 minutes. Add carrots and celery; continue cooking for about 45 minutes, or until meat and vegetables are tender. Meantime, prepare corn meal pastry by stirring corn meal into sifted flour and salt and then proceeding as for plain pastry; roll out into a circle large enough to fit over top of a two-quart casserole and set aside. When meat, carrots, and celery are tender, add peas; correct seasoning; pour into the casserole. Cover with the rolled pastry; cut gashes in pastry to permit escape of steam. Bake in a hot oven (450° F) for 25 to 30 minutes, or until crust is browned. Serves four to six.

2 pounds round steak, cut 1 inch thick
⅓ cup flour
¼ cup bacon drippings or salad oil
1 medium-sized onion, chopped
1 cup dry red table wine
1 cup water
1 tablespoon soya sauce
Pinch of thyme
Salt and pepper to taste
1½ cups diced raw carrots
1 cup diced raw celery
Corn meal pastry (1 cup sifted all-purpose flour, ½ teaspoon salt, ¼ cup yellow corn meal, 6 tablespoons shortening, and approximately 3 to 4 tablespoons cold water)
1 cup cooked peas

Stew with a foreign accent, you might call this:

HUNGARIAN GOULASH

Heat butter and oil in a large, heavy skillet; add onions and sauté gently, stirring frequently, for five minutes. Push onions to one side of pan; add meat and sauté until browned. Add remaining ingredients. Bring to a boil, then cover and simmer very gently, stirring occasionally, for about two and one-half hours, or until meat is fork-tender. Before serving, taste and add salt, if needed. Serves four to six. Buttered noodles are a "must" with this dish.

2 tablespoons butter
2 tablespoons salad oil
1 pound onions, peeled and thinly sliced
2 pounds lean beef stew meat, cubed
1 cup dry red table wine
1 cup diced fresh or well-drained canned tomatoes
1 teaspoon caraway seeds
1 teaspoon paprika
Dash each of thyme and marjoram
Salt and pepper to taste

The familiar Swiss steak tastes better than ever when there's wine in the ingredient list. Try it this way:

SWISS STEAK BURGUNDY

Trim excess fat from meat. Mix flour, one and one-half teaspoons salt, and one-half teaspoon pepper. Pound mixture into both sides of meat with a meat tenderizer or the edge of a heavy saucer. Cut meat in serving-sized portions. Heat bacon drippings in a large, heavy skillet or a Dutch oven; brown meat nicely on both sides. Blend beef stock, wine, and tomato paste; pour over meat. Add vegetables. Season with sugar, thyme, marjoram, salt, and pepper. Cover and simmer gently for one and one-half to two hours, or until meat is tender, turning meat occasionally. Serves four to six. Elegant with mashed or baked potatoes and a green vegetable or a salad.

2 pounds round steak, cut 1 inch thick
½ cup flour
Salt and pepper
4 tablespoons bacon drippings or salad oil
1 cup beef stock or canned consommé
½ cup dry red table wine
1 (6 oz.) can tomato paste
1 large onion, chopped
1 green pepper, chopped
1 cup diced carrots
1 cup diced celery
1 teaspoon sugar
Dash each of thyme and marjoram

Yorkshire pudding is so good that it's a shame to make it the exclusive property of roast beef! I like it with any "gravied" meat or chicken dish such as:

BRAISED BEEF WITH YORKSHIRE PUDDING

2 pounds round steak, cut 1 inch thick
½ cup flour
¼ cup bacon drippings or salad oil
1 (10½ oz.) can condensed consommé
½ cup dry red table wine
1 tablespoon tomato paste
1 large onion, chopped
1 bay leaf
Dash each of thyme and marjoram
Salt and pepper to taste
1 (8 oz.) can mushroom stems and pieces, drained
2 tablespoons chopped parsley
2 tablespoons dry or medium Sherry

Trim excess fat from meat. Pound flour into both sides of meat with a meat tenderizer or the edge of a heavy saucer. Cut meat into strips about one-half inch wide and two inches long. Heat bacon drippings in a large, heavy skillet or Dutch oven; brown strips of meat nicely on all sides. Add consommé, red wine, tomato paste, onion, bay leaf, thyme, marjoram, salt, and pepper. Cover and simmer gently for about one and one-half hours, or until meat is fork-tender. Stir frequently and add a little water if gravy becomes too thick. Before serving, stir in mushrooms, parsley, and Sherry; correct seasoning. Serve with *Yorkshire Pudding*. Serves four to six.

Yorkshire Pudding: Mix one cup sifted all-purpose flour and one-half teaspoon salt. Combine two well-beaten eggs with one cup milk; add gradually to flour, beating just until smooth. Heat one-fourth cup beef or bacon drippings sizzling hot in a 9 x 9 x 2 inch baking dish. Pour batter into this hot dish. Bake at once in a hot oven (450° F) for 25 to 30 minutes, or until puffed and browned. Cut in squares and serve immediately.

SWISS STEAK WITH MUSHROOMS

Trim excess fat from meat. Mix flour, one and one-half teaspoons salt, and one-half teaspoon pepper. Pound mixture into both sides of meat, using a meat tenderizer or the edge of a heavy saucer. Cut meat into serving-sized portions. Heat bacon drippings in a large, heavy skillet or a Dutch oven; brown pieces of meat nicely on both sides. Add all remaining ingredients (including mushroom liquid); season with salt and pepper. Cover and bake in a moderate oven (350° F) (or cook gently over low heat) from one and one-half to two hours, or until meat is tender. Turn and baste meat occasionally, and add a little water if needed to keep gravy from becoming too thick. Serves four to six.

2 pounds round steak, cut 1 inch thick
½ cup flour
Salt and pepper
3 tablespoons bacon drippings or salad oil
1 medium-sized onion, chopped
1 clove garlic, chopped or put through garlic press
1 cup diced celery
1 cup tomato catsup
½ cup dry or medium Sherry
1 (8 oz.) can mushroom stems and pieces (undrained)

There's a very good-to-eat surprise inside these beefsteak rolls.

BEEF ROLL-UPS

Wrap a strip of bacon around each dill pickle quarter. Roll each steak around a bacon-wrapped pickle; secure with skewers or toothpicks. Roll steaks in flour seasoned with salt and pepper. Heat bacon drippings in a large, heavy skillet; brown rolls nicely on all sides. Add catsup, wine, and onion. Cover and simmer gently for about one hour, or until meat is tender. Turn rolls occasionally during cooking and add a little water if necessary to keep gravy from becoming too thick. Remove skewers or toothpicks before serving. Serves four.

4 slices bacon
1 dill pickle, quartered lengthwise
4 serving-sized cube steaks
Flour
Salt and pepper
3 tablespoons bacon drippings or salad oil
½ cup catsup
½ cup dry red table wine
2 tablespoons minced onion

Here thin slices of round steak are rolled around a well-seasoned bread stuffing and simmered to tenderness in a wine-flavored gravy.

BRAISED BEEFSTEAK ROLLS

2 pounds round steak, cut ¼ inch thick
Salt and pepper
2 cups grated soft bread crumbs
¼ cup melted butter
2 tablespoons minced onion
¼ teaspoon poultry seasoning
Flour
¼ cup bacon drippings or salad oil
1 cup dry red table wine
1 cup beef stock or water
2 tablespoons chopped parsley

Cut round steak into 12 pieces about four by two inches. Sprinkle with salt and pepper and pound with a meat tenderizer or the edge of a heavy saucer to flatten pieces slightly. Mix bread crumbs, butter, onion, and poultry seasoning; season to taste with salt and pepper. Spread mixture on pieces of meat; roll up; tie securely with string or fasten with skewers or toothpicks. Dredge rolls with flour. Heat bacon drippings in a large, heavy skillet; brown rolls nicely on all sides. Remove rolls from skillet. Add two tablespoons flour to drippings and blend well; add wine and beef stock; cook, stirring constantly, until gravy boils and thickens; season to taste with salt and pepper. Return rolls to skillet. Cover tightly and simmer gently for one to one and one-half hours, or until meat is very tender, turning rolls occasionally. Remove string, skewers, or toothpicks and place rolls on a heated platter. Add parsley to gravy; pour over rolls. Serves six.

P.S. Sautéed fresh or drained canned mushrooms may be added to the gravy before serving, if desired.

———◄►———

Stuffed flank steak is one of my favorite braised meat dishes. Try it this delicious way.

BRAISED STUFFED FLANK STEAK

Have meat dealer score flank steak. Mix crumbs, onion, pickle relish, and melted butter; season with salt and pepper. Spread this stuffing evenly over steak. Roll up, from one wide side to the other, tucking in the ends as you roll. Fasten roll securely with skewers or string. Dredge with flour. Heat bacon drippings in a large, heavy skillet or a roasting pan; brown steak slowly on all sides. Add tomato sauce, wine, and salt and pepper to taste. Cover and simmer gently (or bake at 350° F) from one and one-half to two hours, or until meat is tender, turning steak occasionally. To serve, remove skewers or string from steak and place on a heated platter; carve crosswise in one-inch slices. Pour a little gravy over steak and pass remainder separately. Serves five or six.

1 flank steak (1½ to 2 pounds)
2 cups grated soft bread crumbs
½ cup very finely chopped onion
½ cup well-drained sweet pickle relish
¼ cup melted butter
Salt and pepper to taste
Flour
3 tablespoons bacon drippings or salad oil
2 (8 oz.) cans tomato sauce
½ cup dry red table wine

BARBECUED SHORTRIBS

Dredge shortribs with flour seasoned with salt and pepper. Heat bacon drippings in a Dutch oven or other heavy kettle; brown shortribs nicely on all sides. Mix tomato sauce, wine, stock, wine vinegar, onion, garlic, sugar, Worcestershire sauce, thyme, and marjoram; add salt and pepper to taste; pour over shortribs. Cover and simmer gently, stirring occasionally, for one and one-half to two hours, or until shortribs are almost tender. Add carrots; continue cooking for about one-half hour, or until meat and carrots are tender. Remove meat and carrots from kettle.

3 pounds beef shortribs, cut in pieces for serving
Flour
Salt and pepper
2 tablespoons bacon drippings or salad oil
1 (8 oz.) can tomato sauce
½ cup dry Vermouth
½ cup beef stock or water
2 tablespoons red wine vinegar
1 large onion, chopped
1 clove garlic, chopped or put through garlic press
1 tablespoon brown sugar
1 teaspoon Worcestershire sauce
Dash each of thyme and marjoram
4 carrots, sliced
2 tablespoons chopped parsley

To make gravy: Pour liquid from kettle into a bowl or measuring pitcher; skim off fat. Measure liquid and add stock or water, if necessary to make two cups. Measure two tablespoons fat back into the kettle; blend in two tablespoons flour; add the two cups liquid and cook, stirring constantly, until gravy boils and thickens. Season to taste with salt and pepper. Add parsley. Return shortribs and carrots to kettle. Heat thoroughly before serving. Serves four.

Here is another wonderful way to prepare flank steak:

FLANK STEAK WITH SPINACH STUFFING

Have meat dealer score flank steak. Mix bread crumbs, spinach, cheese, egg, two tablespoons olive oil, sage, thyme, marjoram, salt, and pepper. Spread mixture evenly over steak; roll up from one wide side to the other, tucking in the ends as you roll. Tie or skewer securely. Dredge rolled steak with flour. Heat bacon drippings in a large, heavy skillet or a roasting pan; brown steak slowly on all sides. Mix tomato sauce, wine, beef stock, onion, and garlic; add a dash of thyme and marjoram and salt and pepper to taste; pour over browned steak. Cover tightly and simmer gently (or bake at 350° F) for one and one-half to two hours, or until meat is very tender. Turn steak occasionally during cooking, and add a little water if necessary to keep gravy from becoming too thick. Remove string or skewers; place steak on heated platter and garnish with parsley or watercress; slice, cutting across fibers. Serve gravy separately. Serves five or six.

1 flank steak (1½ to 2 pounds)
1 cup grated soft bread crumbs
1 (10 oz.) package frozen chopped spinach, cooked and well drained
¼ cup grated Parmesan cheese
1 egg, slightly beaten
2 tablespoons olive oil
¼ teaspoon sage
Dash of thyme and marjoram
Salt and pepper to taste
Flour
3 tablespoons bacon drippings or olive oil
1 (8 oz.) can tomato sauce
½ cup dry red table wine
½ cup beef stock
1 small onion, chopped
1 clove garlic, chopped or put through garlic press

My first choice in pot roasts is a boned beef chuck, rolled and tied.

These two recipes are my favorites:

FRENCH POT ROAST

Cook bacon slowly in a Dutch oven or other heavy kettle for five minutes. Add meat and brown slowly and thoroughly on all sides. Add all remaining ingredients. Bring to a boil, then cover tightly and simmer very, very gently for three to four hours, or until meat is tender, turning meat occasionally. Remove meat from kettle and if it's to be served in the near future, set it where it will keep warm. If dinner is still a while away, simply set the roast aside and reheat it gently in the gravy before serving.

4 slices bacon, "diced" with scissors
4 to 5 pounds beef chuck, rolled and tied
1 (10½ oz.) can condensed consommé
1 cup dry red table wine
2 carrots, diced
1 large onion, diced
1 clove garlic, halved
6 whole allspice
8 whole peppercorns
1 bay leaf, crushed
Several sprigs parsley
Pinch of thyme
Salt and pepper to taste

To make gravy: Strain broth and skim off as much of the fat as possible. Measure three cups broth, adding beef stock or water if necessary to make that amount; pour back into kettle and heat to boiling. Blend one-third cup flour and one-half cup cold beef stock or water until smooth; stir slowly into boiling broth; continue cooking and stirring until mixture is thickened and smooth, then simmer five minutes longer. Add two tablespoons Brandy (if you like) and salt and pepper to taste. Serve gravy piping hot with the roast. Serves eight or more.

ITALIAN POT ROAST

Dredge meat with flour seasoned with salt and pepper. Heat bacon drippings in a Dutch oven or other heavy kettle; brown meat slowly and thoroughly on all sides. Add all remaining ingredients; season to taste with salt and pepper. Cover and simmer gently for three to four hours, or until meat is tender, turning occasionally. Remove from kettle. Make gravy as directed in the recipe for *French Pot Roast*, omitting Brandy. Serves eight or more.

4 to 5 pounds beef chuck, rolled and tied
Flour
Salt and pepper
2 tablespoons bacon drippings or olive oil
1 cup dry red table wine
1 (8 oz.) can tomato sauce
½ cup finely chopped onion
½ cup finely chopped celery
¼ cup finely chopped parsley
¼ teaspoon oregano
¼ teaspoon sweet basil

P.S. Another very fine-flavored roast can be prepared using one cup of dry or medium Sherry in place of the red table wine called for in the recipe for *Italian Pot Roast*.

———◆———

While we're on the subject of pot roasts, we musn't forget *sauerbraten*, the spicily delicious German specialty that depends for much of its flavor and tenderness on a red wine-wine vinegar marinade.

SAUERBRATEN

Place meat in a large bowl. Combine all remaining ingredients except bacon drippings; pour over meat. Cover and let stand in the refrigerator for three or four days, turning meat each day. Remove meat from marinade. Dry meat thoroughly with paper towels. Strain marinade. Heat bacon drippings in a Dutch oven or other large, heavy kettle; brown meat *slowly* and thoroughly on all sides. Pour strained marinade over meat. Cover and simmer very gently for about three hours, or until meat is tender, turning meat occasionally. Remove meat to a platter and keep warm, or set aside to be reheated later in the gravy.	4 to 5 pounds beef chuck, rolled and tied 1 cup dry red table wine ½ cup red wine vinegar ½ cup water 2 onions, sliced 3 bay leaves 10 whole peppercorns 10 whole cloves 1 tablespoon sugar 1 teaspoon dry mustard ¼ teaspoon each: thyme and powdered ginger 1 teaspoon salt 3 tablespoon bacon drippings or salad oil

To make gravy: Pour broth from kettle and skim off as much of the fat as possible. Measure three cups broth, adding beef stock or water if necessary to make that amount; pour back into kettle and heat to boiling. Blend one-third cup flour with one-half cold beef stock or water until smooth; stir slowly into boiling broth; continue cooking and stirring until mixture is thickened and smooth, then simmer five minutes longer. Add two tablespoons tomato paste, two tablespoons dry or medium Sherry, and salt to taste. Serve piping hot. Serves eight or more. Potato pancakes are traditional with this.

———◆———

If I have a pound of ground beef in the refrigerator, my menu worries are over! Maybe it will appear on the table as broiled hamburger steak for two, maybe as a tempting casserole of meat balls for five or six. In any case, the main dish will be good.

HAMBURGER STEAKS

Combine these ingredients *lightly* but thoroughly. (A fork is best for this.) Shape into two nice fat steaks (or three, if your appetites aren't as hearty as ours). Broil or panbroil until they're done to your liking. While steaks are cooking, heat together three tablespoons butter, two tablespoons dry red table wine, two teaspoons Worcestershire sauce, and one to two tablespoons chopped parsley. Place cooked steaks on dinner plates and spoon some of the butter-wine sauce over each one. Serves two or three.

1 pound ground beef (I like chuck)
1 teaspoon salt
¼ teaspoon coarse black pepper
¼ cup dry red table wine
1 to 2 tablespoons grated onion (if you like)

And now some variations on the hamburger-steak theme.

SALISBURY STEAKS WITH MUSHROOM SAUCE

Mix beef lightly with cream, onion, one teaspoon salt, and one-fourth teaspoon pepper. Shape into three or four thick patties. Heat butter in a large, heavy skillet; brown patties quickly on both sides. Remove patties from skillet. Add flour to the drippings and blend well; add consommé and wine; cook, stirring constantly, until mixture boils and thickens. Add Worcestershire sauce, parsley, and mushrooms (including liquid). Season to taste with salt and pepper. Return patties to sauce; simmer until meat is as done as desired. (If you like your meat rare, just heat the patties through.) Place on toast and pour sauce over all. Serves three or four.

1 pound ground beef
½ cup cream or rich milk
1 tablespoon grated onion
Salt and coarse black pepper
2 tablespoons butter or bacon drippings
2 tablespoons flour
½ cup canned consommé
½ cup dry red table wine
1 teaspoon Worcestershire sauce
2 tablespoons chopped parsley
1 (4 oz.) can mushrooms (undrained)
3 or 4 slices toast

Lemon juice and peel give the sauce for these patties real "character."

BEEF PATTIES BUENA VISTA

Lightly mix beef, crumbs, milk, onion, one teaspoon salt, and one-fourth teaspoon pepper; shape into eight little fat patties. Heat butter in a large, heavy skillet; brown patties nicely on both sides. Pour off almost all the drippings. Meantime, mix remaining ingredients in a saucepan; heat, stirring, until bouillon cubes are dissolved; add salt to taste. Pour sauce over browned patties; cover and simmer 30 minutes, turning and basting patties occasionally. Serve on toast so that none of the good sauce will be wasted. Serves four.

1 pound ground beef
1 cup (firmly packed) grated soft bread crumbs
½ cup milk
2 tablespoons grated onion
Salt and pepper
2 tablespoons butter or bacon drippings
1 cup dry red table wine
½ cup catsup
¼ cup lemon juice
1 tablespoon Worcestershire sauce
2 beef bouillon cubes (or 2 teaspoons beef stock base)
¼ cup chopped parsley
1 teaspoon grated lemon peel
2 tablespoons sugar

These next three meat-ball recipes are special pets of mine. They're good to eat, and they make a little meat go a long way! All of them call for buttered noodles, rice, or mashed potatoes as an accompaniment.

MEAT BALLS WITH ONION SAUCE

Mix beef, bread crumbs, cream, egg, one teaspoon salt, and one-fourth teaspoon pepper. Take up mixture by rounded teaspoonfuls and shape into balls. Heat butter in a large, heavy skillet; add meat balls and brown nicely on all sides. Remove balls from pan. Add flour to pan drippings and blend well; add onion soup and water; cook, stirring constantly, until mixture is thickened and smooth; add Sherry, parsley, and salt and pepper to taste. Return balls to sauce; cover tightly and simmer gently for 20 minutes, shaking pan occasionally to turn balls. Serves five or six.

1 pound ground beef
1 cup (firmly packed) grated soft bread crumbs
½ cup cream
1 egg, slightly beaten
Salt and pepper
4 tablespoons butter or bacon drippings
3 tablespoons flour
1 (10½ oz.) can condensed onion soup
¾ cup water
½ cup dry or medium Sherry
2 tablespoons chopped parsley

SWEDISH MEAT BALLS

Combine beef, cornflake crumbs, milk, egg, onion, mace, allspice, one teaspoon salt, and one-fourth teaspoon pepper; mix lightly but thoroughly. Shape mixture into small balls, using one level tablespoonful per ball. Heat butter in a large, heavy skillet; brown balls nicely on all sides, shaking pan gently from time to time to turn balls and brown them evenly. Remove balls from skillet. Pour off all fat; measure three tablespoons and return to skillet. Blend in flour; add stock and cream; cook, stirring, until mixture boils and thickens; add wine; season with salt and pepper. Return meat balls to pan. Cover and simmer for 25 minutes, shaking pan gently several times to turn balls. Just before serving, stir in parsley. Serves five or six.

1   pound ground beef
1   cup cornflake crumbs
½   cup milk
1   egg, slightly beaten
¼   cup very finely chopped onion
¼   teaspoon each: mace and all spice
    Salt and pepper
3   tablespoons butter or bacon drippings
3   tablespoons flour
1½ cups beef or chicken stock
½   cup cream or rich milk
½   cup dry white table wine
2   tablespoons chopped parsley

NELL'S MEAT BALLS

Mix beef, corn chips, milk, egg, one teaspoon salt, and one-eighth teaspoon pepper. Shape mixture into balls the size of large marbles. Heat butter in a large skillet; brown balls nicely on all sides. Remove balls from skillet. Pour off all but three tablespoons drippings from skillet. Add onion and garlic to drippings in skillet; sauté gently until golden. Add flour and blend well; add tomatoes and wine; cook, stirring constantly, until sauce boils and thickens. Season to taste with salt and pepper. Return balls to sauce. Cover and simmer gently, stirring occasionally, for 30 minutes. Serves four or five.

1   pound ground beef
½   cup finely crushed corn chips
½   cup milk
1   egg, slightly beaten
    Salt and pepper
2   tablespoons butter or bacon drippings
1   medium-sized onion, minced
1   clove garlic, minced or put through garlic press
2   tablespoons flour
1   (1 lb.) can stewed tomatoes
½   cup dry red table wine

I love to share recipes, but it was a long time before I could bring myself to part with this one. Friends raved about these meat balls when I served them at supper parties, and then when they asked me for the how-to's I couldn't bear to admit that I hadn't been slaving over the proverbial hot stove all day! Finally my conscience, or maybe my ego, forced me to divulge the secrets of this delectable and easy dish.

MEAT BALLS STROGANOFF

In a heavy skillet or saucepan, blend sour cream and flour; stir in liquid from mushrooms. Add mushrooms and meat balls with their gravy; mix gently (with a wooden spoon or rubber spatula), taking care not to break the tender balls. Add remaining ingredients. Cover and simmer very, very slowly for 15 to 20 minutes, stirring often. Remove from heat and let stand, uncovered, for at least an hour so that flavors can blend. Cover and reheat gently before serving. Serves four. With some simple arithmetic (and very little additional effort) you can increase this recipe to serve 16 to 24 or more. A grand dish for a crowd, and men seem to love it!

½ cup dairy sour cream
1 tablespoon flour
1 (4 oz.) can mushrooms stems and pieces
2 (10½ oz.) cans meat balls in gravy
2 tablespoons dry or medium Sherry
1 teaspoon Worcestershire sauce
1 tablespoon chopped parsley
Salt, garlic salt, and pepper to taste

A meat-loaf-with-glamour dish is:

CHEESEBURGER PIE

In a mixing bowl combine the beef, bread crumbs, eggs, onion, green pepper, wine, horseradish, and salt. Mix well, preferably with the hands. Pack mixture into an ungreased baking dish 8 x 8 x 2 inches. Spread tomato sauce over the top. Bake in a moderate oven (350° F) for one hour. Remove from oven and arrange cheese slices over pie. Return to oven just long enough to melt the cheese. Serves six.

2 pounds ground lean beef
2 cups (firmly packed) grated soft bread crumbs
2 eggs, slightly beaten
1 onion, minced or ground
1 green pepper, minced or ground
⅓ cup dry red table wine
1 tablespoon prepared horseradish
2 teaspoons salt
1 (8 oz.) can tomato sauce
¼ pound process American or Cheddar cheese, thinly sliced

I once sent a slightly different version of this pie to a recipe contest, hoping it would win me $10,000! It didn't, but to my palate it has a ten thousand-dollar flavor. With a vegetable salad, it makes a perfect supper dish.

BEEF PIE VIENNA

Line a nine-inch pie plate with pastry, making a nice high, fluted rim, because this is going to be a generously filled pie. Prick shell thoroughly on bottom and sides to prevent puffing during baking. Bake in a hot oven (425° F) for ten minutes, then let it cool while you prepare the filling as follows:

Heat butter in a large, heavy skillet; sauté onions and garlic about ten minutes, or until tender. Don't let them brown! Add meat; cook until it is no longer red, stirring with a fork to separate it into bits. Sprinkle flour over meat; stir well. Add seasonings. Remove skillet from heat. Blend eggs, sour cream, and Sherry; add to meat and mix well. Add parsley. Pour into prepared crust. Bake in a moderate oven (350° F) about 35 minutes, or until a knife inserted in the center comes out clean. Remove from oven and let stand ten minutes or so before cutting. Serves four to six, depending on appetites and the rest of the menu.

FILLING

- 3 tablespoons butter
- 1 cup very thinly sliced onions
- 1 small clove garlic, chopped or put through garlic press (if you like)
- 1 pound lean ground beef
- 2 tablespoons flour
- 1½ teaspoons Worcestershire sauce
- 1½ teaspoons salt
- ¼ teaspoon pepper
- 3 eggs, slightly beaten
- 1 cup dairy sour cream
- 3 tablespoons dry or medium Sherry
- 3 tablespoons chopped parsley

P.S. For *Tuna or Crab Pie Vienna,* follow the recipe above for *Beef Pie Vienna* with these changes: Substitute two (6½ oz.) cans chunk-style tuna or two cups flaked crabmeat for the beef. Reduce salt to one teaspoon. Cook onions; stir in tuna or crabmeat, then flour and seasonings. Remove from heat and proceed as directed above. With a salad, either of these pies makes a very good main dish for a buffet luncheon.

A pork chop, well prepared, is food for a king. Treated indifferently it will come to the table dry and tasteless—a deplorable dish! I hope you'll agree with me that the pork chop recipes given here all produce regal results.

BRAISED PORK CHOPS IN TOMATO SAUCE

Sprinkle pork chops with salt and pepper; dredge with flour. Brown slowly on both sides in a large, heavy skillet, using a little fat trimmed from the chops. Pour off excess fat. Mix tomato paste, water, and wine; add carrot, green pepper, onion, garlic, sugar, thyme, marjoram, and salt and pepper to taste. Pour sauce over chops. Cover tightly and cook slowly for one hour or longer, until chops are tender, turning chops occasionally. Before serving, taste and correct seasoning. Serves four. Buttered rice, with lots of chopped parsley added, is good with these.

4 pork chops, cut 1¼ to 1½ inches thick
Salt and pepper
Flour
1 (6 oz.) can tomato paste
1 cup water
½ cup dry red table wine
1 medium-sized carrot, scraped and grated
2 tablespoons grated green pepper
2 tablespoons grated onion
1 clove garlic, grated or put through garlic press
1 teaspoon sugar
Dash each of thyme and marjoram

HUNGARIAN PORK CHOPS

Sprinkle pork chops with salt and pepper; dredge with flour. Brown slowly on both sides in a large, heavy skillet, using a little fat trimmed from the chops. Pour off excess fat. Mix remaining ingredients; add salt and pepper to taste; pour over chops. Cover and simmer gently for one hour or longer, until chops are tender, turning and basting chops occasionally. Serves four.

4 pork chops, cut 1¼ to 1½ inches thick
Salt and pepper
Flour
½ cup dairy sour cream
⅓ cup dry or medium Sherry
¼ cup catsup
½ teaspoon Worcestershire sauce
¼ teaspoon paprika

BAKED PORK CHOPS MOANA

Place chops in a single layer in a shallow baking pan. Mix wine and soya sauce; pour over chops. Let stand at room temperature one hour or so, turning three or four times. Bake, uncovered, in a moderate oven (350° F) for one hour, turning and basting chops occasionally. Meantime, cut a thin slice from the stem end of each pepper; remove seeds and fibrous portion; parboil peppers in boiling water for five minutes. Drain thoroughly and cut each pepper crosswise into three rings. At end of the one hour baking time, remove chops from oven. Place a ring of pineapple on each chop; top pineapple with a green pepper ring and fill the ring with rice. Pour pineapple syrup over all. Return to 350° F oven and continue baking, uncovered, for 30 minutes, basting chops three or four times with the pan juices. To serve, place chops on a platter or dinner plates and pour some of the juices over each one. Serves six. Green peas and a tossed salad are good accompaniments.

6 pork chops, cut about 1¼ inches thick
⅔ cup dry or medium Sherry
¼ cup soya sauce
2 green peppers
6 rings canned pineapple
2 cups cooked white rice (approximately)
1 cup syrup from canned pineapple

Stuffed pork chops are a perfect dinner-party dish, not too hard to prepare and so simple to serve. Try them this way:

STUFFED PORK CHOPS IN ORANGE SAUCE

Have chops slit from fat side to bone to form a pocket. Mix bread crumbs, onion, and three tablespoons of the melted butter; season with salt and pepper. Fill pockets of pork chops with this stuffing; fasten openings securely with skewers or toothpicks. Heat a large, heavy skillet; grease it with a bit of fat trimmed from the chops; brown chops slowly on both sides. Pour off fat from skillet. In a saucepan blend remaining three tablespoons melted butter with the flour; add orange juice, wine, and water; cook, stirring, until mixture boils and thickens. Add brown sugar, orange peel, lemon peel, and salt to taste; pour sauce over browned chops. Cover and simmer gently about one and one-quarter hours, or until chops are tender. Turn and baste chops occasionally, and add a little additional water if gravy becomes too thick. Serves four. Fluffy mashed sweet potatoes and a spinach ring filled with buttered whole-kernel corn are perfect with these.

4 pork chops, cut about 1¼ inches thick
2 cups (firmly packed) grated soft bread crumbs
2 tablespoons grated onion
6 tablespoons melted butter
Salt and pepper to taste
3 tablespoons flour
1 cup orange juice
½ cup dry white table wine
¼ cup water
¼ cup brown sugar
2 tablespoons grated orange peel
1 teaspoon grated lemon peel

Just thinking about how good baked spareribs can be makes my mouth water! Here are three ways to do them, the first two simplicity itself, the other a little longer on ingredients, but still easy.

SIMPLE SIMON SPARERIBS

Arrange spareribs in a single layer in a large, shallow baking pan. Mix remaining ingredients; pour over ribs. Bake, uncovered, in a moderate oven (350° F) for one and three-quarters to two hours, turning and basting ribs frequently. When the ribs are done, most of the fat will have cooked out of them and they will be deliciously glazed, tender, and flavorful. Serves four or five. Suggested menu: *Simple Simon Spareribs*, baked potatoes, green peas, and hot applesauce.

4 pounds meaty spareribs, cut in pieces for serving
⅔ cup dry or medium Sherry
3 tablespoons red wine vinegar
⅔ cup (firmly packed) brown sugar
¼ cup soya sauce

SPARERIBS WAIKIKI

Sprinkle spareribs with salt and pepper. Arrange, meaty side up, in a single layer in a shallow baking pan. Mix cornstarch and brown sugar in a saucepan; stir in pineapple, vinegar, wine, and soya sauce; stir over medium heat until mixture boils and thickens. Pour sauce over spareribs. Bake, uncovered, in a moderate oven (350° F) for one and one-quarter hours, basting occasionally. Arrange sweet potatoes around spareribs. Continue baking about one-half hour, basting occasionally. Serves four or five.

3½ pounds spareribs, cut in pieces for serving
Salt and pepper
1 tablespoon cornstarch
¼ cup (firmly packed) brown sugar
1 (9 oz.) can crushed pineapple (undrained)
⅓ cup red wine vinegar
½ cup dry or medium Sherry
2 tablespoons soya sauce
4 or 5 servings boiled sweet potatoes

SAVORY SPARERIBS

4 pounds meaty spareribs, cut in pieces for serving
1 cup chili sauce
½ cup dry Vermouth
½ cup water
¼ cup chopped onion
    Bit of chopped or pressed garlic (if you like)
1 teaspoon Worcestershire sauce
    Salt and pepper to taste

Arrange spareribs in a single layer in a large, shallow baking pan. Mix remaining ingredients; pour over ribs. Bake, uncovered, in a moderate oven (350° F) for one and three-quarters to two hours, turning and basting ribs frequently. Serves four or five. Good with mashed potatoes and buttered green beans to which a generous sprinkling of celery seed has been added.

The dessert wines make wonderful "basters" for baked ham during the glazing period. Here are some good illustrations:

WINE-BASTED BAKED HAM

Place ham, fat side up, on a rack in a shallow roasting pan. Bake, uncovered, in a slow oven (325° F). If your ham is labeled *Fully-Cooked*, allow approximately three hours for a whole 12- to 15-pound ham, two and one-quarter hours for a six-pound half-ham (to internal temperature of 130° F on a meat thermometer). If it is labeled *Cook-Before-Eating*, allow approximately three and one-half to four hours for a 10- to 12-pound whole ham, four to four and one-half hours for a 12- to 15-pound one, three and one-quarter hours for a six-pound half-ham (to 160° F on meat thermometer).

Half an hour before the ham is finished baking, remove it from the oven. Pour off the drippings from the pan. Remove the skin from the ham. With a sharp knife, score the fat in diamond shapes, one-quarter inch deep. Then proceed in one of these ways:

Honey-Port Glazed Ham: Spread prepared mustard thinly over ham and stick with whole cloves. Mix one cup strained honey, one-half cup Port, and one-half teaspoon cinnamon; pour over ham. Continue baking for 30 minutes, basting frequently.

Baked Ham Muscatel with Peaches: Spread ham with a mixture of one cup brown sugar, two tablespoons cornstarch, and one-half teaspoon ground cloves. Around ham arrange canned peach halves, cut side up;

place a spoonful of currant or grape jelly in the hollow of each half. Mix one cup Muscatel and one-half cup syrup from canned peaches; pour over ham and peaches. Continue baking 30 minutes, basting ham and peaches frequently.

Orange-Sherry Glazed Ham: Mix one cup (firmly packed) brown sugar, one teaspoon dry mustard, one-half cup sweet Sherry, one-half cup orange juice, and two tablespoons grated orange peel. Spread mixture over ham. Continue baking 30 minutes, basting often.

◆

If you're hungry for ham but not in the mood for a whole one or even a half, a nice, thick, center-cut slice, baked in an interesting sauce is just the ticket.

BAKED HAM SLICE WITH FRUIT SAUCE

1 (2-inch) center-cut slice smoked ham
1 tablespoon prepared mustard
1 (1 lb.) can fruit cocktail
1 tablespoon cornstarch
¼ cup (firmly packed) brown sugar
¼ teaspoon cinnamon
¼ teaspoon ground cloves
½ cup Port, Muscatel, or sweet Sherry

Cut gashes at two-inch intervals in the ham fat to prevent slice from curling during cooking. Place ham in a baking pan; spread with prepared mustard. Drain and reserve syrup from fruit cocktail. Mix cornstarch, brown sugar, and spices in a saucepan; gradually stir in fruit-cocktail syrup and wine. Stir over medium heat until mixture boils and thickens, then continue cooking for a minute or two until clear. Pour sauce over ham. Cover and bake in a moderate oven (350° F) for one and one-quarter hours. Pour drained fruit cocktail over ham. Continue baking, uncovered, 15 to 20 minutes longer, basting frequently. Serves six. With sweet potatoes and a green vegetable, this is really a "super" dish!

P.S. For an added good-eating touch, arrange peeled bananas around the ham when the fruit cocktail is poured over it.

◆

Here's ham loaf baked in a ring mold, with its own delicious built-in glaze. Good with broccoli and spoon bread or buttered canned hominy.

GLAZED HAM RING

Mix meats, cracker crumbs, onion, eggs, wine, milk, mustard, salt, and pepper, blending thoroughly. Mix brown sugar and cloves; sprinkle evenly over bottom of a one and one-half-quart ring mold; arrange pieces of pineapple in the sugar-clove mixture. Pack the meat mixture into the mold, patting it down gently but firmly. Bake in a moderate oven (350° F) for two hours. Remove from oven and let stand five minutes or so. Unmold on a heated platter and garnish with sprigs of parsley or watercress. Serves six.

1 pound ground smoked ham
1 pound ground fresh pork
1 cup cracker crumbs
2 tablespoons grated onion
2 eggs, slightly beaten
½ cup dry red table wine
½ cup milk
½ teaspoon dry mustard
¼ teaspoon of salt
  Dash of pepper
½ cup (firmly packed) brown sugar
¼ teaspoon ground cloves
4 rings canned pineapple, cut in thirds

HAM AND MUSHROOM PATTIES

Drain mushrooms, reserving liquid. Melt butter; add onion and mushrooms; sauté, stirring frequently for five minutes. Sprinkle in flour; stir well. Add chicken stock and one cup of the reserved mushroom liquid; cook, stirring until mixture boils and thickens. Remove from heat. Add sour cream, cheese, wine, Worcestershire sauce, paprika, salt, and pepper. Stir in ham and parsley. Heat *gently*, just until piping hot. (Do *not* let mixture boil!) Heat patty shells in a moderate oven (350° F) for five minutes or so. Place shells on individual plates; fill with the hot ham mixture; dust with paprika. Serve at once. Serves eight to ten.

2 (8 oz.) cans sliced mushrooms
6 tablespoons butter
1 tablespoon minced onion
6 tablespoons flour
1 cup chicken stock
1 cup dairy sour cream
⅓ cup grated Parmesan cheese
¼ cup dry or medium Sherry
½ teaspoon Worcestershire sauce
¼ teaspoon paprika
  Salt and pepper to taste
2 cups diced, cooked ham
3 tablespoons chopped parsley
8-10 patty shells
  Paprika

◄————————►

Chunks of tender lamb and succulent vegetables in a wine-flavored gravy—what a good dish lamb stew can be! For instance:

HARVEST LAMB STEW

Dredge meat with flour by shaking them together in a paper bag. Heat bacon drippings in a large, heavy skillet or a Dutch oven; add meat and any flour remaining in bag; sauté, stirring frequently until meat is nicely browned. Add wine and water; cook, stirring constantly until gravy is thickened and smooth; add onion, garlic, parsley, thyme, bay leaf, salt, and pepper. Cover tightly and simmer very gently for two hours, stirring occasionally. Add carrots and celery; continue cooking for one-half hour, or until vegetables are tender. Just before serving, add peas and correct seasoning as necessary. Serves five or six.

2 pounds lamb stew meat, cut in 1-inch cubes
½ cup flour
4 tablespoons bacon drippings or salad oil
2 cups dry white table wine
2 cups boiling water
1 large onion, chopped
1 clove garlic, chopped or put through garlic press (if you like)
2 tablespoons chopped parsley
Dash of thyme
1 bay leaf
Salt and pepper to taste
6 medium-sized carrots, scraped and sliced
1 cup sliced celery
1 cup cooked peas

P.S. Substitute red table wine for the white and you'll have another very good stew.

————————◆————————

Shoulder of lamb, boned and rolled, makes a delicious, easy-to-serve pot roast.

BRAISED SHOULDER OF LAMB

Dredge lamb with flour seasoned with salt and pepper. Heat butter in a Dutch oven or other heavy kettle; brown lamb slowly on all sides. Add onion, garlic, wine, water, bay leaf, peppercorns, thyme and salt to taste. Cover tightly and simmer gently for two to two and one-half hours, or until meat is tender, turning meat occasionally. Place lamb on a heated platter.

4 to 5 pounds lamb shoulder, boned and rolled
Flour
Salt and pepper
2 tablespoons butter or bacon drippings
1 large onion, chopped
1 clove garlic, chopped or put through garlic press
1 cup dry red table wine
1 cup boiling water
1 bay leaf
3 or 4 peppercorns
Pinch of thyme
2 tablespoons chopped parsley
1 to 2 tablespoons dry or medium Sherry

To make gravy: Pour off liquid from kettle and skim off as much of the fat as possible. Measure liquid; add canned consommé or water, if necessary, to make three cups; heat to boiling. Blend one-third cup flour with one-half cup cold consommé or water to make a smooth paste; add gradually to the boiling liquid; cook, stirring constantly until mixture is thickened and smooth. Simmer five minutes. Taste and add salt and pepper, if needed. Add parsley and Sherry. Serve piping hot. Serves six to eight.

———————◆———————

Sherry and sour cream give this gravy a flavor that's really "something."

LAMB RAGOUT

Heat butter in a Dutch oven or other heavy kettle. Add lamb and onion; sauté, stirring frequently, until lamb is nicely browned. Sprinkle flour over meat and blend well; add stock and wine; cook, stirring constantly, until sauce boils and thickens. Season with Worcestershire sauce, paprika, salt, and pepper. Add carrots. Cover and simmer very gently, stirring occasionally for one and one-quarter to one and one-half hours, or until lamb is very tender. Add sour cream. (If sauce is now a little thinner than you like it, blend one tablespoon or so of flour with an equal amount of soft butter, add to contents of Dutch oven, and simmer until sauce thickens.) Add onions, peas, and parsley. Taste and add additional salt, if needed. Heat thoroughly before serving. Serves five or six. Good with buttered noodles and a tomato salad.

2 tablespoons butter or bacon drippings
2 pounds boneless lamb shoulder, cubed
½ cup chopped onion
3 tablespoons flour
1 cup beef stock
½ cup dry or medium Sherry
1 teaspoon Worcestershire sauce
¼ teaspoon paprika
   Salt and pepper to taste
4 carrots, diced
1 cup dairy sour cream
1 (1 lb.) can small whole onions, drained
1 (10 oz.) package frozen peas, cooked and drained
2 tablespoons chopped parsley

———————◆———————

Years ago in *Sunset Magazine* there appeared a recipe called, "L'Ambrosia," starring lamb shanks in brown gravy. This truly ambrosial dish was my introduction to these meaty morsels and they have been favorites with me ever since. The simplest, and to me the best, way of preparing them is to simmer them to tenderness in a flavorful sauce. Here are some good examples:

SPANISH LAMB SHANKS

Dredge lamb shanks with flour seasoned with salt and pepper. Heat bacon drippings in a large, heavy skillet; brown lamb shanks slowly on all sides. Add onion, garlic, celery, tomato sauce, wine, bay leaf, and salt and pepper to taste. Cover and simmer (or bake at 350° F) for one and one-half to two hours, or until meat is very tender, turning and basting shanks occasionally. Add a little more wine if gravy thickens down too much. Before serving, taste and correct seasoning. Serves four. Good with baked potatoes and a green vegetable.

4 lamb shanks
Flour
Salt and pepper
4 tablespoons bacon drippings or salad oil
½ cup chopped onion
Chopped or pressed garlic to taste
½ cup chopped celery
1 (8 oz.) can tomato sauce
½ cup dry red table wine
1 bay leaf

BRAISED LAMB SHANKS

Heat oil in a large, heavy skillet; brown lamb shanks slowly on all sides. Remove shanks from pan. Add flour to drippings and blend well; add wine and stock; cook, stirring, until mixture is thickened and smooth. Add remaining ingredients. Cover and simmer gently (or bake in a 350° F oven) for one and one-half to two hours, or until meat is fork-tender. Turn shanks occasionally and add a little more stock or water if gravy becomes too thick. Before serving, taste and correct seasoning as necessary. Serves four.

4 tablespoons salad oil or bacon drippings
4 lamb shanks
4 tablespoons flour
1 cup dry white or red table wine
1 cup beef stock or water
1 large onion, chopped
1 clove garlic, chopped or put through garlic press
2 to 3 tablespoons chopped parsley
1 teaspoon Worcestershire sauce
1 bay leaf, crumbled
Pinch each of thyme and rosemary
Salt and pepper to taste

P.S. My pet side dish with these is *kasha:* Put one cup whole buckwheat groats in a dry skillet or wide-bottomed saucepan; toast lightly over *very* low heat, stirring often. Add two cups boiling stock or water and salt to taste. Clap on the lid and cook as *slowly as possible* for 15 to 20 minutes until *kasha* is tender and liquid is absorbed. With a fork, gently stir in a generous lump of butter before serving. Serves four.

———◆———

A very good lamb curry that makes the most of an inexpensive cut is:

EAST INDIAN LAMB

3 pounds lamb neck, cut in 8 or 9 pieces
Flour
Salt and pepper
⅓ cup bacon drippings **or salad oil**
3 cups boiling water
2 cups dry white table wine
1 large onion, minced
1 clove garlic, minced or put through garlic press
1 tart apple, peeled and chopped
1 cup finely cut celery
¼ cup flaked coconut
2 teaspoons sugar
1 teaspoon (or more) curry powder
1 teaspoon Worcestershire sauce

Dredge lamb with flour seasoned with salt and pepper. Heat bacon drippings in a Dutch oven or other heavy kettle; brown lamb slowly on all sides. Remove lamb. Add one-half cup flour to drippings and blend well. Add water and wine; cook, stirring constantly, until sauce boils and thickens. Add all remaining ingredients; season to taste with salt and pepper. Return lamb to sauce. Cover and simmer gently, stirring occasionally, for two hours, or until lamb is tender and almost ready to fall from bones. Remove lamb from sauce, separate meat from bones, and cut meat in good-sized pieces with kitchen shears. Return meat to sauce and reheat before serving. Serves six generously, eight modestly. Delicious with rice and a green vegetable such as broccoli or spinach. And don't forget the chutney —a "must" with any curry!

P.S. This dish may be prepared ahead of time and reheated before serving. The flavor really improves as it mellows.

———◆———

In this variation on the stew theme, the potatoes are cooked with the meat and you can serve whatever vegetables you like with it. My choice is a small whole pattypan squash, cooked, slightly hollowed out, and filled with green peas.

LAMB CAPRI

Dredge lamb with flour seasoned with salt and pepper. Heat bacon drippings in a Dutch oven or a large, heavy skillet; add lamb, onion, and garlic; sauté, stirring frequently until lamb is nicely browned. Add all remaining ingredients except potatoes; season to taste with salt and pepper. Cover and simmer very gently for one hour. Add potatoes. Cover and cook 20 to 30 minutes longer until lamb and potatoes are tender. Stir occasionally during cooking and add a little more wine if gravy becomes too thick. Serves five or six.

2 pounds boneless lamb shoulder, cut in small cubes
Flour
Salt and pepper
4 tablespoons bacon drippings or salad oil
1 large onion, thinly sliced
1 clove garlic, minced or put through garlic press
¼ cup chopped parsley
Pinch each of rosemary and thyme
2 cups boiling water
1 cup dry white table wine
4 medium-sized potatoes, pared and cubed

———————◆———————

Another favorite in our house is baked breast of lamb. In fact, it's such a favorite that three-quarters pound per person is none too much! Try it these ways:

BAKED BREAST OF LAMB SONOMA

Arrange pieces of lamb, fat side up, in a single layer in a shallow baking pan. Mix remaining ingredients; pour over lamb; cover (using aluminum foil if the pan has no cover of its own) and let stand at room temperature for an hour or so. Bake, covered, in a hot oven (400° F) for 45 minutes; uncover and continue baking for about 45 minutes, basting frequently. Delicious with rice and a green vegetable. Serves four.

3 pounds breast of lamb, cut in 2- to 4-rib portions
1 cup dry white table wine
½ cup chili sauce
1 large onion, chopped
1 clove garlic, chopped or pressed
½ green pepper, chopped
1 tablespoon soya sauce
Salt and pepper to taste

BAKED BREAST OF LAMB, SPECIAL SAUCE

Place lamb, fat side down, on a rack in a shallow baking pan; sprinkle with salt and pepper. Bake, uncovered, in a hot oven (400° F) for one hour. Remove from oven and pour off all fat from pan. Place lamb fat side up on the rack; sprinkle with salt and pepper; pat a generous amount of crumbs into fat surface of meat. Continue baking at 400° F for about 30 minutes, or until lamb is tender. Meantime, heat beef gravy with jelly until jelly melts; stir in Sherry; add salt if needed. Remove baked lamb to a platter and pass the hot sauce separately. Serves four.

3 pounds breast of lamb, cut in 2- to 4-rib portions
Salt and pepper
Very fine, dry bread crumbs (packaged ones are best)
1 (10¾ oz.) can beef gravy
¼ cup currant jelly
3 tablespoons dry or medium Sherry

OVEN-BARBECUED BREAST OF LAMB

Place meat, fat side down, in a shallow baking pan; sprinkle with salt and pepper. Bake, uncovered, in a hot oven (400° F) for 45 minutes. While meat is baking, combine remaining ingredients for sauce. At the end of the 45 minutes, remove meat from oven and pour off all fat from pan. Turn meat fat side up and pour sauce over it. Return to oven and continue baking at 400° F for about 45 minutes, basting the meat frequently with the sauce. Serves four. Baked potatoes and green beans or asparagus are good accompaniments to this dish.

3 pounds breast of lamb, cut in 2- to 4-rib portions
Salt and pepper
1 cup catsup
1 cup dry red table wine
2 tablespoons wine vinegar
2 tablespoons brown sugar
1 medium-sized onion, minced

It's hard to improve on a nice, thick lamb chop, broiled so the fat is deliciously crisp and the meat tender and juicy. But variety is the spice that whets the appetite, so try one of these:

ELEGANT STUFFED LAMB CHOPS

12 rib lamb chops, cut about 1¼ inches thick
1 (3 oz.) can liver pâté or spread
1 (3 oz.) can chopped broiled mushrooms, drained and chopped very fine
1 tablespoon finely chopped onion
1 tablespoon finely chopped parsley
Garlic salt and pepper
1 cup dry red table wine
3 or 4 tablespoons butter
Additional chopped parsley

With a very sharp paring knife, slit each chop all the way through from fat side to bone to make a pocket for stuffing. Mix liver pâté, mushrooms, onion, and parsley; season with garlic salt and pepper. Spread mixture in pocket of each chop, using a scant measuring-teaspoonful per chop. Sprinkle both sides of chops with garlic salt and pepper. Place chops on rack in broiling pan. Broil until nicely browned on one side, then turn and brown the other side. Reduce heat to 350° F and bake chops, uncovered, for ten to 15 minutes, or until they're done as you like them. Remove chops to a heated platter. Remove rack from broiling pan and pour off fat. Swish wine around in the broiling pan and heat to simmering, stirring to scrape up any little brown bits. Add butter and parsley. Pour this sauce over the chops or pass it separately. Serves six. I can't recommend these too highly. They're marvelous for a company dinner!

LAMB CHOPS ARMENIAN

Arrange chops in a shallow baking dish; cover with onion slices and green pepper strips. Mix remaining ingredients; pour over chops. Let stand in the refrigerator several hours or overnight, turning chops occasionally. Remove chops from marinade and place on rack in broiler pan. Strain marinade. Broil chops to the desired degree of doneness, basting several times with the strained marinade. Serves four. Brown rice and stewed tomatoes go well with these.

4 shoulder lamb chops, cut about 1½ inches thick
1 medium-sized onion, thinly sliced
1 small green pepper, cut in thin strips
½ cup dry white table wine
¼ cup salad oil
1 clove garlic, chopped or put through garlic press
½ teaspoon oregano
½ teaspoon salt
¼ teaspoon coarse black pepper

Shish kebab is an elegant dish to eat and an easy one to prepare.

OVEN SHISH KEBAB

Put meat, onion, garlic, and green peppers in a bowl; add seasonings, oil, and wine; mix well. Let stand in the refrigerator for several hours or overnight, stirring occasionally. An hour or so before serving time, remove from refrigerator and string meat cubes on metal skewers alternately with pieces of green pepper. Lay filled skewers on a rack in a shallow baking pan, or suspend them between the sides of a loaf pan. Broil for 20 to 30 minutes, until meat is well browned and tender, turning to brown evenly. Or, bake in a hot oven (450° F) for 35 to 40 minutes. Serve on the skewers. Serves four. Rice and broiled or baked tomatoes are best with this.

3 pounds boneless lamb shoulder, cut in 1½-inch cubes
1 large onion, thinly sliced
1 clove garlic, chopped or put through garlic press
2 green peppers, cut in 1-inch squares
1 teaspoon salt
½ teaspoon coarse black pepper
¾ teaspoon oregano
¼ cup salad oil
¾ cup dry or medium Sherry

There are dozens of good recipes for Veal Scallopine. I like this one because it's simple to prepare and really delectable.

VEAL SCALLOPINE

Using a meat tenderizer or the edge of a heavy saucer, pound veal until one-quarter-inch thick. Cut veal in pieces about one-inch wide and three-inches long. Dredge with flour. In a skillet heat butter and oil with garlic; add veal and brown slowly on both sides. Remove garlic; add all remaining ingredients except Sherry. Cover and simmer gently for 30 minutes, or until veal is fork-tender, stirring frequently. Just before serving, stir in Sherry. Taste and correct seasoning. Serves four to six. A rice ring filled with peas is a nice accompaniment to the *scallopine*.

1½ pounds veal steak, cut ½ inch thick
Flour
2 tablespoons butter
2 tablespoons olive oil
1 clove garlic, crushed
¾ cup dry white table wine
¾ cup chicken or beef stock
2 tablespoons chopped parsley
½ teaspoon grated lemon peel
Dash each of thyme and marjoram
Salt and pepper to taste
2 tablespoons dry or medium Sherry

P.S. Sautéed fresh mushrooms or drained canned ones may be added to the veal just before serving, if desired.

◆

Veal chops, cooked gently in a savory sauce, make good eating:

BAKED VEAL CHOPS

Heat butter in a large, heavy skillet; brown chops slowly on both sides. Remove chops from skillet. Add flour to drippings and blend well; add beef gravy and wine; cook, stirring until mixture boils and thickens. Blend in tomato paste; add mushrooms and seasonings. Return chops to skillet. Cover and bake in a moderate oven (350° F) for one hour, or until chops are tender, turning and basting chops several times. Serves four.

3 tablespoons butter or bacon drippings
4 thick veal rib chops
3 tablespoons flour
1 (10¾ oz.) can beef gravy
⅓ cup dry or medium Sherry
1 tablespoon tomato paste
1 (3 oz.) can sliced broiled mushrooms, drained
Dash each of thyme and marjoram
Garlic salt, salt, and pepper to taste

This version of Veal Paprika is an excellent main dish for a buffet supper party. With it serve buttered noodles to which some poppy seeds and toasted, slivered almonds have been added. A salad, any relishes you like, and hot rolls can round out the main course.

VEAL PRINCESS

Heat butter in a Dutch oven or other heavy kettle; add veal and onion; brown meat nicely on all sides. Sprinkle flour over meat and stir well. Add all remaining ingredients except sour cream; cook, stirring constantly until mixture boils. Cover and simmer gently for one hour, or until meat is fork-tender, stirring frequently. Just before serving, stir in sour cream. Taste and add additional salt and pepper, if needed. Serves six to eight.

3 tablespoons butter or bacon drippings
3 pounds boneless veal shoulder, cubed
1 large onion, minced
¼ cup flour
1 cup dry white table wine
½ cup water
1 (4 oz.) can mushroom stems and pieces (undrained)
2 tablespoons chopped parsley
2 tablespoons chopped pimiento
1 clove garlic, chopped or put through garlic press
1 teaspoon Worcestershire sauce
1 teaspoon paprika
Salt and pepper to taste
1 cup dairy sour cream

Brown rice cooked in the wine-flavored veal stock makes a flavorful accompaniment for the veal here.

BRAISED VEAL WITH BROWN RICE

Melt butter in a large, heavy skillet; add veal and onion; cook, stirring frequently until meat is no longer pink. Add wine and water; season with salt and pepper. Bring to a boil, then cover and simmer very gently, stirring occasionally for about one hour or until veal is fork-tender. Pour off and reserve stock. To the veal add the chicken soup, one-half cup of the reserved stock, and the mushrooms (including their liquid); mix well; taste and correct seasoning. Set aside while cooking rice (below), then reheat gently before serving.

3 tablespoons butter or bacon drippings
2 pounds boneless veal shoulder, cut in small cubes
1 medium-sized onion, minced
1½ cups dry white table wine
1½ cups water
Salt and pepper to taste
1 (10½ oz.) can condensed cream of chicken soup
1 (4 oz.) can sliced mushrooms (undrained)
1½ cups uncooked brown rice
Parsley

To cook rice: Measure remaining stock and add water to make three cups; season with salt to taste. Heat stock to boiling; slowly sprinkle in rice. Cover tightly, turn heat very low, and steam for 45 minutes, or until rice is tender and liquid is absorbed. To serve, arrange rice in a ring on a heated platter; pour veal and sauce in center. Garnish with parsley. Serves five or six.

These veal birds, with their savory stuffing and wine-flavored sauce are an elegant dish.

VEAL BIRDS

Pound meat with a meat tenderizer or the edge of a heavy saucer until very thin. Cut in six even-sized pieces. Prepare stuffing: Melt four tablespoons of the butter; add bread crumbs, onion, thyme, marjoram, salt, and pepper; mix well. Place some of the stuffing on each piece of veal; roll up and tie with string or secure with toothpicks. Roll birds in flour. Melt remaining two tablespoons butter in a heavy skillet; brown birds lightly on all sides. Add wine, stock, parsley, and salt and pepper to taste; cover tightly and simmer gently for about 45 minutes, or until meat is tender, turning birds occasionally. Remove birds to a heated platter and spoon pan juices over them. (If juices are on the scant side, add a little wine.) Serves six.

1½ pounds veal steak, cut ¼ inch thick
6 tablespoons butter
2 cups (firmly packed) grated soft bread crumbs
2 tablespoons minced onion
⅛ teaspoon each: thyme and marjoram
Salt and pepper to taste
Flour
½ cup dry white table wine
½ cup chicken or beef stock
2 tablespoons chopped parsley

P.S. If you'd like a creamy gravy with the birds, add a can of condensed cream of mushroom or cream of celery soup to the pan juices. Blend well, heat to simmering, and season to taste. Pour gravy over birds or serve separately.

Here's a roast that's really at its best served cold. It's festive enough for the dressiest warm-weather menu! But it's good hot, too, with a gravy made from the pan drippings.

ROAST STUFFED SHOULDER OF VEAL

Rub veal all over with the cut clove of garlic; sprinkle inside and out with salt and pepper. Melt butter in a large, heavy skillet; sauté onion and celery gently for about five minutes. Add crumbs, applesauce, parsley, poultry seasoning, nutmeg, three-fourths teaspoon salt, and one-fourth teaspoon pepper. Fill veal cavity with this stuffing; sew or skewer opening securely. Place in a shallow baking pan; lay bacon on top of roast and pour wine over it. Bake, uncovered, in a slow oven (325° F), allowing 40 minutes per pound (to 180° F on meat thermometer). Baste frequently with the wine in the pan. Serve hot with gravy (see below), or serve cold with chutney, cranberry sauce, or a sauce made of sour cream seasoned to taste with lemon juice, salt, and a bit of prepared horseradish. Makes about ten generous servings.

5 pounds (approximately) boned veal shoulder
1 clove garlic, halved
Salt and pepper
½ cup butter or bacon drippings
1 medium-sized onion, finely chopped
½ cup finely cut celery
4 cups (firmly packed) grated soft bread crumbs (use day-old bread)
1 cup canned applesauce
¼ cup chopped parsley
½ teaspoon poultry seasoning
¼ teaspoon nutmeg
4 slices bacon
1 (4/5 qt.) bottle dry white table wine

To make the gravy: Pour off all liquid from roasting pan. Skim off and reserve as much of the fat as possible. (This is easier when the liquid has been chilled so the fat is solid.) Add beef, or chicken stock, or water to the liquid to make three cups. Melt one-fourth cup of the reserved fat; blend in one-fourth cup flour. Gradually add the three cups liquid and cook, stirring constantly, until mixture is thickened and smooth. Simmer five minutes, stirring often. Add some canned or sautéed fresh mushrooms, if you like. Season with salt and pepper; add one to two tablespoons dry or medium Sherry. Serve hot as hot!

Like the little girl with the curl in the middle of her forehead, liver, when it's good, can be very, very good. Poorly cooked, it's better relegated to oblivion! These two ways of preparing it are favorites of mine, delicious for brunch or dinner:

LIVER AND BACON BROCHETTES

Remove skin from liver slices. Cut liver into small pieces (36 is the ideal number); cut each strip of bacon into six pieces. String alternate pieces of liver and bacon on six wooden or metal skewers, beginning and ending with bacon. Mix wine, oil, onion, salt, and pepper in a shallow baking dish. Lay filled skewers in the dish and let stand one hour or longer, turning the skewers occasionally. Remove skewers from marinade and suspend between the sides of a loaf pan. Bake in a hot oven (450° F) for 15 to 20 minutes, basting several times with the marinade. Or broil, about five inches from heat source for 15 minutes, turning to cook evenly. To serve, lay skewers on crisp toast and pour some of the pan drippings over all. Garnish with parsley. Serves three.

1 pound sliced liver (calf, lamb, or baby beef)
7 slices bacon
½ cup dry red table wine
½ cup salad oil
2 tablespoons grated onion
½ teaspoon salt
¼ teaspoon coarse black pepper

LIVER SAUTÉ WITH MUSHROOMS

Remove skin from liver slices; cut slices in strips or squares; roll in flour. Heat three tablespoons of the butter in a large skillet; add liver and onion; sauté quickly just until liver is nicely browned (no longer!), stirring frequently. Remove liver from skillet. Add remaining one tablespoon butter to drippings in skillet; blend in three tablespoons flour; add consommé and liquid from mushrooms; cook, stirring until mixture is thickened and smooth. Add wine, Worcestershire sauce, thyme, salt, pepper, mushrooms, and parsley. Add liver to sauce and heat just until piping hot. Serve at once on toast or with rice. Serves four.

1 pound sliced liver (calf, lamb, or baby beef)
   Flour
4 tablespoons butter
2 tablespoons grated onion
1 (10½ oz.) can condensed consommé
1 (4 oz.) can sliced mushrooms
¼ cup dry or medium Sherry
1 teaspoon Worcestershire sauce
   Dash of thyme
   Salt and pepper to taste
2 tablespoons chopped parsley

Young venison, properly aged, is a treat. Prepare this game meat as you would beef, but take care not to overcook it. Because it lacks fat, the meat dries faster under heat than beef. If venison is cooked too much, there's a loss of flavor and the fibers harden and become tough.

Bacon, herbs, and wine contribute good flavor to:

HUNTER'S ROAST VENISON

1 venison roast
2 or 3 slices bacon
Crumbled rosemary or oregano
Lemon
Salt and pepper
1 cup canned bouillon (beef broth) or consommé
1 cup dry red table wine

Trim the meat, removing any skin, fat, or dry pieces; wipe meat with cloth wrung out in vinegar. Sprinkle bacon slices with herbs; roll up like jelly roll. Cut each strip crosswise, making two or three smaller rolls. Cut deep slits in surface of meat and push bacon rolls inside; press cuts together to enclose bacon. Squeeze lemon over meat and season with salt and pepper. Set venison in roasting pan and sear on all sides in very hot oven (500° F) about 10 to 15 minutes. Lower heat to 425° F. Combine bouillon and wine; pour about one-third over meat. Cover loosely with foil and roast to desired degree of doneness; allow about 20 minutes per pound for medium-rare meat. Baste venison often with remaining wine mixture. If necessary, additional wine or bouillon may be used. When meat is done, skim excess fat from pan drippings. Serve the rich brown drippings as a natural gravy or thicken slightly, if you prefer. A five-pound roast will serve about eight.

———◆———

This way of cooking venison insures fine flavor and tender meat even if the deer is not too young. This is almost a pot-roasting treatment.

SPICY ROAST VENISON

Trim meat, discarding any skin, fat, or dry pieces. Wipe meat with cloth wrung out in vinegar. Combine wine, vinegar, water, garlic salt, and dill. Pour over meat. Cover and refrigerate overnight, turning several times. Drain meat well, saving marinade. Brown venison on all sides in heated oil (use a little more oil if meat has a tendency to stick to pan). Add chili sauce and onion to marinade; pour half over meat. Cover and cook until tender in a hot oven (425° F), basting with remaining marinade now and then. Allow about 20 minutes per pound of meat. Skim any excess fat from pan juices; thicken remaining liquid, if desired, or serve "as is." A five-pound roast will serve about eight.

1 venison roast
1 cup dry red table wine
2 tablespoons red wine vinegar
⅓ cup water
½ teaspoon garlic salt
½ teaspoon dried dill
2 tablespoons salad oil
½ cup chili sauce
¼ cup chopped green onion

❖ VII ❖

Featuring Poultry And Game Birds

There are lots of wonderful ways to cook chicken with wine—some with white table wine, some with red, some with Sherry or Vermouth.

Probably the simplest way to introduce the two to each other is to brown plump pieces of chicken to a golden turn in butter and oil, then cook them in a little wine gently (very gently!) until tender. Served as is, or with a sauce made by swishing a little more wine around in the pan or a nice rich, creamy gravy, Chicken Sauté is marvelous eating!

For this dish (and for all the frying-chicken recipes), I'm partial to a meaty bird of two and one-half to three pounds, ready-to-cook weight. I like it disjointed, but you can have it quartered, if you prefer. Or you can use two smaller chickens, one and one-half to one and three-quarters pounds each, disjointed, quartered, or halved. If you use the smaller birds, you'll undoubtedly find the cooking time a little shorter than I've indicated, so watch carefully lest you end up with overcooked chicken!

Now for the recipe:

CHICKEN SAUTÉ

Dredge pieces of chicken with flour. (Roll them in flour or shake with flour in a paper bag.) Heat butter and oil in a large, heavy skillet; add chicken and sauté slowly until golden brown, turning the pieces frequently and adding a little more butter or oil, if necessary. Add onions, garlic, parsley, thyme, paprika, salt, pepper, and wine. Cover tightly and simmer *very, very* gently for 30 to 45 minutes, or until chicken is tender, turning pieces occasionally. Remove chicken to a heated platter. If you'd like a little wine sauce to pour over it, swish another one-half cup or so of wine around in the skillet; heat to bubbling and stir well to capture any tasty little brown bits. Spoon sauce over the chicken and serve at once. Serves three or four. Good accompaniments: a casserole of scalloped or *au gratin* potatoes and buttered asparagus or broccoli.

1 frying chicken (2½ to 3 pounds), cut in pieces for serving
Flour
2 tablespoons butter
2 tablespoons salad oil
2 green onions, very finely chopped
Bit of chopped or pressed garlic (if you like)
2 tablespoons chopped parsley
Sprinkling of thyme and paprika
Salt and pepper to taste
½ cup dry white table wine, dry or medium Sherry, or dry Vermouth

CHICKEN ÉLÉGANCE

If you're having company and want something really superb in the way of a main dish, serve chicken breasts cooked "*à la Chicken Sauté.*" Substitute four whole, serving-sized chicken breasts (or two large ones, halved) for the cut-up fryer in the *Chicken Sauté* recipes. Have the breasts boned and flatten them slightly by pounding gently with the edge of a heavy saucer. Then choose from these delectable ideas:

Chicken Breasts in Wine: Cook breasts according to the recipe for *Chicken Sauté.* When they are tender, make the wine pan sauce as direct and spoon it over them. If you like, you can add some sautéed fresh or drained canned mushrooms to the sauce. Serves four.

Chicken and Ham Supreme: Cook breasts according to the recipe for *Chicken Sauté with Cream Gravy.* Have ready four slices of broiled ham (cut the same size as the chicken breasts) and four slices of crisp buttered toast. Place ham on toast, top with the cooked chicken breasts, and cover with the hot cream gravy. Dust with paprika and garnish with sautéed fresh or canned whole mushroom caps. Serve *at once!* Serves four.

Baked Chicken Breasts with Broccoli: Cook breasts according to the recipe for *Chicken Sauté with Cream Gravy.* Arrange four servings of cooked broccoli in four shallow individual baking dishes or in one large baking dish. Arrange cooked chicken breasts over broccoli and pour the cream gravy over all. Sprinkle liberally with grated Parmesan cheese and dust with paprika. Bake at 375° F for 15 to 20 minutes, or until bubbly and delicately browned. Serves four.

CHICKEN SAUTÉ WITH CREAM GRAVY

Brown the chicken and cook it until tender as directed above in the recipe for *Chicken Sauté,* using white table or dry or medium Sherry. When it's done, remove it to a platter, set it where it will keep warm, and make gravy as follows:

CREAM GRAVY

- 3 tablespoons flour
- 2 cups rich milk
- 2 tablespoons dry or medium Sherry
- Dash of nutmeg or mace
- Salt and pepper to taste

Blend flour with drippings remaining in skillet; add milk gradually and cook, stirring constantly until mixture is thickened and smooth. Continue cooking and stirring for another minute or two. Add Sherry, nutmeg, salt, and pepper. Spoon gravy over chicken or serve separately. Either way, be sure it's really hot! Serves three or four. Rice or mashed potatoes are a good accompaniment here, along with succotash (corn and baby lima beans).

P.S. For a curried version of this dish, omit the nutmeg or mace and blend one to two teaspoons curry powder with the flour and skillet drippings. Serve with rice and peas or green beans, and pass a bowl of chutney.

Seedless grapes add a subtle and delicious note of flavor to this dish.

CHICKEN VERONICA

Heat butter and oil in a large, heavy skillet; brown chicken slowly on all sides. Sprinkle onion, parsley, salt, pepper, and paprika over chicken; add white wine and chicken stock. Cover and simmer very gently for 30 to 45 minutes, or until chicken is tender, turning and basting pieces frequently. Remove cooked chicken from skillet. Pour off and reserve liquid from skillet; skim off and reserve the fat. Measure one-half cup of the liquid, adding chicken stock or water if needed to make that amount. Return three tablespoons of the fat to the skillet (use a little butter if there isn't enough fat); blend in the flour; add the one-half cup liquid and the milk; cook, stirring constantly, until mixture is thickened and smooth. Add Sherry, nutmeg, and salt and pepper to taste; stir in grapes. Return chicken to skillet and heat *very* gently for a few minutes before serving. Serves three or four.

2 tablespoons butter
2 tablespoons salad oil
1 frying chicken (2½ to 3 pounds), cut in pieces for serving
2 tablespoons chopped onion
2 tablespoons chopped parsley
Salt, pepper, and paprika
½ cup dry white table wine
½ cup chicken stock
3 tablespoons flour
1½ cups milk (part cream for a richer sauce)
2 tablespoons dry or medium Sherry
Dash of nutmeg
1 cup fresh or thoroughly drained canned seedless grapes

P.S. For a simplified version of *Chicken Veronica* (and an excellent one) do this: Cook the chicken as directed. Remove it from the skillet, pour off the liquid, and skim off the fat. Measure the one-half cup liquid and combine it in the skillet with one (10¾ oz.) can white sauce. Add Sherry, seasonings, and grapes to sauce, then add chicken and heat very gently before serving.

When I'm in a chicken-with-white-wine mood, this is a favorite:

CHICKEN CARMELO

Follow the recipe for *Chicken Burgundy,* substituting dry white table wine for the red wine and omitting the can of whole onions. Cook and drain a (9 oz.) package of frozen artichoke hearts. Add these to the chicken shortly before serving, along with the drained mushrooms.

———◆———

Tomatoes are teamed with the chicken and wine in this recipe.

CHICKEN, HUNTER'S STYLE

Dredge pieces of chicken with flour. Heat four tablespoons butter and the oil in a large, heavy skillet or a Dutch oven; add chicken and brown slowly on all sides. Sauté onion, garlic, and green pepper slowly in remaining one tablespoon butter for five minutes; add to browned chicken. Mix tomato sauce, wine, consommé, mushrooms (including liquid), parsley, thyme, rosemary, salt, and pepper; pour over chicken. Cover and simmer very gently for 30 to 45 minutes, or until chicken is tender, basting chicken occasionally with the sauce. Before serving, taste and add salt and pepper if needed. Serves six to eight. Good with this: macaroni or spaghetti and buttered zucchini that has been liberally sprinkled with grated Parmesan cheese.

2 frying chickens (2½ to 3 pounds each), cut in pieces for serving
Flour
5 tablespoons butter
4 tablespoons olive oil
1 medium-sized onion, minced
1 clove garlic, minced or put through garlic press
1 green pepper, minced
1 (8 oz.) can tomato sauce
½ cup dry red or white table wine
½ cup canned consommé
1 (4 oz.) can sliced mushrooms (undrained)
2 tablespoons chopped parsley
Pinch each of thyme and rosemary
Salt and pepper to taste

———◆———

There's a surprise ingredient in this recipe—orange marmalade. It isn't detectable as such in the finished dish; rather, it combines with the tomato sauce, Sherry, and seasonings to produce a most appealing flavor.

CHICKEN BERNARDINO

Dredge chicken with flour. Heat oil in a large, heavy skillet; brown chicken slowly on all sides. Pour off almost all the drippings. Mix remaining ingredients; pour over chicken. Cover and simmer 30 to 45 minutes until chicken is tender, turning and basting chicken several times. Add a little chicken stock or water toward end of cooking time if gravy seems a bit too thick. Before serving, taste to see whether more salt and pepper are needed. Serves three or four.

1 frying chicken (2½ to 3 pounds), cut in pieces for serving
Flour
⅓ cup salad oil
1 (8 oz.) can tomato sauce
½ cup dry or medium Sherry
⅓ cup orange marmalade
¼ cup chopped onion
1 tablespoon Worcestershire sauce
Salt and pepper to taste

Pineapple and soya sauce contribute the oriental touch to:

CHICKEN CHINESE

Dredge pieces of chicken with flour. Heat oil in a large, heavy skillet; brown chicken slowly on all sides. Sprinkle onions over chicken; add soya sauce, wine, and chicken stock. Cover and simmer gently for 30 to 45 minutes, or until chicken is tender, turning and basting chicken occasionally. Remove chicken to a heated platter and keep warm. Add undrained pineapple to drippings in skillet; heat thoroughly. Pour sauce over chicken or pass separately. Rice, and peas or green beans mixed with canned or sautéed fresh mushrooms, go well with this. Serves three or four.

1 frying chicken (2½ to 3 pounds), cut in pieces for serving
Flour
⅓ cup salad oil
½ cup thinly sliced green onions (include some of the green tops)
¼ cup soya sauce
½ cup dry or medium Sherry
½ cup chicken stock
1 (9 oz.) can crushed pineapple

A long time ago I gave up broiling halves of chicken in favor of baking them. Now a died-in-the-wool lover of broiled chicken may not agree, but to me baking is a more "relaxed" method, with equally delicious (if not better) results. There's less need for watching and turning, and the chicken always comes to the table juicy, tender, and temptingly browned.

◄────

Buttered noodles, liberally sprinkled with poppy seeds, and green beans with a few mushrooms added go very well with:

CHICKEN PAPRIKA

2	tablespoons butter
2	tablespoons salad oil
1	frying chicken (2½ to 3 pounds), cut in pieces for serving
1½	teaspoons paprika
	Salt to taste
¼	cup chopped onion
½	clove garlic, chopped or put through garlic press
½	cup dry or medium Sherry or dry white table wine
½	cup chicken stock
1	cup dairy sour cream
3	tablespoons flour
1	tablespoon dry or medium Sherry
2	tablespoons chopped parsley

Heat butter and oil in a large, heavy skillet; brown chicken slowly on all sides. Sprinkle paprika and salt over chicken; add onion, garlic, the one-half cup wine, and stock; cover and simmer very gently for 30 to 45 minutes, or until chicken is tender, turning and basting chicken frequently. Remove chicken to a heated platter and keep warm. Pour off and reserve liquid from skillet; skim off the fat. Measure liquid and add chicken stock or water as necessary to make one and one-half cups; pour back into skillet. Blend sour cream and flour until smooth; add to liquid in skillet; cook very gently, stirring constantly until mixture is thickened and smooth. Add the one tablespoon Sherry and parsley; taste and adjust seasoning. Pour gravy over chicken or serve separately. Serves three or four.

The French *coq au vin* was the inspiration for this:

CHICKEN BURGUNDY

Heat oil in a large, heavy skillet; brown chicken slowly on all sides. Remove chicken from skillet. Add flour to drippings and blend well; add stock and wine; cook, stirring until mixture is smooth. Add all remaining ingredients except mushrooms and onions; return chicken to skillet. Cover and simmer very gently for 30 to 45 minutes, or until chicken is tender, turning and basting chicken frequently. Before serving, add mushrooms and onions; taste and correct seasoning, if necessary. Serves three or four. My favorite accompaniment to this is steamed rice that has been cooked in chicken stock along with a little grated carrot and grated green pepper to give it extra flavor and color.

3 tablespoons salad oil or bacon drippings
1 frying chicken (2½ to 3 pounds), cut in pieces for serving
1½ tablespoons flour
1 cup chicken stock
½ cup Burgundy or other red table wine
1 small onion, chopped
1 clove garlic, chopped or pressed
Several sprigs parsley, chopped
1 bay leaf, crumbled
Pinch of thyme and paprika
Salt and pepper to taste
1 (4 oz.) can sliced mushrooms, drained
1 (1 lb.) can small whole onions, drained (optional)

This is definitely one of my recipe favorites, as easy to do for ten as for two:

BEST BAKED BROILERS

Allow half of a one and one-half to two pound chicken per person. Spread generously with softened butter; sprinkle with salt and pepper. Place, skin side down, in a shallow baking pan that has been lined with aluminum foil. In the cavity of each chicken half put two or three tablespoons of wine (red or white table wine, dry or medium Sherry, or dry Vermouth) and, if you like, a bit of chopped green onion. Lay strips of bacon over the chicken, allowing one and one-half strips per chicken half. Bake, uncovered, in a very hot oven (450° F) for 15 minutes, then reduce heat to moderate (350° F) and continue baking for 35 to 45 minutes, or until chicken is tender, basting several times with the juices in the pan. Before serving, turn skin side up and brown under the broiler, if desired. If by chance dinner is delayed, you can cover the chicken securely with aluminum foil and keep it warm in a *very* slow oven. It doesn't mind waiting!

P.S. If you do decide to broil your broilers, marinate them for an hour or two beforehand in a mixture of equal parts of dry white table wine (or dry Sherry or dry Vermouth) and salad oil, seasoned to taste, then use this to baste them during broiling. Good flavor!

———————◆———————

A bit of white table wine does nice things for a roast chicken this way.

ROAST CHICKEN WITH RAISIN-WALNUT STUFFING

6 tablespoons butter
½ cup finely cut celery
2 tablespoons finely chopped onion
4 cups (firmly packed) grated soft bread crumbs (use day-old bread)
½ cup seedless raisins, rinsed with boiling water and drained
½ cup chopped walnuts
2 tablespoons chopped parsley
Salt
¼ teaspoon pepper
½ teaspoon poultry seasoning
6 tablespoons dry white table wine (approximately)
1 roasting chicken (4 to 5 pounds)
Salad oil or melted fat

Melt butter in a saucepan; add celery and onion; cook gently for three or four minutes. Mix bread crumbs, raisins, walnuts, parsley, one teaspoon salt, pepper, and poultry seasoning; add butter mixture and just enough wine to moisten the stuffing slightly. Rub cavity of chicken with salt; stuff and truss; brush bird all over with salad oil or melted fat. Place, breast up, on a rack in a shallow pan. Cover loosely with a clean piece of cheese-cloth dipped in salad oil or melted fat. Roast in a moderately slow oven (325° F) for three to three and one-half hours, or until drumstick-thigh joint breaks or moves easily when leg is grasped at bone end. Moisten cheese-cloth with fat in pan during roasting, if necessary. Serve with *Giblet Gravy*. Serves four or five.

What would we do without the faithful stewing hen? It's delicious by itself in a fricassee and provides the meat for many another good chicken dish. When I make a fricassee, I like to brown the pieces of chicken first for extra flavor, but you can omit this step, if you prefer.

SUNDAY CHICKEN FRICASSEE

Heat butter in a Dutch oven or other deep, heavy kettle; brown pieces of chicken nicely on all sides, adding a little more butter, if needed. Add onion, carrot, celery, parsley sprigs, bay leaf, cloves, two teaspoons salt, peppercorns, white wine, and boiling water. Cover tightly and simmer very gently for one and one-half to two and one-half hours, or until chicken is fork-tender. Remove chicken from kettle. Strain broth; skim off and reserve as much of the fat as possible. Measure two cups broth, adding canned chicken broth or water, if needed, to make that amount. Measure one-third cup of the chicken fat back into the kettle; blend in the flour. Gradually add the two cups broth and the cream; cook, stirring constantly, until mixture is thickened and smooth, then continue cooking (very gently!) and stirring for another minute or two. Add Sherry, nutmeg, pepper, salt to taste, and parsley. Return chicken to gravy and heat thoroughly before serving. Serves five or six. Mashed potatoes, a carrot ring filled with peas, and hot biscuits go beautifully with this.

4 tablespoons butter or bacon drippings
1 stewing chicken (4 to 5 pounds), cut in pieces for serving
1 onion, sliced
1 carrot, sliced
1 stalk celery, sliced
Several sprigs parsley
1 bay leaf (if you like)
2 whole cloves
Salt
3 or 4 peppercorns
1 cup dry white table wine
2 cups boiling water
⅓ cup flour
1 cup cream
2 or 3 tablespoons dry or medium Sherry
Dash each of nutmeg and pepper
2 tablespoons chopped parsley

Giblet Gravy: While chicken is roasting, simmer gizzard and heart in salted water to cover until tender (one to two hours). For extra flavor, add a bit of celery, onion, and parsley to the water. Add liver during last ten minutes of cooking. Drain giblets, reserving broth. Strain broth; measure one cup, adding canned chicken broth or water if necessary to make that amount. Chop giblets fine. When chicken is done, pour off fat from roasting pan. Return three tablespoons of the fat to the pan; blend in three tablespoons flour; cook gently for a minute or so. Add the 1 cup giblet broth, one-half cup dry white table wine, and one-half cup cream; cook, stirring constantly, until mixture boils and thickens, then simmer for five minutes. Add chopped giblets. Season with salt and pepper to taste. Serve very hot!

———

There's something very "party-fied" about a curry. Served with an array of condiments, it looks festive and it's a natural for buffet service, because part of the fun of a curry dinner is helping oneself to a little of this and that.

ABOUT CURRY CONDIMENTS

The more condiments the merrier and the tastier! Chutney, of course, is a "must," and any or all of the following will add flavor interest:

Flaked coconut
Diced banana
Sieved hard-cooked egg
Crumbled crisp bacon
Tiny whole cocktail onions
Canned French-fried onions

Chopped salted peanuts
Seedless raisins
Sliced ripe or stuffed olives
Drained canned crushed pineapple
Finely chopped green pepper
Diced fresh tomato

And now two recipes for the star of the meal.

CHICKEN CURRY

Place a whole stewing chicken (four to five pounds) in a large kettle. Add one onion (sliced), one carrot (sliced), one stalk celery (sliced), several sprigs parsley, one bay leaf (if you like), two whole cloves, two teaspoons salt, a few whole peppercorns, one cup dry white table wine, and enough boiling water so that chicken is barely covered. Cover and simmer *gently* for two to three hours, or until chicken is fork-tender. Let cool in broth, then remove skin and separate meat from bones.

Cut meat in not-too-small pieces. Strain broth; skin off and reserve fat. For remainder of recipe, proceed as follows:

In the top of a double boiler over direct heat, sauté onion and garlic gently in chicken fat and butter until golden. Blend in curry powder, ginger, and flour. Gradually add chicken broth and cream; cook, stirring constantly, until mixture is thickened and smooth. Add sugar and salt. Add chicken. Place over hot (but not boiling) water, cover, and let stand for 15 to 20 minutes before serving so that flavors can mellow. Just before serving, add Sherry. Serve with rice, chutney, and whatever condiments you like from the list above. Serves 6.

1   medium-sized onion, chopped
1   clove garlic, chopped or put through garlic press
3   tablespoons each: chicken fat and butter
1   tablespoon curry powder
½   teaspoon ground ginger
½   cup flour
2   cups strained chicken broth
1½ cups cream or rich milk
¼   teaspoon sugar
    Salt to taste
2   tablespoons dry or medium Sherry

PINEAPPLE CHICKEN CURRY

Cook, cool, and cut up a four to five pound stewing chicken as directed above in the recipe for *Chicken Curry*. Strain broth; skim off and reserve fat. Finish dish as follows:

Sauté onion gently in chicken fat and butter until golden. Blend in curry powder and flour. Gradually add broth and cook, stirring constantly, until mixture is thickened and smooth; simmer five minutes, stirring frequently. Stir in cream; add pineapple, raisins, chicken, Sherry, and salt. Heat gently but thoroughly. Serve with rice, and be sure that your condiment list includes chutney, coconut, and bacon. (Omit raisins and pineapple from the condiment tray, since they're part and parcel of the curry mixture.) Serves eight.

1 large onion, chopped
⅓ cup each: chicken fat and butter
1 tablespoon curry powder
⅔ cup flour
4 cups strained chicken broth (add canned chicken broth or water, if needed, to make that amount)
1 cup cream
1 (9 oz.) can crushed pineapple, well drained
½ cup seedless raisins
2 tablespoons dry or medium Sherry
  Salt to taste

A good chicken pie is a soul-satisfying dish. Try this one:

CHICKEN CASSEROLE PIE

Cook, cool, and cut up a four to five pound stewing chicken as directed in the recipe for *Chicken Curry* but save the chicken skin and put it through the food grinder. Strain broth; skim off fat. Then

Blend chicken fat and flour; stir over low heat for a minute or two. Add chicken broth and cream; cook, stirring constantly, until sauce boils and thickens. Add nutmeg, salt, and pepper. Stir in ground chicken skin, then add chicken, peas, and carrots. Turn hot mixture into a two-quart casserole. Cover casserole with rolled pastry; cut several gashes in pastry to permit escape of steam. Bake immediately in a hot oven (450° F) for 15 minutes. Serves five or six.

¼ cup chicken fat or butter
¼ cup flour
1 cup strained chicken broth
1 cup cream
Dash of nutmeg or mace
Salt and pepper to taste
1 cup cooked peas
1 cup diced, cooked carrots
Pastry for top of pie (1¼ cups flour, ½ teaspoon salt, ⅓ cup shortening, and about 3 tablespoons cold water)

P.S. Sautéed fresh mushrooms, or drained canned ones, are good added along with the peas and carrots.

———◆———

Cubes of tender cooked chicken in an interesting sauce make a main dish that can be served with equal success at brunch, lunch, or dinner. What's an "interesting" sauce? Maybe it's a cream sauce, maybe a tomato sauce, maybe one in which chicken stock plays the leading part. But one thing is certain—there's wine in it!

In the chart that follows you'll find a baker's-dozen delicious ways to "sauce" chicken, plus suggestions for accompaniments to set off the featured dish to best advantage. Turkey, of course, can be used in these same ways.

Stuffing Ring (for *Chicken in the Nest*): Sauté one-fourth cup minced onion and one-half cup finely cut celery in one-third cup butter for five minutes. Mix with six cups (firmly packed) grated soft bread crumbs (two-day-old bread), one-half teaspoon baking powder, one teaspoon

GOOD WAYS TO USE

THE DISH	*Melt*	*Add & cook gently for 5 minutes*	*Blend in*	*Add & cook, stirring constantly until mixture thickens*
CHICKEN-CHEESE SHORTCAKE *Serves 4 to 6*	4 tbs. butter		4 tbs. flour	1 cup cream ½ cup chicken stock ⅓ cup dry white table wine
CREAMED CHICKEN TARTS *Serves 8*	6 tbs. butter		6 tbs. flour	1¼ cups cream 1 cup chicken stock
CHICKEN IN THE NEST *Serves 3 or 4*	2 tbs. butter		2 tbs. flour	1 cup milk 1 (10½ oz.) can condensed cream of chicken soup
CHICKEN CANTON *Serves 5 or 6*	4 tbs. butter	1 medium-sized onion, chopped 1 cup diced celery	4 tbs. flour	1½ cups chicken stock ½ cup dry white table wine
CHICKEN HAVANA *Serves 4 or 5*	3 tbs. butter	1 medium-sized onion, chopped 1 green pepper, chopped 1 clove garlic, chopped or pressed	3 tbs. flour	1 (8 oz.) can tomato sauce ¾ cup chicken stock ½ cup dry or medium Sherry
CHICKEN À LA QUEEN *Serves 4 or 5*	4 tbs. butter		5 tbs. flour	1 cup cream 1 cup chicken stock ⅓ cup dry or medium Sherry
CHICKEN AND HAM PRINCESS *Serves 6*	3 tbs. butter	1 small onion, chopped 1 green pepper, chopped	3 tbs. flour	1 (10½ oz.) can condensed cream of chicken soup ⅔ cup milk ⅓ cup dry white table wine

COOKED CHICKEN (OR TURKEY)

Stir in	*Add & heat very gently (do not boil!)*	*Serve*
1 tb. dry or medium Sherry ¼ tsp. paprika Dash of nutmeg or mace Salt & pepper to taste	2 cups cubed, cooked chicken 2 tbs. chopped parsley	over hot cheese biscuits (prepare baking powder biscuits, using 2 cups flour, etc., cut in ½ cup grated Cheddar cheese with the shortening) or over servings of Cheese Soufflé
¼ cup dry or medium Sherry ⅛ tsp. nutmeg Salt & pepper to taste	2 cups cubed, cooked chicken ¼ cup chopped pimiento 1 (8 oz.) can sliced mushrooms, drained	in 4-inch baked tart shells, or in patty shells
2 tbs. dry or medium Sherry Salt & pepper to taste	1½ to 2 cups cubed, cooked chicken 1 (4 oz.) can sliced mushrooms, drained 2 tbs. chopped parsley	in a nest of heated canned shoestring potatoes, or in the center of *Stuffing Ring*
1 tb. soya sauce Salt & pepper to taste	2 cups cubed, cooked chicken 1 (4 oz.) can mushrooms, drained ½ green pepper, slivered	over canned crisp Chinese noodles or with rice
¼ cup grated Cheddar cheese (let it melt) Salt & pepper to taste	2 cups cubed, cooked chicken 2 tbs. chopped parsley	with rice
¼ cup grated Cheddar cheese (let it melt) ¼ tsp. Worcestershire sauce Dash of mace Salt & pepper to taste	2 cups cubed, cooked chicken 1 (4 oz.) can mushrooms, drained 1 pimiento, chopped	in patty shells, on toast, or with noodles
¼ cup grated Cheddar cheese (let it melt) Salt & pepper to taste	1½ cups cubed, cooked chicken 1 cup cubed, cooked ham 2 pimientos, chopped	in patty shells, on toast, or with noodles or rice

GOOD WAYS TO USE

THE DISH	Melt	Add & cook gently for 5 minutes	Blend in	Add & cook, stirring constantly until mixture thickens
CREAMED CHICKEN ALBERTO *Serves 4 or 5*	4 tbs. butter		5 tbs. flour	1⅓ cups chicken stock ⅔ cup cream
CHICKEN GOURMET *Serves 6*	4 tbs. butter		5 tbs. flour	1 cup cream ⅔ cup chicken stock ½ cup dry white table wine
CHICKEN STROGANOFF *Serves 6*	4 tbs. butter	2 tbs. finely chopped onion	5 tbs. flour	⅔ cup chicken stock ½ cup dry white table wine
CHICKEN CELESTE *Serves 5 or 6*	4 tbs. butter	1 (4 oz.) can mushrooms, drained 1 tb. each: chopped green pepper & pimiento 2 tbs. chopped parsley	4 tbs. flour	1 cup cream ⅔ cup chicken stock ⅔ cup dry white table wine
CHICKEN SORRENTO *Serves 6*	4 tbs. butter	2 tbs. each: chopped onion and green pepper	4 tbs. flour	1 (10½ oz.) can condensed tomato soup 1 cup chicken stock
CHICKEN CREOLE *Serves 4 or 5*	3 tbs. butter	1 medium-sized onion, chopped ¼ cup chopped green pepper 1 clove garlic, chopped or pressed	2 tbs. flour	1 (1 lb.) can stewed tomatoes ⅔ cup dry red table wine

P.S. When a recipe calls for chicken stock, use homemade or canned stock, or make it

COOKED CHICKEN (OR TURKEY)

Stir in	Add & heat very gently *(do not boil!)*	*Serve*
¼ cup dry or medium Sherry ⅓ cup grated Parmesan cheese 1 tsp. each: lemon juice & Worcestershire sauce Salt, pepper, & paprika to taste	2 cups cubed, cooked chicken 1 (4 oz.) can mushrooms, drained 2 tbs. chopped parsley	in patty shells or tart shells, or over waffles or toast
1 small can deviled ham ⅓ tsp. each: scraped onion & Worcestershire sauce Salt & pepper to taste	2 cups cubed, cooked chicken 1 (4 oz.) can mushrooms, drained 2 tbs. chopped parsley	over stalks of cooked broccoli, or in patty or tart shells
1 cup dairy sour cream 2 tbs. dry or medium Sherry ⅓ tsp. each: Worcestershire sauce & paprika Salt and pepper to taste	2½ cups cubed, cooked chicken 2 tbs. chopped parsley	over waffles or toast, or with rice or noodles
1 tb. dry or medium Sherry ¼ tsp. Worcestershire sauce Salt & pepper to taste	2 cups cubed, cooked chicken	in piping hot popovers, patty shells, or tart shells
¼ cup dry or medium Sherry Salt & pepper to taste	2 cups cubed, cooked chicken 1 (4 oz.) can mushrooms, drained	over mounds of *Polenta* or over buttered macaroni or noodles to which a generous amount of grated Parmesan cheese has been added
1 tsp. Worcestershire sauce Salt & pepper to taste	2 cups cubed, cooked chicken 1 cup well-drained canned okra	with rice

with bouillon cubes or chicken stock base.

poultry seasoning, and salt and pepper to taste. Add three slightly beaten eggs blended with one and one-half cups milk. Turn into well-greased eight and one-half-inch ring mold. Bake at 350° F about 45 minutes, or till firm. Let stand five to ten minutes before unmolding.

Polenta (for *Chicken Sorrento*): In top of double boiler mix one cup corn meal, one-third cup instant mashed potato powder, and one and one-half teaspoons salt. Stir in one cup cold water till smooth; add three cups boiling water. Stir over low heat until mixture boils and thickens; cover; cook over boiling water one hour, stirring occasionally. Add one cup grated process American cheese and three tablespoons butter; stir till melted and blended with polenta mixture.

For other interesting ways to use cooked chicken (or turkey), see Chapter V, "Stars at Lunch and Supper."

———◆———

Here is another recipe that makes excellent use of cooked chicken or turkey:

CHICKEN CREAM HASH

4	tablespoons butter
5	tablespoons flour
1	cup cream or rich milk
½	cup chicken stock
½	cup dry white table wine
1	teaspoon grated onion
	Salt, celery salt, and pepper to taste
1½	cups diced, cooked chicken (or turkey)
1½	cups diced, cooked potatoes
2	tablespoons chopped parsley
2	to 3 tablespoons grated Parmesan cheese
	Paprika

Melt butter and stir in flour; add cream, chicken stock, and wine; cook, stirring constantly until sauce boils and thickens. Add onion, salt, celery salt, and pepper. Stir in chicken, potatoes, and parsley. Turn mixture into a greased, shallow baking dish 10 x 6 x 2 inches is a good size. Sprinkle with Parmesan cheese and paprika. Bake in a moderately hot oven (375° F) about 25 minutes, or until bubbly and delicately browned. Serves four or five. Good for luncheon or dinner with a vegetable (perhaps asparagus, peas, or green beans), a sliced tomato salad, and hot rolls. Also nice for brunch with a pickled peach or apricot and hot biscuits or toasted English muffins.

Chicken livers are good at any meal, from breakfast right through dinner. Here they are, served forth with two different sauces. Both of these are good with rice, on toast, or as the filling for a chicken liver omelet.

CHICKEN LIVERS ANNA

Melt butter in a large, heavy skillet; sauté onion until tender and golden. Add chicken livers; sauté gently about five minutes, or until lightly browned, turning frequently. Remove livers from pan. Add flour to drippings and blend well; add gravy and wine; cook, stirring, until mixture boils and thickens. Blend in tomato paste; season with salt and pepper. Just before serving, add livers, mushrooms, and parsley to sauce; heat gently but thoroughly. Serves four.

4 tablespoons butter
2 tablespoons chopped onion
1 pound chicken livers, halved
2 tablespoons flour
1 (10¾ oz.) can beef gravy
¼ cup dry or medium Sherry
1 tablespoon tomato paste
  Salt and pepper to taste
1 (4 oz.) can sliced mushrooms, drained
2 tablespoons chopped parsley

CHICKEN LIVERS GRANADA

Cook bacon, onion, and green pepper together slowly in a large, heavy skillet until bacon begins to brown. Add chicken livers; sauté over medium heat for about five minutes, turning livers often. Sprinkle in flour; add stock and red wine; cook, stirring gently until mixture boils and thickens. Add olives, parsley, Sherry, salt, and pepper. Serve piping hot, without delay! Serves four.

3 slices bacon, diced
¼ cup chopped onion
¼ cup chopped green pepper
¾ pound chicken livers, cut in bite-sized pieces
2 tablespoons flour
½ cup chicken stock
½ cup dry red table wine
½ cup sliced ripe olives
¼ cup chopped parsley
1 tablespoon dry or medium Sherry
  Salt and pepper to taste

I can remember when turkey seldom appeared on the table except at Thanksgiving and Christmas, and in our house the stuffing never varied. Bread, butter, celery, onions, and seasonings were tossed together with nary another ingredient allowed in the mixing bowl. Nowadays we enjoy turkey the year around with all sorts of stuffings, including the two flavorful ones I'm giving you here.

Choose a turkey weighing 12 to 14 pounds, ready-to-cook weight. Rinse with cold water; pat dry. Stuff neck lightly with *Prune and Apple*

ROAST TURKEY WITH PRUNE AND APPLE STUFFING

Stuffing (below). Pull neck skin over stuffing and skewer to back. Bring wing tips up and over back, shaping them "akimbo" fashion. Rub body cavity with salt; pack stuffing in *loosely*. Place skewers across opening and lace shut with string. Tie drumsticks securely to tail, or push them under band of skin at tail. Place bird on a rack in a shallow pan, breast side up. Brush entire surface of bird with melted fat. Cover loosely with a clean piece of cheesecloth dipped in melted fat or salad oil. (As the cloth dries during roasting, moisten it with the pan drippings.) Roast in a slow oven (325° F) about four and one-half to five hours. When turkey is two-thirds done, cut string or band of skin between drumstick and tail, then continue roasting. To test for doneness, press fleshy part of drumstick; meat should feel very soft. Or, move drumstick up and down; the joint should give readily or break. Remove skewers and string. Place bird on a hot platter. Serve with *Giblet Gravy* (below). Serves about 12 to 14, with leftovers.

Rinse prunes and place in a saucepan; cover with water; bring to a boil, then cover and simmer for ten minutes. Drain. Cut prunes from pits in small pieces. Sauté celery and onion gently in fat for five to ten minutes. Add bread crumbs, apple, prunes, poultry seasoning, salt, and pepper; mix lightly but thoroughly. Gradually add enough wine to moisten stuffing nicely. Makes enough stuffing for a 12- to 14-pound turkey. If your bird is larger or smaller, increase or decrease the amount of stuffing, allowing about one cup stuffing per pound of turkey. Extra stuffing may be baked in a separate pan during the last 45 minutes or so the turkey is in the oven. Baste with pan drippings or broth from giblets.

PRUNE AND APPLE STUFFING

1   pound dried prunes
2   cups diced celery
½   cup chopped onion
1   cup fat (butter, turkey fat, etc.)
3½ quarts (14 cups) grated bread crumbs (use 2-day-old bread)
2   cups chopped, peeled apple
2   teaspoons poultry seasoning
2   teaspoons salt
¼   teaspoon pepper
¾   to 1 cup dry red table wine

To make gravy: While turkey is cooking, place gizzard, heart, and neck in a saucepan; add one cup dry red table wine, three cups boiling water, one stalk celery, two or three slices onion, one bay leaf, three or four peppercorns, and one teaspoon salt. Cover and simmer about two and one-half hours, or until giblets are tender. Add liver; continue cooking 15 to 20 minutes. Drain, reserving the liquid; discard neck and chop giblets fine.

When turkey is done, lift it onto a heated platter and set it aside while you finish the gravy. (A "rest" of 20 to 30 minutes will make the bird easier to carve.) Pour off drippings from roasting pan; let fat rise to the top, then skim it off. Add liquid that remains to reserved giblet broth; add water to make four cups liquid. Measure six tablespoons of the fat into a saucepan; blend in six tablespoons flour; add the reserved four cups liquid and cook, stirring constantly until mixture boils and thickens. Pour this gravy into the roasting pan; add chopped giblets and salt and pepper to taste. Continue cooking gently for five minutes, stirring to capture any little brown bits left in the roaster. Serve very hot with the turkey.

ROAST TURKEY WITH RAISIN-WALNUT STUFFING

Choose a turkey weighing 12 to 14 pounds, ready-to-cook weight. Follow recipe above for *Roast Turkey with Prune and Apple Stuffing,* but substitute this stuffing:

Sauté celery and onion gently in fat for five to ten minutes. Add bread crumbs, raisins, walnuts, parsley, poultry seasoning, salt, and pepper; mix lightly but thoroughly. Gradually add enough wine to moisten stuffing nicely. Makes enough stuffing for a 12- to 14-pound turkey.

RAISIN-WALNUT STUFFING

2 cups diced celery
½ cup chopped onion
1 cup fat (butter, turkey fat, etc.)
3½ quarts (14 cups) grated bread crumbs (use 2-day-old bread)
2 cups seedless raisins, rinsed with boiling water and drained
1½ cups chopped walnuts
½ cup chopped parsley
2 teaspoons poultry seasoning
2 teaspoons salt
¼ teaspoon pepper
¾ to 1 cup dry red table wine

Domestic duck comes to the table richly flavored and browned in this version of:

WINE-GLAZED DUCK

Have your meat dealer cut duck into quarters. Trim off any excess fat. Place duck in shallow baking pan. Roast, uncovered, in a hot oven (400° F) for one-half hour. Remove from oven and drain off fat in pan. Season duck well with salt, paprika, and ginger; sprinkle with the grated onion and pour one-fourth cup of the wine in bottom of pan. Cover pan closely with foil. Continue roasting until duck is tender, about 40 to 45 minutes. Combine sugars, cornstarch, salt, orange peel, and remaining three-fourths cup wine in a saucepan; bring to boil; pour over duck. Roast, uncovered, about ten minutes longer, or until duck is nicely glazed, basting frequently. Sprinkle with toasted sesame seeds before serving, if desired. Serves four.

1 large domestic duck
Salt
Paprika
Powdered ginger
2 tablespoons grated onion
1 cup dry red table wine
⅓ cup brown sugar
⅓ cup granulated sugar
1 tablespoon cornstarch
¼ teaspoon salt
1 teaspoon grated orange peel
Toasted sesame seeds (if you like)

Rock Cornish game hens, roasted to a golden brown, are handsome and succulent fare. They're delicious stuffed or *au naturel,* as you prefer.

CASHEW STUFFING

Bring butter, broth (or wine), and onion to boil; add stuffing mix. Remove from heat and stir lightly to blend; add nuts. Pack loosely into cavity of birds. (Wrap any extra stuffing lightly in foil and bake along with the birds the last 15 to 20 minutes they are in the oven.)

¼ cup butter
½ cup broth from giblets (or dry white table wine)
3 tablespoons finely chopped green onion
2 cups prepared stuffing mix half an 8 oz. package)
½ cup cashew nuts, coarsely chopped

STUFFED ROCK CORNISH GAME HENS

Remove giblets from game hens. (Cook giblets in seasoned water to make broth for stuffing, if desired.) Fill cavity of each bird with *Cashew Stuffing;* truss birds. Place in a shallow baking pan; pour butter over birds and season with salt and pepper. Roast in a very hot oven (450° F) about 25 minutes. Add orange juice and wine. Continue roasting in a moderate oven (350° F) 35 to 40 minutes longer, or just until birds are tender, basting frequently with the orange-wine sauce in the pan. Serves four.

4 (about 14 oz.) Rock Cornish game hens
 Cashew Stuffing (page 144)
⅓ cup melted butter
 Salt and pepper
1 cup orange juice
1 cup dry white table wine

ROCK CORNISH GAME HENS, GOURMET

Remove giblets from game hens. (Cooked in seasoned water, the giblets make a good-tasting broth.) Sprinkle inside of each hen with seasoned salt; tuck a sprig of rosemary or mint into the cavity of each one (or sprinkle with dried herb); truss. Place in a shallow baking pan; pour butter over birds. Roast in a very hot oven (450° F) about 25 minutes. Add wine. Continue roasting in a moderate oven (350° F) 35 to 40 minutes longer, or just until birds are tender, basting frequently with the butter-wine sauce in the pan. When ready to serve, sprinkle birds lightly with seasoned salt and chopped parsley. The pan drippings may be used as a thin sauce, or thickened slightly, if desired. Serves four.

4 (about 14 oz.) Rock Cornish game hens
 Seasoned salt
4 small sprigs fresh rosemary or mint (or ¼ teaspoon dried rosemary or mint)
½ cup melted butter
2 cups dry white table wine
 Chopped parsley

Plump, sweet cherries in a wine-and-jelly sauce add the "supreme" touch here.

WILD DUCK SUPREME

Cut ducks in half. Remove necks and backbone; simmer these with the giblets in seasoned water to make stock, if desired. Season duck halves with salt and pepper. Place in a shallow baking pan; roast in a hot oven (425° F) about 20 minutes. Combine stock and wine; pour over duck. Cover pan closely with foil and continue roasting until duck is tender, about ten to twenty minutes longer. Remove foil and skim off any excess fat. Blend jelly, mustard, orange peel, and lemon juice into pan drippings; stir in flour. Roast, uncovered, a few minutes longer, basting duck several times until glazed. Add drained cherries and let stand in oven a few minutes to heat. Serves four to six.

2 or 3 wild ducks
  Salt and pepper
½ cup duck or chicken stock (or water or syrup drained from canned cherries)
½ cup Port
½ cup currant jelly
1 teaspoon dry mustard
1 teaspoon grated orange peel
1 teaspoon lemon juice
1 tablespoon flour
1 (8¾ oz.) can pitted, dark, sweet cherries

P.S. If the ducks are large, additional stock or wine may be added, and roasting time can be increased as necessary for birds to become tender before glazing.

———————◆———————

I was brought up with the idea that there was only one way to cook wild duck. Twelve minutes in a very hot oven and it was ready to be rushed to the table on a platter too hot to handle, there to be carved, bathed with lemon juice, and dusted liberally with paprika. I still think duck done this way makes good eating, but my enthusiasm for it has been tempered somewhat by my fondness for duck cooked with wine. Nothing could be simpler than:

ROAST WILD DUCK WITH RED WINE

Clean the ducks; wash and dry them well. Sprinkle inside and out with salt. Stuff with slices of apple and onion, and put in a few celery tops, too. Lay slices of bacon over the breast. Place in a shallow baking pan. Roast, uncovered, in a very hot oven (450° F-500° F), basting often with dry red table wine (about one-half cup per duck). Allow 15 to 20 minutes for rare duck, 45 minutes if you like yours well done. Remove the "stuffing" before serving. Wild rice, peas, and hot biscuits with currant jelly are wonderful companions here.

P.S. If you like your duck well done, you may also like it stuffed. Use your favorite bread-and-butter stuffing, adding the usual chopped onion and celery, and maybe a bit of chopped apple. (A stuffing of cooked wild rice plus a bit of sautéed onion and celery is also good.) Stuff the ducks *loosely*, then truss them and roast them as directed above for well-done duck.

Fortunately you don't have to be a hunter or know one to enjoy pheasant these days. Game farms have taken care of the situation nicely. Wine pairs happily with pheasant in numerous ways, such as:

ROAST PHEASANT WITH RICE-MUSHROOM STUFFING

1	pheasant (about 2 lbs., ready-to-cook weight)
	Rice-Mushroom Stuffing
2	slices bacon
½	cup dry or medium Sherry
¼	cup melted butter
3	tablespoons flour
1½	cups chicken stock
2	tablespoons dry or medium Sherry
	Salt and pepper to taste

Fill cavity of pheasant loosely with stuffing; truss; place in a baking pan and lay slices of bacon over bird. Roast in a moderate oven (350° F) for about one hour, or until pheasant is tender, basting frequently with a mixture of the one-half cup wine and the melted butter. Remove pheasant to a serving platter and keep warm. To prepare gravy: Pour off drippings from pan; measure three tablespoons and return to pan. Blend in flour; add stock and cook, stirring, until mixture boils and thickens. Add the two tablespoons wine; season with salt and pepper. Serve hot with the pheasant. Serves two.

Rice-Mushroom Stuffing: Sauté two tablespoons chopped onion in two tablespoons butter five minutes. Measure liquid from one (4 oz.) can mushroom stems and pieces; add water to make one cup liquid; add this to sautéed onion. Bring to a boil; slowly sprinkle in one-half cup rice; cover and cook very slowly for about 25 minutes, or until rice is tender and liquid is absorbed. Stir in drained mushrooms and two tablespoons chopped parsley; season with salt and pepper. (Extra stuffing may be baked, covered, during the last 20 minutes or so the bird is in the oven. A spoonful or two of the pan drippings will give it added flavor.)

PHEASANT BAKED IN SOUR CREAM

Season pheasant with salt and paprika mixed together. Beat eggs with one-fourth cup of the wine. Dip each piece of pheasant into egg mixture, then roll in bread crumbs, patting crumbs firmly onto surface. Brown pieces gently in heated oil. Arrange browned pheasant in large shallow casserole or baking pan. Combine stock with remaining one-half cup wine; pour over pheasant. Cover and bake in moderately hot oven (375° F) about 30 minutes. Stir in sour cream. Cover and continue baking 15 to 20 minutes longer, or until meat is tender. Serve pheasant with surrounding gravy; garnish each serving with rings or crescents of avocado, if you like. Serves six to eight.

6 to 8 good-sized, meaty pieces of pheasant, cut for frying (or 12 to 16 pieces, if birds are small)

1 teaspoon seasoned salt

1 teaspoon paprika

2 eggs

¾ cup dry white table wine

1 cup fine, dry bread crumbs

⅓ cup salad oil (or half butter and half salad oil)

½ cup chicken stock or water

1 cup dairy sour cream

BAKED PHEASANT WITH RED WINE

Rub skin side of pheasant halves with butter; sprinkle with salt and pepper. Place, skin side down, in a shallow baking pan; lay strips of bacon over pheasant. Bake, uncovered, in a moderately hot oven (375° F) for 15 minutes. Pour wine over pheasant. Continue baking at 375° F for 30 minutes, or until pheasant is tender, basting frequently with the pan juices. Remove pheasant and bacon to a platter or dinner plates; garnish with triangles of toast. Add parsley to pan juices; pour over pheasant or serve separately. Serves two. (Don't forget to catch every last drop of the delicious juices with those triangles of toast!)

1 pheasant (about 2 pounds, ready-to-cook weight), split in half
¼ cup soft butter
Salt and pepper to taste
4 slices bacon
¾ cup dry red table wine
2 slices crisp toast, cut diagonally in quarters
2 tablespoons chopped parsley

Even mature birds become tender and juicy when cooked as:

QUAIL EN CASSEROLE

Rub whole birds with seasoned salt. Brown them nicely in heated oil in a deep skillet. Remove birds to a heated casserole. Sauté vegetables about five minutes slowly in remaining oil until soft but not brown. Blend in flour; gradually stir in stock; cook, stirring until mixture is thickened and smooth. Taste and season with additional salt, if needed. Pour sauce over quail; add wine. Cover and bake in a moderate oven (350° F) about one-half to three-quarters of an hour until birds are tender. Serves four.

4 quail
Seasoned salt
⅓ cup salad oil (or half butter and half salad oil)
1 carrot, finely chopped
¼ cup chopped green onion
1 cup sliced fresh mushrooms
2 tablespoons flour
1½ cups chicken stock
½ cup dry white table wine

Treat goose to a spicy wine marinade before roasting.

ROAST GOOSE, CALIFORNIA STYLE

Place prepared goose in marinade made by combining wine, vinegar, juice of orange and lemons, onion, bay leaf, celery leaves, nutmeg, and brown sugar. Let stand three or four hours or overnight in refrigerator; turn and baste often. Drain goose, reserving marinade. Season bird with salt and pepper; place apples and celery stalks inside cavity. Truss goose; place, breast-side up, in roasting pan. Sear in a very hot oven (450° F) for about 15 minutes; drain off excess fat from pan. Spoon on part of marinade; cover pan. Lower heat to 350° F and roast one to one and one-half hours, or just until bird is tender, basting frequently with remaining marinade and pan drippings. Serves four to six.

1   young goose
1½ cups dry white table wine
⅓   cup wine vinegar
1   orange
2   lemons
1   small onion, sliced
1   bay leaf
    Few sprigs celery leaves
⅛   teaspoon nutmeg
2   tablespoons brown sugar or honey
    Salt and pepper
2   tart apples, quartered
2 or 3 stalks celery

✤ VIII ✤

If Fish Is The Dish

How do you like your fish? Baked to tender perfection . . . sautéed to a delicate brown . . . simmered ever so gently and served with a piquant sauce? Whatever your choice, it will be all the more delectable if somewhere along the line a bit of wine enters the picture . . . usually a dry white table wine or dry or medium Sherry, often dry Vermouth. Occasionally a red table wine is found in a fish recipe, but it's the exception, not the rule.

In our house we enjoy fish often. Our favorite "cut" is the fillet, and we like it cooked in lots of different ways. Baking is the most versatile method. You can be plain or fancy as the mood and the occasion demand and you'll be rewarded with good eating every time.

In this first recipe the fillets are marinated briefly in wine, dipped in fine bread crumbs, then drizzled with melted butter and baked quickly to a golden brown. The result is a nice crisp crust and a wonderful flavor. In this and any of the fillet recipes to come you can use whatever fish your market affords—sole, sea bass, cod, halibut, perch, salmon, and so on—fresh or frozen. If you use frozen fillets, thaw and separate them before cooking.

CRUSTY BAKED FISH FILLETS

Arrange fish fillets in a single layer in
a shallow pan or baking dish. Mix
wine and salt; pour over fish; let stand
30 minutes or so. Remove fillets from
wine and roll in bread crumbs, turning until well coated. Place fillets on a
well-greased baking sheet or shallow
baking pan. Drizzle melted butter
evenly over them; dust with paprika.
Bake in a very hot oven (500° F) for
ten to 12 minutes, or until tender and
nicely browned. Serve at once with
Tartar Sauce or *Cucumber Sauce.*
Serves two if you enjoy fish as much
as we do, three if your appetites are
more modest.

1 pound fish fillets
1 cup dry white table wine or
  dry Vermouth
2 teaspoons salt
1 cup very fine, dry bread
  crumbs (toast dry bread and
  roll your own, or use packaged crumbs)
2 or 3 tablespoons melted butter
  or salad oil
  Paprika

Here's baked fish with a "built-in" sauce. Instead of being given the
crumb treatment as in the recipe above, the marinated fish is spread
with one of several savory mixtures before baking.

BAKED FISH FILLETS PIQUANT

Arrange fish fillets in a single layer in
a shallow pan or baking dish. Mix
wine and salt; pour over fish; let stand
30 minutes or so. Remove fillets from
wine and pat as dry as possible with
paper towels. Place in a well-greased
shallow baking dish. Spread evenly
with one of these toppings:

1 pound fish fillets
1 cup dry white table wine or
  dry Vermouth
2 teaspoons salt
  Topping (see below)
  Fine, dry bread crumbs
  Paprika

1. Mix one-half cup mayonnaise, one-half cup dairy sour cream, and
two tablespoons finely chopped green onion (including some green
tops).
2. Mix one cup dairy sour cream and one tablespoon anchovy paste.
3. Mix three-fourths cup mayonnaise, one-half cup grated Parmesan

cheese, two tablespoons finely chopped onion, and two teaspoons lemon juice.

Sprinkle bread crumbs over topping and dust with paprika. Bake in a very hot oven (500° F) for ten to twelve minutes, or until fish flakes when tested with a fork. Remove from oven and let stand a few minutes, just long enough to let any juices settle. Serve with lemon wedges. Serves two or three.

—————◆—————

The sturdy flavors of onion, garlic, green pepper, and tomato contribute to the succulent goodness of:

FISH FILLETS IMPERIAL

Arrange fish fillets in a single layer in a shallow baking dish; tuck tomato wedges around fish. Mix onion, garlic, and green pepper; spread evenly over fish. Sprinkle with salt, pepper, and oregano. Mix wine and melted butter; pour over all. Bake in a moderately hot oven (375° F) for 25 to 30 minutes, or until fish is tender, basting occasionally. Serves three or four. Rice and green beans are admirable companions to this dish, and for an extra note of flavor pass a bowl of grated Parmesan cheese to be sprinkled over the fish at the table.

1½ pounds fish fillets (or steaks)
2 fresh tomatoes, peeled and cut in eighths (or use 2 thoroughly drained canned tomatoes)
1 small onion, chopped
1 clove garlic, chopped or put through garlic press
½ green pepper, grated (if you like)
  Salt and pepper to taste
  Generous pinch of oregano
½ cup dry white table wine, dry or medium Sherry, or dry Vermouth
¼ cup melted butter or salad oil

—————◆—————

Take your choice of canned cream of mushroom soup or frozen cream of shrimp soup in this next recipe. With either one you'll have a wonderful addition to your repertoire of quick-and-easy main dishes.

SIMPLE SOLE

Arrange one pound fillets of sole (or other fish) in a single layer in a greased shallow baking dish. Over it spread one of the following sauces:

Mushroom Sauce: Mix one (10½ oz.) can condensed cream of mushroom soup, three tablespoons dry or medium Sherry or dry Vermouth, two tablespoons chopped parsley, and one tablespoon chopped onion.

Shrimp Sauce: Thaw one (10 oz.) can frozen condensed cream of shrimp soup by letting it stand, unopened, in a pan of hot water for about 30 minutes. Mix thawed soup with four tablespoons dry or medium Sherry, one-half teaspoon grated lemon peel, and a dash of cayenne.

Sprinkle with one-half cup shredded Cheddar cheese or one-fourth cup grated Parmesan cheese. Dust with paprika. Bake in a moderately hot oven (375° F) about 25 minutes, or until fish flakes when tested with a fork. Serves two or three.

———————◆———————

There are lots of good fish dishes in which fillets are covered with a sauce, cream or otherwise, and then baked. These are easy to do and they're dressy enough for your fanciest dinner party. Here are some of my favorites:

BAKED FISH FILLETS IN CHEESE SAUCE

1½ pounds fish fillets
¼ cup butter
¼ cup flour
1 cup milk
⅓ cup dry white table wine or dry or medium Sherry
1 cup grated Cheddar cheese (natural or process)
½ teaspoon Worcestershire sauce
Dash of nutmeg
Salt, celery salt, and pepper to taste
¼ cup grated Parmesan cheese
Paprika

Arrange fish in a single layer in a greased shallow baking dish. Melt butter and stir in flour; add milk and cook, stirring constantly, until mixture boils and thickens. Blend in wine; add Cheddar cheese and stir over lowest possible heat until melted. Add seasonings. Pour sauce over fish; sprinkle with the Parmesan cheese and dust with paprika. Bake in a hot oven (450° F) for ten to 15 minutes, or until fish flakes when tested with a fork. Serves four.

P.S. Substitute one-half cup chicken stock and one-half cup cream or rich milk for the milk in the above recipe and, *voilà*, another good dish!

An interesting cream sauce with shrimp added teams deliciously with the fillets here.

BAKED SOLE WITH SHRIMP SAUCE

Arrange fillets in a single layer in a shallow baking dish. Melt butter and stir in flour; add milk and cream; cook, stirring, until mixture boils and thickens. Blend in mayonnaise and Sherry; add parsley, lemon peel, salt, and pepper; stir in shrimp. Pour sauce over fish; dust with paprika. Bake in a moderately hot oven (375° F) about 25 minutes, or until fish flakes when tested with a fork. Serves four.

1½ pounds fillets of sole (or other fish)
4 tablespoons butter
4 tablespoons flour
¾ cup milk
¾ cup light cream (or milk, for a less rich sauce)
2 tablespoons mayonnaise
3 tablespoons dry or medium Sherry
2 tablespoons chopped parsley
½ teaspoon grated lemon peel
Salt and pepper to taste
¾ to 1 cup cooked or canned small shrimp
Paprika

Intriguing in appearance and delicious to eat is this next dish featuring sole spread with a shrimp-filled cream sauce and baked in foil.

SOLE BAKED IN FOIL

To serve four, allow four good-sized fillets of sole. Cut four pieces of aluminum foil large enough so that when the fillet is laid on it and wrapped up, the package can be sealed with a double fold all the way around. Crease each piece of foil down the center, then spread it out flat again. Lay a fillet on each piece of foil, placing it so that one side of the fillet is next to the crease.

Cover each fillet with some of the *Shrimp Sauce* (below). Fold foil over sole so that edges of foil meet; seal wide side with a double fold, then seal ends the same way. Place packages on a baking sheet. Bake in a hot oven (425° F) for 20 minutes. Remove from oven and make a short slit in the center of the top of each package with a sharp paring knife. Serve packages as is, and let each person open his own. Serves four.

SHRIMP SAUCE

Sauté onion gently in butter for five
minutes. Blend in flour; add cream
and cook, stirring, until mixture boils
and thickens. Blend in Sherry, then
add all remaining ingredients except
paprika. Spread sauce over sole; dust
with paprika. Bake as directed above.

2 tablespoons chopped onion
¼ cup butter
¼ cup flour
¾ cup light cream or rich milk
¼ cup dry or medium Sherry
½ teaspoon grated lemon peel
Salt, celery salt, and pepper
to taste
1 cup cooked or canned shrimp
(whole if small, cut up if large)
2 tablespoons chopped parsley
Paprika

Company fare indeed is this dish combining sole and creamed crabmeat. It's another of my fish favorites. Since this is a perfect party dish,
the recipe is planned to serve eight. It's a simple matter to halve it to
serve four.

CRAB-STUFFED FILLETS OF SOLE

Divide sole into 16 even portions. Arrange eight of these in eight shallow
individual baking dishes (or in two 12
x 8 x 2-inch baking dishes). Melt
butter and stir in flour; gradually add
milk and cook, stirring constantly until mixture boils and thickens. Add
Sherry, lemon peel, Worcestershire
sauce, mustard, salt, pepper, and nutmeg. Mix sauce, crabmeat, and spinach; spread mixture over sole in
dishes; cover with remaining fillets.
Brush with melted butter; sprinkle
with Parmesan cheese. Bake in a hot
oven (400° F) for 20 minutes. Before
serving, dust with paprika. Serves
eight. Good with shoestring potatoes
and green beans to which toasted
slivered almonds have been added.

3 to 3¼ pounds fillet of sole
6 tablespoons butter
6 tablespoons flour
2 cups rich milk
3 tablespoons dry or medium
Sherry
1 teaspoon grated lemon peel
1 teaspoon Worcestershire sauce
½ teaspoon prepared mustard
Salt and pepper to taste
Dash of nutmeg
1 pound cooked or canned crabmeat
1 (10 oz.) package frozen
chopped spinach, cooked and
thoroughly drained
Melted butter
Grated Parmesan cheese
Paprika

Some Thoughts on Poaching Fish

Poaching fish, simmering it in a seasoned liquid just until tender, is an excellent way to cook either a large piece or the smaller slices and fillets. The secrets of success here are to be sure that the poaching liquid (court bouillon) is a happy symphony of flavors, and that once the fish is added it is cooked ever so gently, *never* boiled.

A good basic recipe for the poaching liquid includes equal parts of dry white table wine (or dry Vermouth) and water, plus seasonings to taste—salt, peppercorns, bay leaf, sliced or chopped onion, and perhaps a few slices of carrot and celery, several sprigs of parsley, and a pinch of thyme.

Use a large kettle for poaching a sizeable chunk of fish, a skillet for fillets or slices. In the kettle or skillet prepare the amount of court bouillon you think you'll need so the fish will be barely covered.

If it's a large piece you're cooking, wrap it loosely in cheesecloth so you'll be able to remove it from the kettle without having it break apart. Place the fish in the simmering liquid, and, if necessary, add a little more wine so the fish is barely covered. Cover the kettle or skillet and simmer ever so gently until the fish is done, allowing five to ten minutes for fillets or slices, eight to twelve minutes per pound for a large piece. Test for doneness with a fork.

Lift the cooked fish onto a heated platter, garnish with sprigs of watercress or parsley, and serve hot with your favorite sauce. (*Shellfish Sauce*, *Egg Sauce*, and *Hollandaise Sauce* are especially good here) or, for a fine hot-weather dish, chill the fish and serve it with *Tartar Sauce*, *Cucumber Sauce* or mayonnaise. To my palate, there's nothing more delightful in salmon season that a chilled, poached coral-pink fillet on a bed of watercress or butter lettuce, with a few slices of tomato and cucumber for garnish and a bowl of caper-decked mayonnaise to top it off!

Trout poached in wine is delicious hot or cold.

TROUT POACHED IN WINE
(Served hot)

Remove heads from trout. Slash flesh of fish two or three times on the diagonal. Season inside and out with seasoned salt and pepper. Melt butter in a shallow, wide skillet or baking pan. When butter bubbles, remove pan from heat and lay trout in it, side by side. Pour wine and mushroom liquid over fish; sprinkle on the mushrooms. Cover pan with foil and poach fish in a moderately hot oven (375° F) about 25 minutes, or just until tender-firm. Place fish on a heated platter and sprinkle with parsley. Thicken remaining pan liquid slightly, if desired, and serve as a sauce. Serves four or five.

4 or 5 medium-large trout
Seasoned salt and pepper
3 tablespoons butter
½ cup dry white table wine
½ cup liquid from canned mushrooms (or chicken stock)
½ cup sliced canned mushrooms
Finely chopped parsley

TROUT POACHED IN WINE
(Served cold)

Remove heads from trout. Slash flesh of fish two or three times on the diagonal. Season fish inside and out with lemon juice, dill, salt, and pepper. Let stand 15 minutes. In a shallow, wide skillet bring wine, stock, and onion to a gentle bubble. Add trout and simmer just until fish is tender, about 15 minutes. Cool fish in liquid; remove skin. Chill fish and liquid until ready to serve. Arrange fish on a platter; spoon a little of the liquid over it. Serve with watercress mayonnaise, made by blending finely chopped watercress into mayonnaise. Serves four or five.

4 or 5 medium-large trout
Fresh lemon juice
Dried dill or rosemary
Salt and pepper
1 cup dry white table wine
1 cup chicken stock
¼ cup chopped green onion

Here's a real party dish. Portions of sole wrapped around oysters are poached, then baked in a creamy crab-filled sauce. Frozen oyster stew makes a wonderfully flavorful base for the sauce.

SOLE AND OYSTER ROLLS IN CRABMEAT SAUCE

1	(10 oz.) can frozen condensed oyster stew
1½	pounds fillets of sole
12	medium-sized oysters
1½	cups water
1	cup dry white table wine or dry Vermouth
1	slice onion
	Pinch of thyme
3 or 4	whole peppercorns
	Salt to taste
⅓	cup butter
⅓	cup flour
¼	cup cream or rich milk
2	tablespoons dry or medium Sherry
	Pepper to taste
1½	cups cooked or canned crabmeat (or shrimp)
⅓	cup grated Parmesan cheese
	Paprika

Thaw oyster stew by letting the can stand, unopened, in a pan of hot water for about 30 minutes. Cut fillets of sole in 12 pieces; wrap each one around an oyster; fasten with toothpicks. Combine water, white table wine, onion, thyme, peppercorns, and salt in a large skillet; heat to simmering. Place fish in liquid; cover and simmer gently for five to ten minutes, or just until fish is tender. Carefully remove fish to six greased shallow individual casseroles or to a shallow baking dish 12 x 8 x 2 inches. Remove toothpicks. Strain fish liquid and boil rapidly until reduced to one cup. Melt butter and stir in flour; add reduced fish liquid, thawed oyster stew, and cream; cook, stirring constantly, until mixture boils and thickens. Add Sherry; season to taste with salt and pepper; add crabmeat. Pour sauce over fish; sprinkle with Parmesan cheese and paprika. Bake in a hot oven (450° F) about ten minutes, or just until bubbly and delicately browned. Serves six.

If you would like to taste pan-cooked fish that is wonderfully moist and well-flavored, a sort of vinous cousin to the usual fried fish, try this:

FISH SAUTE

Arrange steaks in a single layer in a shallow dish; pour wine over them. Let stand in the refrigerator for an hour or so, turning once. Remove steaks from wine, sprinkle with salt and pepper, and roll in flour. Heat butter and oil in a large skillet; add floured steaks and sauté quickly to a golden brown on one side, then turn carefully and brown the other side. Add wine in which fish was marinated; cover and simmer very gently for five minutes or so, just until fish flakes when tested with a fork. Place fish on a heated platter or dinner plates; sprinkle with paprika and/or parsley. Serve at once with *Tartar Sauce*. Serves four.

4 servings fish steaks or fillets
¾ cup dry white wine or dry Vermouth
Salt and pepper
Flour
2 tablespoons butter
2 tablespoons salad oil
Paprika and/or chopped parsley

Striped bass, stuffed and baked in wine, is a fisherman's delight.

STUFFED BAKED BASS

Scale fish; remove head and tail. Place fish in a hot oven (425° F) for about five minutes to loosen skin; carefully remove skin and discard. Sprinkle fish with salt and pepper; squeeze on lemon juice. Combine bread crumbs with all remaining ingredients except wine. Stuff fish lightly and fasten together with small skewers. Place fish in a buttered baking dish; spoon on half the wine. Bake in a moderately hot oven (375° F) until fish is tender-firm, 45 to 60 minutes, basting with remaining wine and pan juices. Serve garnished with thin slices of fresh tomato and a sprinkling of finely chopped parsley, if desired. Serves about six.

4- to 5-pound striped bass (or salmon or other fish)
Salt and pepper
Lemon juice
1½ cups fine, dry bread crumbs
¼ cup finely chopped green onion
1 teaspoon chopped fresh basil or rosemary (or ¼ teaspoon dried basil or rosemary)
2 tablespoons chopped parsley
¼ cup chopped or sliced mushrooms (fresh or canned)
¾ teaspoon seasoned salt
½ cup melted butter
1 cup dry white table wine

P.S. For a quick sauce, dilute a 10½ oz. can condensed cream of mushroom soup with the juices from the fish. Serve very hot.

———◆———

A delicious variation on the sauté theme is:

FISH FILLETS MEUNIÈRE

Marinate, flour, and cook four servings fish fillets as described above in the recipe for *Fish Sauté*. Remove cooked fish to a heated platter. Have ready a mixture of:

Heat sauce to simmering and pour over fish fillets. Serve at once. Serves four.

¼ cup butter, melted and cooked gently until slightly browned
1 tablespoon lemon juice
1 tablespoon chopped parsley

FISH FILLETS AMANDINE

Marinate, flour, and cook four servings fish fillets as described in the recipe for *Fish Sauté* (above). Remove cooked fish to a heated platter. Have ready a sauce made as follows:

AMANDINE SAUCE

Melt butter; add almonds and sauté gently until almonds are golden brown. Add lemon juice and parsley. Heat to simmering and pour over fish. Serve at once. Serves four.

½ cup butter
½ cup shaved or slivered unblanched almonds
2 tablespoons lemon juice
1 tablespoon chopped parsley

SOME THOUGHTS ON BROILING FISH

Basting fish during broiling with a mixture of butter and dry white table wine or dry Vermouth is a wonderful way to ensure juiciness and good flavor. Whether you are cooking small whole fish (with or without heads and tails), split and boned medium-sized fish, or slices or fillets of large fish, the procedure is the same:

Line a shallow baking pan with aluminum foil and brush the foil with salad oil or melted butter. Lay the fish in the pan. (Split fish should be skin-side down.) Dot *generously* with butter; sprinkle with salt, pepper, and (if you like) a bit of finely chopped onion. Place in a preheated broiler. When the butter starts to melt, begin basting with dry white table wine or dry Vermouth, using enough wine so you can spoon it generously over each piece of fish. Broil until fish flakes easily with a fork, basting frequently and adding wine to the pan as needed. No need to turn the fish; if it begins to get too brown before it's tender, simply move the pan lower down in the oven. Remove the cooked fish carefully to a heated platter or dinner plates (two broad spatulas are handy here). Spoon any pan juices over it and sprinkle with chopped parsley, or serve with *Amandine Sauce*. Serve at once.

———◆———

I couldn't keep house without canned tuna! It's indispensable as a sandwich filling, good in salads, and most versatile as a hot-dish ingredient. Here are some tuna recipes I think you'll enjoy:

TUNA DIABLE

Melt butter and stir in flour; add milk and cook, stirring constantly, until mixture boils and thickens. Add wine, lemon juice, mayonnaise, mustard, onion juice, salt, and pepper; blend well. Stir in tuna and parsley. Heat gently but thoroughly before serving. Serve over mounds of rice or in patty shells. Serves four or five.

¼ cup butter
⅓ cup flour
1¾ cups milk
⅓ cup dry white table wine
2 tablespoons lemon juice
¼ cup mayonnaise
1 tablespoon prepared mustard
1 teaspoon onion juice
Salt and pepper to taste
2 (6½ or 7 oz.) cans tuna, drained and flaked
2 tablespoons chopped parsley

TUNA EN COQUILLE

Mix sour cream, wine, lemon juice, Worcestershire sauce, mustard, and eggs. Stir in tuna, cracker crumbs, parsley, and onion. Add salt and pepper. Spoon mixture into six greased baking shells or individual casseroles. Top each with a lemon slice and sprinkle with paprika. Bake in a moderate oven (350° *F*) for 30 minutes. Serves six.

¾ cup dairy sour cream
¼ cup dry or medium Sherry
1 tablespoon lemon juice
1 teaspoon Worcestershire sauce
½ teaspoon dry mustard
2 eggs, slightly beaten
2 (6½ or 7 oz.) cans tuna, drained and flaked
⅓ cup fine cracker crumbs
¼ cup chopped parsley
1 tablespoon chopped onion
Salt and pepper to taste
6 thin slices lemon
Paprika

SAVORY CREAMED TUNA

Mix all ingredients except tuna and eggs in a saucepan; heat gently to simmering. Add tuna and eggs; continue heating just until piping hot. Serve on toast, with rice, or over servings of hot, cooked broccoli or asparagus. Serves four.

1 (10½ oz.) can condensed cream of celery soup
3 tablespoons mayonnaise
¼ cup dry or medium Sherry
¼ cup grated Parmesan cheese
2 tablespoons chopped parsley
1 teaspoon grated lemon peel
¼ teaspoon Worcestershire sauce
1 (6½ or 7 oz.) can tuna, drained and flaked
3 hard-cooked eggs, quartered lengthwise and halved crosswise

P.S. This delectable sauce is also good with chicken, crabmeat, or shrimp. Wonderful, and so easy!

———————◆———————

Serve this delicately-flavored dish in little individual casseroles, or in tart shells or patty shells.

CREAMED FISH FLAKES

Melt butter and stir in flour; add milk and cook, stirring, until mixture boils and thickens. Add Sherry, lemon peel, and seasonings. Carefully stir in fish and parsley. Heat gently before serving. Spoon into casseroles, tart shells, or patty shells, and dust each portion with paprika. Serves four.

4 tablespoons butter
4 tablespoons flour
1½ cups rich milk
4 tablespoons dry or medium Sherry (or 2 tablespoons each: Sherry and Brandy)
¾ teaspoon grated lemon peel
½ teaspoon Worcestershire sauce
   Dash of nutmeg
   Salt, celery salt, and pepper to taste
2 cups flaked, cooked fish (halibut, haddock, cod, or salmon)
2 tablespoons chopped parsley
   Paprika

P.S. This is an excellent way to use leftover poached fish. Or, you can "start from scratch" with one pound of fish and simmer it, covered, for five to ten minutes in a mixture of one cup dry white table wine, one cup water, and seasonings to taste. Drain and flake the fish then proceed as directed. One (1 lb.) can of salmon or two (6½ or 7 oz.) cans of tuna may also be used in this recipe.

———————◄►———————

This has been a favorite luncheon-party main dish in my family for as long as I can remember. Fill the center with any sauce you like— *Egg Sauce, Shellfish Sauce,* and *Hollandaise Sauce* are especially recommended—or fill the center with peas mixed with mushrooms and pass the sauce separately.

MIMI'S FISH TIMBALE RING

Combine wine, water, onion, celery, and salt in a large skillet; bring to a boil. Add fish; cover and simmer five to ten minutes, or just until fish is tender. Drain and flake fish. Simmer bread crumbs and cream together gently for five minutes, stirring constantly. Remove from heat; cool slightly. Add fish and parsley; beat with a fork until ingredients are well blended. Season to taste. Add the slightly beaten egg yolks, then gently fold in the stiffly beaten egg whites. Turn into a well-greased ring mold, set in a shallow pan of hot water, and bake in a moderate oven (350° F) for about 50 minutes, or until firm. Remove from oven and let stand out of the water for five minutes or so before unmolding onto a heated platter. Serves five or six.

1 cup dry white table wine
1 cup water
1 small onion, sliced
1 stalk celery, sliced
  Salt to taste
1 pound halibut, cod, haddock, sea bass, or salmon
1 cup (firmly packed) grated soft bread crumbs
1 cup light cream or rich milk
2 tablespoons chopped parsley
  Celery salt, onion salt, and pepper to taste
3 eggs, separated

———————◄►———————

Here's one of the most popular of all crab dishes. It's perfect for a party luncheon with a molded pineapple and cucumber salad and some hot rolls.

DEVILED CRAB

Melt butter and stir in flour; add milk and cook, stirring constantly until mixture is thickened and smooth; continue cooking and stirring for another minute or two. Add lemon juice, Sherry, and seasonings; gently stir in crabmeat and eggs. Turn into four greased baking shells or individual casseroles; top each with a slice of lemon; dust generously with paprika. Bake in a moderately hot oven (375° F) for 20 minutes. Serves four.

4 tablespoons butter
4 tablespoons flour
1½ cups rich milk
2 tablespoons lemon juice
¼ cup dry or medium Sherry
2 teaspoons Worcestershire sauce
1 teaspoon prepared mustard
Salt to taste
Dash of cayenne
1½ cups cooked or canned crab-meat
2 hard-cooked eggs, chopped
4 thin slices lemon
Paprika

P.S. Shrimp or tuna can replace the crabmeat.

Canned salmon is another very versatile and handy ingredient. There are lots of good dishes to be made from it such as:

JUNEAU SALMON CASSEROLE

Soak soft bread crumbs in milk for ten minutes or so; beat well with a fork. Add all remaining ingredients except buttered crumbs; mix well. Turn into a greased baking dish; top with buttered crumbs. Bake in a moderate oven (350° F) for 30 to 40 minutes, or until firm in the center. Serve with fat wedges of lemon, or with *Hollandaise Sauce, Egg Sauce,* or *Shellfish Sauce.* Serves four or five.

1 cup (firmly packed) grated soft bread crumbs
½ cup rich milk
¼ cup dry white table wine
1 (1 lb.) can salmon, drained, boned, and flaked
1 cup grated Cheddar cheese
2 eggs, slightly beaten
1 tablespoon lemon juice
½ teaspoon grated lemon peel
2 tablespoons grated onion
½ teaspoon Worcestershire sauce
Salt, celery salt, garlic salt, and pepper to taste
½ cup buttered fine bread crumbs

This is a distant relative of the French *bouillabaisse*, a flavorful mingling of fish, shellfish, and a tomato-wine sauce. It's a sort of cross between a soup and a stew, best served with lots of hot garlic-buttered French bread (for lapping up the sauce) and a tossed green salad.

FISHERMAN'S CATCHALL

Heat oil in a Dutch oven or other heavy kettle. Add onion, garlic, tomatoes, parsley, celery, green pepper, and bay leaf; cook gently for five minutes. Add wine, clam broth, and seasonings; cover and simmer, stirring occasionally, for 45 minutes. Add fish and shellfish; cover and simmer just until fish is tender, ten minutes or less. Serve piping hot in heated individual casseroles or soup bowls. Serves eight.

⅓ cup olive oil
½ cup chopped onion
1 clove garlic, chopped or pressed
3 fresh tomatoes, peeled and cut up, or 3 well-drained canned tomatoes, cut up
2 tablespoons each: chopped parsley, celery, and green pepper
1 bay leaf, crumbled
1½ cups dry white table wine
1½ cups canned clam broth (or water)
   Pinch each of saffron and rosemary
   Dash of Tabasco sauce
   Salt and pepper to taste
1½ pound fillets of sole, cut in serving-sized pieces
1½ pounds fillets of halibut, haddock, cod, or sea bass, cut in serving-sized pieces
1 cup oysters
1 cup cooked or canned crabmeat
1 cup cooked or canned shrimp

P.S. This dish is even better if the sauce is made the day before and allowed to mellow. Then just before the dish is to be served, the sauce can be heated, the fish and shellfish added, and the dish completed.

◆

All the members of the shellfish family seem to take kindly to a curry sauce. This sauce is pleasantly flavored and not so pungent that it will overpower the personality of the crabmeat.

CURRIED CRABMEAT

Melt butter in the top of a double boiler over direct heat; add onion and sauté until golden. Blend in flour and curry powder; add cream, chicken stock, and white wine; cook, stirring constantly until mixture is thickened and smooth. Add crabmeat, parsley, Sherry, sugar, salt, and garlic salt. Cover and let stand over hot water for 15 to 20 minutes before serving. Serve with rice. Serves four or five.

4 tablespoons butter
2 tablespoons minced onion
4 tablespoons flour
1½ teaspoons curry powder
1 cup light cream or rich milk
½ cup chicken stock
½ cup dry white table wine
2 cups cooked or canned crab-meat
2 tablespoons minced parsley
1 tablespoon dry or medium Sherry
¼ teaspoon sugar
Salt and garlic salt to taste

Shrimp makes an excellent curry. For instance:

SHRIMP CURRY WITH WHITE WINE

Melt butter in a heavy skillet or sauce-pan; add onion, garlic, celery, and apple; cook gently five minutes. Stir in curry powder; continue cooking for five minutes. Blend in flour; add chicken broth and wine; cook, stirring constantly, until mixture is thickened and smooth. Add parsley, salt, and pepper; cover and simmer gently, stirring occasionally, for 30 minutes. Just before serving, add cream and shrimp. Serve piping hot with rice. Serves five or six. Chutney is a "must" with this dish. Other traditional curry condiments (chopped crisp bacon, chopped hard-cooked egg, seedless raisins, flaked coconut, diced banana, etc.) may be added to the menu as desired.

¼ cup butter
1 large onion, chopped
1 clove garlic, chopped or pressed
3 stalks celery, chopped
1 apple, pared, cored, and chopped
1 tablespoon curry powder (or to taste)
¼ cup flour
2½ cups chicken broth
½ cup dry white table wine
2 tablespoons chopped parsley
Salt and pepper to taste
½ cup light cream
4 cups cooked or canned shrimp

Easy to put together and very good to eat is

CRABMEAT FLORENCE

Cook spinach without salt; drain *thoroughly*. In a saucepan combine the mushroom soup, one cup of the cheese, cream, Sherry, Worcestershire sauce, and pepper; stir over low heat until cheese melts and ingredients are nicely blended. Mix one-half cup of this sauce with the spinach; spread in bottom of a greased 10 x 6 x 2-inch baking dish. Arrange crabmeat evenly over spinach; cover with remaining sauce. Mix crumbs and melted butter; sprinkle over contents of casserole. Top with remaining cheese and dust with paprika. Bake in a moderate oven (350° F) for 25 to 30 minutes. Serves six to eight. All you need with this are hot rolls and a salad . . . a bowl of mixed greens, wedges of tomato, and artichoke hearts tossed with French dressing would be a good choice.

2 (10 oz.) packages frozen chopped spinach
1 (10½ oz.) can condensed cream of mushroom soup
2 cups grated Cheddar cheese
¼ cup cream or rich milk
¼ cup dry or medium Sherry
1 teaspoon Worcestershire sauce
Dash of pepper
1 pound crabmeat
½ cup fine, dry bread crumbs
2 tablespoon melted butter
Paprika

If you use the small bay scallops in these next two recipes, leave them whole. The large deep-sea scallops should be halved or quartered. Either variety will give you a tasty dish.

SCALLOPS NEWBURG

In a saucepan combine one pound fresh or thawed frozen scallops, one-half cup dry white table wine, and a dash of salt. Add enough boiling water so scallops are barely covered. Cover and simmer five minutes. Drain. The scallops are now ready to be used in place of the lobster in the recipe for *Lobster Newburg*.

SCALLOP SHELLS

Drain mushrooms, reserving liquid. In a saucepan combine mushroom liquid, wine, and dash of salt; heat to simmering. Add scallops; cover and simmer five minutes. Remove scallops from liquid. Boil liquid rapidly until reduced to three-fourths cup. Sauté mushrooms, onion, and green pepper gently in butter for five minutes. Blend in flour; add cream and the three-fourths cup scallop liquid; cook, stirring until mixture boils and thickens. Add cheese, parsley, thyme, marjoram, salt, and pepper. Add scallops to sauce; turn into four greased baking shells or individual casseroles sprinkle with bread crumbs and paprika. Bake in a moderate oven (350° F) for 15 minutes, then broil just long enough to brown the crumbs. Serves four.

1 (4 oz.) can sliced mushrooms
¾ cup dry white table wine
Salt
1 pound scallops (fresh or thawed frozen ones)
2 tablespoons chopped onion
2 tablespoons chopped green pepper (if you like)
3 tablespoons butter
3 tablespoons flour
¾ cup light cream or rich milk
2 tablespoons grated Parmesan cheese
2 tablespoons chopped parsley
Dash each of thyme and marjoram
Pepper
½ cup buttered fine bread crumbs
Paprika

Oysters adapt themselves nicely to various sauces. Serve one of these oyster specialties with a salad and hot rolls for Sunday night supper, or any night when a supper rather than a hearty dinner is on the agenda.

OYSTERS POULETTE

Melt butter in top of double boiler over direct heat; blend in flour; add stock and wine; cook, stirring constantly, until sauce boils and thickens. Place over boiling water. Mix cream and egg yolks; add to sauce, stirring constantly; season with salt, pepper, and cayenne. Heat oysters in their liquid until edges curl; drain thoroughly; add to sauce. Serve at once in toast cases or patty shells. Serves four.

2 tablespoons butter
3 tablespoons flour
¾ cup chicken stock (or vegetable stock made by dissolving 1 vegetable bouillon cube in ¾ cup water)
¼ cup dry white table wine
⅓ cup light cream
2 egg yolks, slightly beaten
Salt and pepper to taste
Dash of cayenne
1 pint oysters

OYSTERS MEPHISTO

Drain oysters, reserving liquid. Measure liquid; add milk to make one cupful. Melt butter and stir in flour; add oyster liquid-milk mixture; cook, stirring constantly until sauce boils and thickens. Add wine, lemon juice, Worcestershire sauce, onion, beef extract, mustard, salt, and pepper. Let sauce cool slightly, then stir in oysters. Turn mixture into greased baking shells or individual casseroles; sprinkle with Parmesan cheese; dust with paprika. Bake in a hot oven (400° F) for about 15 minutes, or *just* until piping hot and nicely browned. (Do not overcook!) Serves three or four as a main dish, six as the first course at a dinner party.

1   pint oysters
    Milk
¼   cup butter
¼   cup flour
¼   cup dry or medium Sherry
1½ teaspoons lemon juice
1   teaspoon Worcestershire sauce
1   teaspoon grated onion
½   teaspoon beef extract
½   teaspoon prepared mustard
    Salt and pepper to taste
    Grated Parmesan cheese
    Paprika

Canned minced clams have lots of possibilities, recipe-wise. Here they're featured in a light main dish.

BAKED CLAMS AU GRATIN

Drain clams; measure one cup liquid. Melt butter and stir in flour; add the one cup clam liquid, cream and wine; cook, stirring constantly, until mixture boils and thickens. Add seasonings. Remove from heat; blend in egg yolk; add clams, hard-cooked eggs, and parsley. Turn mixture into greased baking shells or individual casseroles; sprinkle with Parmesan cheese and paprika. Bake in a moderately hot oven (375° F) for about 15 minutes, or until bubbly and golden brown on top. Serves four to six.

2   (7 oz.) cans minced clams
3   tablespoons butter
4   tablespoons flour
¼   cup light cream
¼   cup dry white table wine
½   teaspoon Worcestershire sauce
    Salt, onion salt, garlic salt, and pepper to taste
    Dash of cayenne
1   egg yolk, slightly beaten
3   hard-cooked eggs, chopped
2   tablespoons chopped parsley
    Grated Parmesan cheese
    Paprika

A good-to-eat and interesting version of a traditional dish is:

SPECIAL SCALLOPED OYSTERS

Drain oysters. Melt butter and stir in flour; add cream and stock; cook, stirring until mixture boils and thickens. Stir in wine and lemon juice; season with nutmeg, salt, and pepper. In a greased casserole arrange half the oysters, then half the croutons and half the sauce. Repeat layers. Sprinkle Parmesan cheese over the top; dust with paprika. Bake in a hot oven (450° F) for 20 minutes. Serves four.

1 pint oysters
3 tablespoons butter
3 tablespoons flour
½ cup cream
½ cup chicken stock
⅓ cup dry white table wine
1 teaspoon lemon juice
Dash of nutmeg
Salt and pepper to taste
2 cups croutons (you can buy excellent ones "ready made")
¼ cup grated Parmesan cheese
Paprika

Mention "lobster" and the two words that come first to mind (to my mind, anyway) are "Newburg" and "Thermidor." This version of the former should probably be called "nearly Newburg" as it departs somewhat from the classic recipe, thickened only with egg yolks, but it's delicious nonetheless.

LOBSTER NEWBURG

Mix lobster and wine; set aside while preparing sauce. Melt butter in top of double boiler over direct heat; stir in flour; add one cup cream; cook, stirring constantly until mixture boils and thickens. Add lemon juice, Worcestershire sauce, salt, paprika, nutmeg, and cayenne. Stir in lobster-wine mixture. Set over hot water. Blend egg yolks with remaining one-half cup cream; add to contents of double boiler; cook over hot water, stirring frequently, for about ten minutes, just until sauce is thick and creamy. Taste and add salt and pepper, if needed. Serve at once on toast, or in patty shells or toast cases. Serves four.

2 cups diced, cooked lobster, or 2 (6½ oz.) cans lobster, drained
4 tablespoons dry or medium Sherry (or 2 tablespoons each: Sherry and Brandy)
4 tablespoons butter
3 tablespoons flour
1½ cups light cream
1 teaspoon lemon juice
½ teaspoon Worcestershire sauce
Salt and paprika to taste
Dash each of nutmeg and cayenne
2 egg yolks, slightly beaten

P.S. Crabmeat or shrimp may be substituted for the lobster.

A dish of real elegance for great occasions is

LOBSTER THERMIDOR

Split lobsters lengthwise; remove meat and cut in bite-sized pieces. Sauté mushrooms and onion in two tablespoons of the butter for five minutes. Melt remaining four tablespoons butter and blend in flour; add cream and cook, stirring until mixture boils and thickens. Remove from heat. Add Sherry, lemon juice, mustard, cayenne, salt, and pepper; stir in lobster and mushrooms. Fill lobster shells with the mixture; sprinkle with buttered cracker crumbs, Parmesan cheese, and paprika. Bake in a moderately hot oven (375° F) for 15 minutes, then brown quickly under the broiler before serving. Serves four.

2 boiled lobsters (about 2 pounds each)
½ pound fresh mushrooms, scrubbed and sliced, or 1 (6 oz.) can sliced broiled mushrooms, drained
1 tablespoon finely chopped onion
6 tablespoons butter
4 tablespoons flour
1¾ cups light cream or rich milk
¼ cup dry or medium Sherry
2 teaspoons lemon juice
Pinch of dry mustard
Dash of cayenne
Salt and pepper to taste
¼ cup fine cracker crumbs, mixed with 1 tablespoon melted butter
¼ cup grated Parmesan cheese
Paprika

Cream cheese gives richness of texture and flavor to the sauce for

LOBSTER SUPREME

Melt butter and stir in flour; add chicken stock and cream; cook, stirring constantly until mixture boils and thickens. Add cheese and wine; stir over low heat until cheese melts. Season with salt and pepper. Add lobster, mushrooms, and parsley. Heat gently just until piping hot. Serve over mounds of hot, cooked rice. Serves five or six.

4 tablespoons butter
4 tablespoons flour
1 cup chicken stock
½ cup light cream
1 (3 oz.) package cream cheese (pimiento or plain)
¼ cup dry or medium Sherry
Salt and pepper to taste
2 cups diced, cooked lobster, or 2 (6½ oz.) cans lobster, drained
1 (4 oz.) can mushroom stems and pieces, drained
2 tablespoons chopped parsley

P.S. Shrimp and crabmeat are also good prepared this way.

⊕ IX ⊕

Sauces Savory
And Simple

═══════════════════════════

Let's start off with some thoughts about Cream Sauce. (Call it "White Sauce" if you must, but somehow "white" just doesn't make my taste buds quiver.) A good cream sauce is stirred as it cooks so that it's as smooth as satin (a French whip or wire whisk is a wonderful help), it's cooked slowly and carefully in a heavy saucepan over low heat (or in a double boiler) so no raw, starchy taste is detectable when it's served, and it's seasoned with care and imagination.

The surest way I know to give cream sauce a pleasing flavor personality is to stir in a little dry or medium Sherry—one to two tablespoons per cup. Most creamed dishes, chicken, seafood, vegetables, or eggs, are the better for this addition. Other seasonings that may be added with happy results include a little grated lemon peel, a chicken or vegetable bouillon cube or some chicken stock base, a dash of nutmeg or mace, or a few drops of Worcestershire sauce. A spoonful of mayonnaise lends piquancy; it's especially good when the sauce is to go with seafood. And it goes without saying that salt, plain or flavored, and pepper will be in the pot, too. Just don't forget the Sherry!

To review the basic cream sauce recipe . . .

BASIC CREAM SAUCE

Melt butter and stir in flour; add milk gradually and cook, stirring over low heat until mixture boils and thickens. Continue cooking and stirring for another minute or two. Add Sherry; season to taste. Makes about one cup sauce.

2 tablespoons butter
2 tablespoons flour
1 cup milk (the richer the better)
1 to 2 tablespoons dry or medium Sherry
Salt, pepper, and other seasonings (see suggestions above)

P.S. To make *Thin Cream Sauce* (the basis for cream soups), reduce butter and flour to one tablespoon each. To make *Thick Cream Sauce* (the basis for croquettes), increase butter and flour to four tablespoons each.

Now for some variations on the basic theme.

Shellfish Sauce: To *Basic Cream Sauce* add one-half to three-fourths cup cooked or canned shrimp, lobster, or crabmeat. Include a bit of grated lemon peel and a dash of Worcestershire sauce among the seasonings. Serve with poached, broiled, or plain-baked fish.

Egg Sauce: To *Basic Cream Sauce* add two chopped hard-cooked eggs, one tablespoon chopped parsley, and a bit of grated onion. For *Anchovy-Egg Sauce*, stir in one teaspoon anchovy paste. Serve with fish.

Cheese Sauce: To *Basic Cream Sauce* add one-half to one cup grated natural or process Cheddar cheese; stir over low heat until melted. Include Worcestershire sauce among the seasonings. For *French Cheese Sauce*, add three tablespoons *each* grated Parmesan cheese and grated Swiss cheese instead of the Cheddar.

Mushroom Sauce: Prepare *Basic Cream Sauce*, but sauté one-half pound sliced fresh mushrooms or one cup sliced canned mushrooms in the butter before blending in the flour.

Sauce Élégante: Prepare *Basic Cream Sauce*. Blend one slightly beaten egg yolk with one-fourth cup cream; stir into sauce just before serving. Taste and adjust seasoning, if necessary.

Hollandaise is an aristocrat among sauces and is supremely elegant with asparagus, broccoli, spinach ring, poached fish, corned or roast beef hash, and sundry other dishes. A touch of dry Sherry or dry Vermouth gives this luscious sauce an extra bit of flavor that I find very "becoming." Try my version, and remember that the secret of success is to cook the mixture over hot, *never* boiling, water.

HOLLANDAISE SAUCE

½ cup butter
4 egg yolks
⅓ cup boiling water
2 tablespoons dry Sherry, or dry Vermouth
1 tablespoon lemon juice
¼ teaspoon salt
Dash of cayenne

Melt butter in the upper part of a small double boiler. Put egg yolks in a small bowl; beat slightly; gradually stir in melted butter, then boiling water. Pour mixture into top of double boiler; stir constantly over hot (not boiling!) water until mixture is very thick and satin-smooth. Remove double boiler from the heat. Stir in wine, then lemon juice and seasonings. If sauce is not to be served at once, remove top of double boiler from lower part, set aside until shortly before serving, and then reheat sauce over hot (not boiling!) water. Makes about one and one-fourth cups.

P.S. Lacking a small double boiler, you can use a small saucepan set in a larger one.

BÉARNAISE SAUCE

Follow the recipe for *Hollandaise Sauce*, using dry Vermouth. Substitute two teaspoons tarragon white wine vinegar for the lemon juice; add one tablespoon chopped parsley and one teaspoon grated onion. The last word with steak!

When it comes to Brown Sauce, I'll confess that very often I take advantage of the canner's art and use the excellent canned brown gravy that's readily available in most markets.

If mushrooms fit into the dish that's being "sauced," canned brown gravy with mushrooms is my choice. Of course I add a little wine, usually Sherry, and sometimes I add a bit of onion or garlic, a dash of powdered herbs, or whatever suits my mood at the moment.

There are times, however, when I like to concoct my own brown sauce, and this is the recipe I use:

BASIC BROWN SAUCE

Sauté onion and bay leaf gently in butter until butter is golden brown. Blend in flour; gradually add bouillon and cook slowly, stirring constantly, until mixture boils and thickens. Simmer *very* gently for two or three minutes. Strain sauce. Add Sherry and seasonings. Reheat before serving. Use wherever a brown gravy is needed. Makes about one and one-fourth cups.

1   tablespoon minced onion
½   bay leaf
2   tablespoons butter or meat drippings
2½ tablespoons flour
1   (10½ oz.) can condensed bouillon (beef broth)
2   tablespoons dry or medium Sherry
½   teaspoon Worcestershire sauce
    Dash of thyme
    Salt and pepper to taste

Here are some good brown sauce variations.

Currant Lamb Sauce: Stir one-fourth cup red currant jelly into the strained sauce; heat, stirring, until jelly melts. Serve with lamb. (A bit of chopped fresh or dried mint is a good addition to this sauce.)

Mushroom Brown Sauce: Sauté one-half pound sliced fresh mushrooms or one cup canned sliced mushrooms in two tablespoons of butter for five minutes. Add to *Basic Brown Sauce.*

Romanoff Sauce: Add one-half cup dairy sour cream and two tablespoons tomato paste to *Basic Brown Sauce;* blend well. Taste and adjust seasoning as necessary. Very good with hamburgers, meat loaf, and leftover roast beef.

Here are two alternates for *Basic Cream Sauce* that are excellent for creaming chicken, seafood, or vegetables, and that go very well over croquettes, cheese dishes, etc. Any of the variations given for *Basic Cream Sauce* (*Shellfish Sauce, Egg Sauce, Cheese Sauce, Mushroom Sauce,* and *Sauce Élégante*) apply equally deliciously to these two:

EASY BECHAMEL SAUCE

Prepare *Basic Cream Sauce,* substituting one-half cup chicken stock and one-half cup cream for the one cup milk. Add Sherry; season to taste.

WHITE-WINE CREAM SAUCE

Melt butter and stir in flour; gradually add cream and stock and cook, stirring, over low heat until mixture boils and thickens. Continue cooking and stirring for another minute or two. Blend in wine; add remaining ingredients. Makes about one cup sauce.

2 tablespoons butter
2 tablespoons flour
½ cup cream
¼ cup chicken stock
¼ cup dry white table wine
½ teaspoon lemon juice
½ teaspoon Worcestershire sauce
1 tablespoon chopped parsley
   Salt, onion salt, and pepper to taste

———————

Here's one of the best sauces for hamburgers and cheeseburgers that was ever devised. Spread it generously on both bun halves just before you put the meat, or the meat and cheese, between them. If you like onion, include a few thin slices in the sandwich. With this sauce no other relishes or condiments are needed.

HAMBURGER RELISH SAUCE

Blend mayonnaise, mustard, and Vermouth; add remaining ingredients. Cover and store in the refrigerator for several hours before serving so that flavors will have a chance to blend. Makes about one and one-fourth cups sauce.

1 cup mayonnaise
2 tablespoons prepared mustard (the yellow variety)
2 tablespoons dry Vermouth
1 tablespoon well-drained sweet pickle relish
1 teaspoon celery seed
   Chopped or pressed garlic to taste
¼ cup finely shredded process Cheddar cheese
½ teaspoon Worcestershire sauce
   Salt to taste

A red wine-mushroom sauce that's perfect with every kind of steak from hamburger to filet mignon is

MUSHROOM STEAK SAUCE

Sauté onion gently in butter until golden brown. Stir in flour and cook to a deep brown. Add wine and consommé; cook, stirring constantly, until mixture boils. Add remaining ingredients. Simmer, uncovered, for 15 to 20 minutes, or until sauce is quite thick, stirring frequently. Remove garlic. Pour over steak before serving or pass separately. Serves four generously.

2 tablespoons minced onion
4 tablespoons butter
2 tablespoons flour
1 cup dry red table wine
1 (10½ oz.) can condensed consommé
Pinch each of thyme, marjoram, and paprika
Salt and pepper to taste
1 clove garlic, peeled and halved
1 (8 oz.) can mushroom stems and pieces, drained

CUMBERLAND SAUCE

Stir jelly over low heat until melted. Blend remaining ingredients; add to jelly; bring to a boil, then simmer, stirring constantly for two or three minutes. Let stand an hour or more before serving. Serve (at room temperature) with wild or domestic duck, cold turkey or chicken, or hot or cold ham. Makes about one cup.

6 tablespoons red currant jelly
4 tablespoons Port
4 tablespoons orange juice
2 tablespoons lemon juice
2 teaspoons dry mustard
1 teaspoon paprika
½ teaspoon ground ginger
1 teaspoon cornstarch
2 tablespoons grated orange peel

HUNTER'S SAUCE

Combine all ingredients in a small saucepan; stir over low heat until jelly and butter are completely melted and sauce is piping hot. Serve warm with wild duck or baked ham. Makes one cup.

½ cup red currant jelly
¼ cup Port
¼ cup catsup
½ teaspoon Worcestershire sauce
2 tablespoons butter

Serve this sauce piping hot with hamburgers, frankfurters, fried chicken, fried prawns or wherever a flavorful sauce with tomato overtones is indicated.

PATIO RELISH SAUCE

Sauté onion and garlic gently in butter until golden and tender. Add remaining ingredients; mix well and heat to simmering. Serve piping hot. Makes about two cups.

1 medium-sized onion, grated
1 clove garlic, grated or put through garlic press
6 tablespoons butter
¾ cup catsup
½ cup dry or medium Sherry
3 tablespoons lemon juice
1½ teaspoons Worcestershire sauce
   Salt to taste

A tangy butter sauce that's fine with broiled or plain-baked fish is

LEMON-BUTTER SAUCE

Combine all ingredients in a saucepan; let stand over low heat until butter melts. Stir well and let stand at room temperature for an hour or so to allow flavors to blend. Remove garlic and reheat before serving. Makes about three-fourths cup.

6 tablespoons butter
¼ cup dry white table wine
¼ cup lemon juice
2 tablespoons chopped parsley
1 clove garlic, peeled and halved
¼ teaspoon paprika
   Salt to taste

An easy cheese sauce with lots of uses is . . .

QUICK CHEESE SAUCE

Combine cheese and cream in a double boiler; heat, stirring occasionally, until cheese melts. Add Sherry and Worcestershire sauce; blend well. Serve over vegetables (broccoli, asparagus, cauliflower, etc.) or wherever a cheese sauce is needed. Makes about one cup.

½ pound process Cheddar cheese, sliced
¼ cup cream or rich milk
¼ cup dry or medium Sherry
¼ teaspoon Worcestershire sauce

P.S. You'll find a number of other good-tasting sauces in Chapter V, "Stars at Lunch and Supper."

How lonesome fried fish would be without *Tartar Sauce!* This is the way I make it.

TARTAR SAUCE

Mix all ingredients. Cover and chill for several hours so flavors can blend. Makes one generous cupful.

1 cup mayonnaise
2 tablespoons dry Vermouth, or dry Sherry
2 tablespoons each: finely chopped dill pickle, finely chopped pimiento - stuffed olives, and chopped parsley
1 tablespoon each: finely chopped onion and finely chopped drained capers
Dash of Tabasco sauce
Salt to taste

Here is a sauce that's good instead of *Tartar Sauce* for a change:

CUCUMBER SAUCE

Pare cucumber; cut lengthwise in halves and remove seeds. Grate or chop fine; drain thoroughly by pressing between several thicknesses of paper towels. Mix cucumber with all remaining ingredients except paprika. Turn into a small serving bowl; dust with paprika. Chill an hour or so before serving. Makes about one and one-fourth cups. This is elegant with cold poached salmon or any cold fish dish. Also a good alternate for Tartar Sauce with fried fish.

½ medium-sized cucumber
1 cup dairy sour cream
2 tablespoons dry Vermouth
2 teaspoons lemon juice
1 tablespoon chopped, drained capers (if you like)
Bit of fresh or dried dill
Salt and pepper to taste
Paprika

P.S. Another good *Cucumber Sauce:* Follow the recipe above, but instead of one cup sour cream use two-thirds cup sour cream and one-third cup mayonnaise.

I like my barbecue sauces on the light side both in consistency and seasoning. It seems a shame to add anything that will detract from that wonderful cooked-over-the-coals flavor! Some simple sauces that we have enjoyed are:

EASY BARBECUE BASTING SAUCES

1. Equal parts of dry or sweet Vermouth and salad oil, plus salt and pepper to taste- with chicken or turkey

2. Equal parts of dry white table wine and salad oil, plus a bit of chopped onion and/or garlic, maybe a pinch of tarragon or rosemary, and salt and pepper to taste—with chicken or turkey

3. Two parts dry or medium Sherry, one part soya sauce, and one part salad oil, plus a bit of chopped garlic, if you wish—with chicken, turkey, beef, lamb, or seafood

4. Two parts white table wine, one part soya sauce, and one part salad oil, plus a bit of onion or garlic—with chicken, turkey, lamb, or seafood

5. Equal parts of red table wine and salad oil, plus chopped onion and/or garlic, a bit of your favorite herbs, and salt and pepper to taste with beef or lamb

Marinate the meat, chicken, or whatever in the sauce for an hour or more before cooking, and use the sauce for basting during barbecuing. You'll be rewarded with some very good eating!

A steak marinade with a lively and distinctive flavor is *Teriyaki Sauce*. Maybe "Sherriyaki" would be a better name for this version.

TERIYAKI SAUCE

Combine all ingredients in a pint jar. Cover and refrigerate for an hour or more so flavors can blend. Marinate thin steaks, strips of thinly sliced round steak, or strips of scored flank steak in this sauce for one to two hours. Cook on the outdoor grill, or broil or pan-fry indoors.

½ cup soya sauce
¼ cup dry or medium Sherry
2 tablespoons sugar
1 to 2 tablespoons grated onion
1 clove garlic, chopped or pressed
1 tablespoon grated fresh ginger root (or 1 teaspoon of ground ginger)

P.S. We also like *Teriyaki Sauce* as a marinade for lamb. Ask your meat dealer for thick (really *thick!*) shoulder lamb chops. Marinate them as directed, turning them occasionally. Then grill them outdoors, or broil them in the oven.

Excellent for marinating and basting chicken or any meat is

SHERRY-HERB BARBECUE SAUCE

Combine all ingredients in a jar or bowl; shake or beat well before using. Makes about one cup sauce.

½ cup dry or medium Sherry
⅓ cup salad oil
1 medium-sized onion, grated
1½ teaspoons Worcestershire sauce
1 teaspoon dry mustard
1½ teaspoons mixed fresh herbs, or ¾ teaspoon mixed dried herbs (thyme, marjoram, rosemary, oregano)
½ teaspoon garlic salt
¼ teaspoon salt
½ teaspoon coarse black pepper

If you enjoy a "tomato-y" basting sauce with a robust flavor, try this:

EL RANCHO BASTING SAUCE

Cook onion and garlic gently in oil for five minutes. Add remaining ingredients. Simmer, uncovered, for 15 minutes. Use as a basting sauce when barbecuing or oven-broiling meat or poultry. Makes about two and one-half cups. This sauce keeps well in the refrigerator.

1 small onion, grated
1 clove garlic, grated or put through garlic press
½ cup salad oil
½ cup catsup
½ cup sweet Vermouth
1 cup water
1 tablespoon lemon juice
2 teaspoons Worcestershire sauce
½ teaspoon oregano
  Salt to taste

To Round Out
The Main Course

A perfectly cooked vegetable served *au naturel* is hard to improve on. Fresh in color, true in flavor, tender yet pleasantly firm, it's a real joy to the palate. Add anything except butter, and a mere sprinkle of seasoning and you'll be gilding the lily.

But sometimes lily-gilding brings rewards and often dressing up a vegetable is a good idea, especially when the rest of the main course is un-sauced or won't offer too much competition flavor-wise. For instance, a creamed vegetable and shrimp curry are hardly a happy twosome, while a broiled lamb chop is perfectly at home on a plate with rich and "cheesey" potatoes *au gratin*.

It's usually in the dressing up that wine enters the vegetable-cookery picture. A bit of white wine in the sauce for creamed cauliflower, a spoonful of Sherry in the spinach ring, a little red wine in the tomato sauce that's teamed with eggplant—this is how wine can be used to give many vegetable dishes a touch of intriguing flavor.

When fresh asparagus is in season we enjoy it often as a first course at dinner, all by itself, so we can appreciate every last vestige of its glorious flavor. We like it "sauced" with plain melted butter, or with a Sherry-flavored cheese sauce, or (on state occasions) with Hollandaise. But I think our favorite is this wine-butter-Parmesan combination which adds piquancy and richness of flavor without dwarfing the personality of the vegetable.

ASPARAGUS PARMESAN

While asparagus cooks, combine butter, wine, lemon juice, and parsley in a small saucepan; heat slowly until butter melts. Lift cooked asparagus carefully onto heated plates. Spoon some of the hot butter-wine sauce over each serving. Sprinkle with grated Parmesan cheese and dust with paprika. Serve at once. Serves four to six.

4 to 6 servings hot, cooked asparagus (fresh or frozen)
½ cup butter
¼ cup dry Vermouth (or dry white table wine, but preferably Vermouth)
2 teaspoons lemon juice
2 tablespoons chopped parsley
Grated Parmesan cheese
Paprika

ARTICHOKES PARMESAN

Substitute two (9 oz.) packages of frozen artichoke hearts for the asparagus in *Asparagus Parmesan* and you'll have a delicious artichoke dish for six. Simply cook and drain the artichokes, mix them gently with the sauce, then turn them into a heated serving dish and sprinkle with Parmesan cheese and paprika.

———————◆———————

Another good way with these frozen hearts is:

ARTICHOKE HEARTS WITH MUSHROOMS

Cook and drain artichoke hearts. Drain mushrooms, reserving liquid. Mix cornstarch and Sherry in a saucepan, stirring until perfectly smooth; add mushroom liquid. Cook, stirring over medium heat until mixture is thickened and clear. Add remaining ingredients. Combine this sauce with the artichoke hearts and mushrooms. Heat gently before serving. Serves three or four.

1 (9 oz.) package frozen artichoke hearts
1 (4 oz.) can sliced mushrooms
1½ teaspoons cornstarch
2 tablespoons dry or medium Sherry
2 tablespoons butter
½ teaspoon lemon juice
Salt, onion salt, garlic salt, and pepper to taste
1 tablespoon chopped parsley

P.S. A package of frozen peas, lima beans, or French-style green beans may be substituted for the artichoke hearts in this recipe. Or, a one-pound can of any of these vegetables, well drained, will do the trick nicely.

Green beans are as versatile a vegetable as you can find. Flavorwise, they combine well with many different ingredients such as cheese, bacon, mushrooms, herbs, and so on. In this easy dish mushroom soup plus Sherry makes the sauce, and canned French-friend onions contribute an interesting note of flavor and texture.

GREEN-BEAN MUSHROOM CASSEROLE

Blend soup and Sherry; combine gently with the beans and one-half of the onions. Bake in a moderate oven (350° F) about 25 minutes. Crumble remaining onions; sprinkle over top; continue baking five minutes. Serves six.

1 (10½ oz.) can condensed cream of mushroom soup
3 tablespoons dry or medium Sherry
3 cups drained cooked or canned French-style green beans
1 (3½ oz.) can French-fried onions

Another good-eating bean idea is

GREEN BEANS PARMESAN

Follow the recipe for *Asparagus Parmesan*, but substitute four to six servings cooked or canned French-style green beans for the asparagus. Mix the hot, drained beans lightly with the butter-wine sauce, then heap in a serving dish and sprinkle with Parmesan cheese and paprika.

If you're a beet fancier, you'll enjoy

BEETS BURGUNDY

Mix cornstarch, sugar, onion salt, and cloves in a saucepan; add Burgundy and wine vinegar, stirring until mixture is perfectly smooth. Stir over medium heat until mixture is thickened and clear. Add butter; gently stir in drained beets. Remove from heat and let stand 30 minutes or so to blend flavors. Reheat gently before serving. Serves three or four.

1½ teaspoons cornstarch
⅓ cup sugar
Dash of onion salt
⅛ teaspoon powdered cloves
¼ cup Burgundy or other red table wine
¼ cup red wine vinegar
2 tablespoons butter
1 (1 lb.) can julienne beets, drained

A Sherry-flavored orange sauce combines flavorfully with the beets here.

BEETS IN ORANGE SAUCE

Mix cornstarch, sugar, and salt in a saucepan; add orange juice, Sherry, and lemon juice, stirring until mixture is perfectly smooth. Stir over medium heat until mixture is thickened and clear. Add butter and orange peel; gently stir in drained beets. Remove from heat and let stand 30 minutes or so to blend flavors. Reheat gently before serving. Serves three or four.

2   teaspoons cornstarch
3   tablespoons brown sugar
¼   teaspoon salt
½   cup orange juice
2   tablespoons dry or medium Sherry
1   tablespoon lemon juice
2   tablespoons butter
1   teaspoon grated orange peel
1   (1 lb.) can baby beets, drained

The ever-faithful carrot becomes quite a glamorous vegetable prepared as

SHERRY-GLAZED CARROTS

Scrub or scrape carrots; slice diagonally, making oval-shaped pieces. Place carrots in saucepan; add all ingredients except parsley. Bring to a boil, then cook fairly rapidly, uncovered, for 15 to 20 minutes, or until liquid has cooked down almost to a syrup and carrots are tender. Reduce heat and continue cooking slowly for five to ten minutes, or until carrots are well glazed, turning carrots frequently. Turn carrots into serving dish and sprinkle with parsley. Serves six.

1½ pounds carrots
1⅔ cups water
⅓   cup dry or medium Sherry
¼   cup sugar
1   teaspoon salt
2   tablespoons butter
1   tablespoon finely chopped parsley or fresh mint

You can fill the center of this ring with another vegetable—peas, green beans, or parslied potato balls—or you can turn it into a main dish by filling it with creamed chicken, tuna, or shellfish.

CARROT RING WITH WHITE WINE

Melt butter and stir in flour; add milk; cook, stirring constantly, until mixture is thickened and smooth. Blend in wine. Add carrots, eggs, onion, parsley, sugar, nutmeg, salt, and pepper. Pour into a well-greased, one-quart ring mold; set in a shallow pan of hot water. Bake in a moderate oven (350° F) for 40 to 50 minutes, or until firm. Remove from oven and let mold stand out of the water for five minutes or so before unmolding on a heated platter. Fill center as desired. Serves six.

2 tablespoons butter
2 tablespoons flour
¾ cup milk
¼ cup dry white table wine
2½ cups mashed, cooked carrots
3 eggs, well beaten
1 tablespoon minced onion
2 tablespoons chopped parsley
½ teaspoon sugar
Dash of nutmeg or mace
Salt and pepper to taste

Here's a quick and simple way to "cream" broccoli. The flavor is delightful.

MUSHROOM-BROCCOLI CRÈME

Cook broccoli without salt until tender; drain thoroughly. Combine soup and wine in the saucepan in which the broccoli was cooked; heat slowly to simmering, stirring constantly. Add broccoli; stir gently until well mixed with the sauce. Add nutmeg; taste and also add salt, if needed. Serve piping hot. Serves three or four, and it's no trick at all to double it for six or eight.

1 (10 oz.) package frozen chopped broccoli
½ cup canned condensed cream of mushroom soup
1-2 tablespoons dry or medium Sherry
Dash of nutmeg
Salt to taste

P.S. The mixture can also be turned into a greased pie plate, or casserole sprinkled with buttered crumbs and/or grated cheese, and baked in a moderate oven (350° F) about 20 minutes, or just until piping hot.

Like asparagus, broccoli takes kindly to a number of sauces, from melted butter on up. Hollandaise and cheese sauce are traditional favorites, and I heartily recommend:

BROCCOLI PARMESAN

Follow the recipe for *Asparagus Parmesan* but substitute four to six servings of hot, cooked broccoli spears for the asparagus.

Mayonnaise adds a piquant note of flavor here. This dish is delicious by itself, or as a "base" for creamed chicken, tuna, or shellfish.

BROCCOLI PUDDING

Cook broccoli and drain thoroughly. Melt butter and stir in flour; add milk and cook, stirring until mixture boils and thickens. Remove from heat. Blend in Sherry, then mayonnaise; add eggs. Combine this mixture with the broccoli; season with onion, salt, and pepper. Turn into a greased nine-inch pie plate; sprinkle with Parmesan cheese and paprika. Bake in a moderate oven (350° F) about 30 minutes, or until firm in the center. To serve, cut in wedges. Serves four or more, depending on the rest of the menu.

1 (10 oz.) package frozen chopped broccoli
2 tablespoons butter
2 tablespoons flour
½ cup milk
2 tablespoons dry or medium Sherry
½ cup mayonnaise
3 eggs, well beaten
Bit of grated onion
Salt and pepper to taste
Grated Parmesan cheese
Paprika

P.S. If you prefer, you can bake this mixture in a well-greased ring mold. Set the mold in a pan of hot water and bake at 350° F about 45 minutes. Fill the center of the ring with creamed chicken or seafood, or with another vegetable.

———◆———

Little white onions, cooked or canned, combine well with a number of sauces. (How good creamed onions are with roast turkey!) Incidentally, it's well to serve these or any other "sauced" vegetable in side dishes ("bird's bathtubs," my father calls them) instead of right on the dinner plate. That way the sauce won't interfere with the rest of the main course and nary a drop of it will be wasted.

HOLIDAY ONION CASSEROLE

Melt butter and stir in flour; add milk and bouillon cube; cook, stirring until mixture boils and thickens and bouillon cube is completely dissolved. Add one-half cup of the cheese and the wine; stir over low heat until cheese melts. Season with salt and pepper. Add onions, nuts, and parsley. Turn into a greased casserole; sprinkle with remaining cheese and dust with paprika. Bake in a hot oven (400° F) about 20 minutes, or until bubbly and browned.

2 tablespoons butter
2 tablespoons flour
¾ cup milk
1 chicken bouillon cube (or 2 teaspoons chicken stock base)
¾ cup grated Cheddar cheese
⅓ cup dry white table wine
Salt and pepper to taste
1 (1 lb.) can small whole onions, drained
½ cup coarsely chopped walnuts or slivered, blanched almonds
2 tablespoons chopped parsley
Paprika

I think this is really my favorite onion recipe. It's perfect with cold turkey, equally good with any not-too-rich meat or chicken dish. Or, you can serve it as a light main dish, accompanied by a green salad.

ALPINE ONION PIE

Prick surface of pastry shell with a fork, then bake in a hot oven (450° F) for 10 minutes. Remove from oven and set aside while preparing filling. Sauté onions gently in butter for 15 minutes, stirring frequently. Stir in flour, then wine. Remove from heat. Beat eggs slightly; blend in sour cream; add parsley, Worcestershire sauce, celery seed, one-fourth teaspoon paprika, salt, and pepper. Pour mixture over onions; mix well. Pour into pastry shell. Sprinkle with Parmesan cheese and dust with paprika. Bake in a moderate oven (350° F) for 40 to 45 minutes, or until firm. Remove from oven and let stand 15 minutes or so before serving. Serves six.

1 (9 inch) unbaked pastry shell
2 heaping cups thinly sliced onions
4 tablespoons butter
2 tablespoons flour
⅓ cup dry or medium Sherry
3 eggs
1 pint dairy sour cream
3 tablespoons chopped parsley
1 teaspoon Worcestershire sauce
1 teaspoon celery seed
Paprika
Salt and pepper to taste
¼ cup grated Parmesan cheese

SAUCY ONIONS

Melt butter and stir in flour; add consommé and wine; cook, stirring constantly, until mixture boils and thickens. Add cheese, parsley, salt, and pepper. Combine this sauce with the onions. Turn into a greased casserole. Mix crumbs with melted butter; sprinkle over onions. Bake in a moderately hot oven (375° F) for 25 minutes. Serves six to eight.

3 tablespoons butter
3 tablespoons flour
1 cup canned consommé
¼ cup dry or medium Sherry or dry Vermouth
¼ cup grated Parmesan cheese
2 tablespoons chopped parsley
Salt and pepper to taste
2 (1 lb.) cans small whole onions, drained
¼ cup fine, dry bread crumbs
2 tablespoons melted butter

The first time I tasted this dish (a fine combination of flavors) it was served as an accompaniment to baked ham at a buffet dinner, so I've always thought of it as a vegetable. However, it would be an excellent light main dish for lunch or supper.

BAKED EGGPLANT WITH CLAMS

Pare eggplants and cut in one-inch cubes. Cook, covered, in boiling salted water for about ten minutes, or just until tender. Drain well and mash. Sauté onion and garlic in butter for five minutes; add to eggplant. Add clams (including liquid), mushrooms, crumbs, eggs, wine, parsley, Worcestershire sauce, salt, and pepper. Turn into a greased baking dish 10 x 6 x 2 inches, or 8 x 8 x 2. Sprinkle with Parmesan cheese and paprika. Bake in a moderate oven (350° F) about 45 minutes, or until firm. Serves five or six.

2 medium-sized eggplants (about 2½ pounds)
1 small onion, chopped
1 clove garlic, pressed or chopped
2 tablespoons butter
1 (7 oz.) can minced clams (undrained)
1 (4 oz.) can sliced mushrooms, drained
½ cup fine, dry bread crumbs
2 eggs, slightly beaten
3 tablespoons dry or medium Sherry, or dry Vermouth
2 tablespoons chopped parsley
½ teaspoon Worcestershire sauce
Salt and pepper to taste
Grated Parmesan cheese
Paprika

This hearty eggplant casserole is an excellent accompaniment to broiled or barbecued steaks, chops, or chicken. Good, too, as the hot dish in a cold cuts-salad menu.

ITALIAN EGGPLANT CASSEROLE

1 small onion, chopped
1 clove garlic, pressed or chopped
2 tablespoons butter
2 (8 oz.) cans tomato sauce
⅓ cup dry red table wine
½ teaspoon sugar
½ teaspoon mixed Italian seasoning
 Salt and pepper to taste
1 medium-sized eggplant (about 1½ pounds)
 Flour
¼ cup (or more) olive oil
6 ounces shredded Mozarella cheese
2 to 3 tablespoons grated Parmesan cheese
 Fine, dry bread crumbs

Sauté onion and garlic gently in butter five minutes. Add tomato sauce, wine, and seasonings; simmer, covered, for ten minutes, stirring occasionally. Pare eggplant and cut crosswise in one-half-inch slices. Dip slices in flour. Heat oil in a large skillet; sauté one layer of eggplant slices at a time until transparent-looking and lightly browned, turning to brown on both sides. Add more oil as needed. Cover bottom of a nine-inch round or square baking dish with half of the eggplant slices, cutting slices to fit as necessary. Sprinkle eggplant with half the cheeses; spoon half of the sauce over all. Repeat layers. Sprinkle with bread crumbs. Bake in a hot oven (450° F) for ten minutes, then reduce heat to moderate (350° F) and continue baking about 20 minutes. Serves five or six.

———

The fresh mushroom is the aristocrat of the vegetable family. It's wonderful by itself, and it adds a touch of elegance and good eating to many another dish. What better companion to steak fillet or hamburger than:

FRESH MUSHROOMS SAUTÉ

To serve four, scrub one pound mushrooms. (Don't peel unless skin is very tough.) Remove tough portion of stems. Leave mushrooms whole or slice them as you wish. Melt four tablespoons butter in a large skillet; add mushrooms. Cover and sauté gently for five minutes, stirring occasionally. Add two or three tablespoons dry or medium

Sherry; continue cooking, uncovered, for another five minutes, stirring often. Season with salt and pepper. Serve piping hot.

P.S. For a deliciously creamy "effect," add one-third cup heavy cream along with the Sherry.

———◆———

Wedges of this crustless pie make a very good vegetable, or you can use them as the base for creamed chicken or seafood.

MUSHROOM TART

Sauté mushrooms and onion together in butter for five minutes. Blend in flour; add milk; cook, stirring until mixture thickens. Remove from heat. Blend in Sherry, then eggs, parsley, and seasonings. Turn into a greased nine-inch pie plate. Bake in a moderate oven (350° F) about 30 minutes, or until firm in the center. Serves four to six, depending on the rest of the menu.

¾ pound mushrooms, scrubbed and chopped
1 small onion, finely chopped
3 tablespoons butter
3 tablespoons flour
¾ cup milk
3 tablespoons dry or medium Sherry
3 eggs, well beaten
2 tablespoons chopped parsley
Dash of nutmeg
Salt and pepper to taste

———◆———

With baked ham or fried chicken this is a very good dish.

CORN AND CHEESE PUDDING

Sauté green pepper and onion gently in butter for five minutes. Blend in flour; add milk and cook, stirring until mixture boils and thickens. Add wine and cheese; stir over low heat until cheese melts. Remove from heat. Add corn and corn meal, then eggs, salt, and pepper. Turn into a nine-inch pie plate and bake in a moderate oven (350° F) for about 40 minutes, or until firm in the center. Serves five or six.

¼ cup finely chopped green pepper (good but not essential)
2 tablespoons chopped onion
3 tablespoons butter
2 tablespoons flour
¾ cup milk
¼ cup dry white table wine
½ cup grated Cheddar cheese
1 (1 lb.) can whole-kernel corn, drained
2 tablespoons corn meal
3 eggs, well beaten
Salt and pepper to taste
Paprika

Rich is the word for

CORN IN SHERRY-CHEESE SAUCE

Combine cheese, butter, cream, and Sherry in a double boiler; heat, stirring occasionally until cheese melts and mixture is nicely blended. Add corn, onion, salt, and pepper. Heat thoroughly over hot water, stirring frequently. Serves six.

¼ pound process Cheddar cheese, sliced
1 tablespoon butter
2 tablespoons cream or evaporated milk
2 tablespoons dry or medium Sherry
2 (12 oz.) cans vacuum-pack Mexican-style whole-kernel corn (with sweet peppers), drained
2 tablespoons finely chopped green onion (if you like)
Salt and pepper to taste

P.S. For a good variation on the succotash theme, substitute a package of frozen French-style green beans or lima beans for one of the cans of corn. Cook the beans and drain them thoroughly before adding them to the sauce.

———————◄———————

Canned celery hearts are luxury fare, and this is a dish worthy of your dressiest menu.

BAKED CELERY HEARTS

Drain celery hearts thoroughly and arrange in a single layer in a greased shallow baking dish. In a small saucepan, mix cornstarch with some of the consommé until smooth; add remaining consommé. Stir over medium heat until mixture is thickened and clear. Add Sherry and butter. Pour sauce over celery hearts; sprinkle *generously* with Parmesan cheese; dust with paprika. Bake in a moderate oven (350° F) about 25 minutes, or until cheese is lightly browned. Serves six to eight.

2 (1 lb.) cans celery hearts
1 tablespoon cornstarch
¾ cup canned consommé
¼ cup dry or medium Sherry
3 tablespoons butter
Grated Parmesan cheese
Paprika

Even people who aren't usually enthusiastic about cauliflower seem to enjoy

BAKED CAULIFLOWER AMANDINE

Trim and wash cauliflower; separate head into flowerets. Drop into boiling salted water and cook for ten to 15 minutes, or just until tender when pierced with a fork. Drain carefully and place in a greased baking dish. Sauté onion gently in butter for five minutes. Stir in flour; add milk and stock; cook, stirring constantly until mixture is thickened and smooth. Add wine, almonds, Worcestershire sauce, salt, and pepper. Pour sauce over cauliflower; sprinkle with grated cheese and paprika. Bake in a moderately hot oven (375° *F*) for about 20 minutes, or until bubbly. Serves five or six.

1 large head cauliflower
2 tablespoons chopped onion
4 tablespoons butter
4 tablespoons flour
1 cup rich milk
⅔ cup chicken stock
⅓ cup dry white table wine
½ cup shredded, blanched almonds
½ teaspoon Worcestershire sauce
  Salt and pepper to taste
½ cup grated Cheddar cheese
  Paprika

———◆———

I like spinach any way as long as it's creamed. Plain spinach, seasoned with butter and a sprinkle of lemon juice, is all very well, but creamed it's a dish of real distinction. Here's one good way to do the creaming:

SPECIAL CREAMED SPINACH

Melt butter and stir in flour; add cream and cook, stirring, until mixture boils and thickens. Add Sherry, then spinach. Season with chicken stock base, lemon peel, nutmeg, salt, and pepper. Cook and stir over *very* low heat for two or three minutes. Serves four or five.

2 tablespoons butter
1½ tablespoons flour
½ cup light cream or rich milk
3 tablespoons dry or medium Sherry
2 cups well-drained, chopped, cooked spinach (2 packages frozen)
½ teaspoon chicken stock base
½ teaspoon grated lemon peel
  Dash of nutmeg
  Salt and pepper to taste

Two quick-to-fix and delicious onion-flavored spinach dishes are

SPINACH-ONION SPECIAL

Cook spinach according to directions on carton; drain *thoroughly*. Combine spinach, onion soup mix, sour cream, and Sherry. Turn into a greased casserole; let stand an hour or two so flavors can blend. Top with onion rings. Bake in a moderate oven (350° F) about 20 minutes, or until bubbly. Serves four or five.

2 (10 oz.) packages frozen chopped spinach
1 (1½ oz.) package dehydrated onion soup mix
½ pint dairy sour cream
2 tablespoons dry or medium Sherry
½ (3½ oz.) can French-fried onions

CONNIE'S BAKED SPINACH

Cook spinach according to directions on carton; drain *thoroughly*. Combine spinach with mushroom soup, wine, and one-half of the onions. Turn into a greased casserole. Bake in a moderate oven (350° F) about 25 minutes. Crumble remaining onions; sprinkle over top; continue baking five minutes. Serves six.

3 (10 oz.) packages frozen chopped spinach
1 (10½ oz.) can condensed cream of mushroom soup
¼ cup dry white table wine
1 (3½ oz.) can French-fried onions

HUNGARIAN SPINACH RING

Cook spinach according to directions on carton; drain *thoroughly* and chop even finer. Combine spinach with remaining ingredients; mix well. Pour into a well-greased one and one-fourth-quart ring mold; set in a shallow pan of hot water. Bake in a moderate oven (350° F) for 40 to 45 minutes, or until firm. Remove from oven and let stand five minutes or so before unmolding. Serves five or six.

2 (10 oz.) packages frozen chopped spinach
1 cup dairy sour cream
¼ cup dry or medium Sherry
3 eggs, well beaten
1 tablespoon grated onion
½ teaspoon Worcestershire sauce
¼ teaspoon nutmeg
Salt and pepper to taste

What's better than a nice freshly baked, fluffy white potato oozing with butter? Here's one delectable answer.

TEXAS BAKED POTATOES

Scrub and bake potatoes as usual. When done, cut a cross in the top of each and squeeze gently to expose the fluffy white interior. Serve immediately, accompanied by a bowl of finely chopped green onions (including some of the green tops), a bowl of crumbled crisp bacon (nice but not absolutely essential), and a bowl of this luscious cheese sauce, all of which are to be spooned over the potato to suit each diner's taste.

Combine all ingredients in a double boiler; heat, stirring occasionally until cheese melts and mixture is nicely blended. Makes enough sauce for four to six potatoes.

CHEESE SAUCE

½ pound process Cheddar cheese, sliced
¼ cup cream or evaporated milk
2 or 3 tablespoons dry or medium Sherry
1 tablespoon butter
½ teaspoon Worcestershire sauce
Dash of pepper

A delicious fix-ahead, heat-later potato dish is

POTATOES AU GRATIN

Sauté onion gently in butter for five minutes. Blend in flour; add milk and cook, stirring, until mixture boils and thickens. Add Sherry and cheese; stir over low heat until cheese melts. Add parsley, Worcestershire sauce, nutmeg, salt, celery salt, and pepper. Combine this sauce with the potatoes. Turn into a greased baking dish; sprinkle with Parmesan cheese and paprika. Bake in a hot oven (400° F) about 20 minutes, or until bubbly and delicately browned on top. Serves four to six.

2 tablespoons chopped onion
3 tablespoons butter
3 tablespoons flour
1¼ cups milk
¼ cup dry or medium Sherry
1 cup grated Cheddar cheese
2 tablespoons chopped parsley
½ teaspoon Worcestershire sauce
Dash of nutmeg or mace
Salt, celery salt, and pepper to taste
1 quart diced cold baked potatoes
Grated Parmesan cheese
Paprika

Sweet potatoes and yams take to the flavor of Sherry like a duck to water. Try one of these with ham or roast pork:

SWEET POTATO PUFF

Boil sweet potatoes in their jackets for 20 to 30 minutes, or until tender, drain, peel, and mash thoroughly. Add melted butter, Sherry, brown sugar, cinnamon, and salt; beat until light and fluffy. (An electric beater is excellent for this purpose.) Pile mixture in a greased casserole and sprinkle with nutmeg. Bake in a hot oven (400° F) for about 15 minutes, or until delicately browned on top. Serves six.

3 pounds sweet potatoes or yams
⅓ to ½ cup melted butter
½ cup medium Sherry
¼ cup brown sugar
½ teaspoon cinnamon
   Salt to taste
   Nutmeg

Zucchini is another accommodating vegetable that takes kindly to various sauces and seasonings. Try it *au gratin* this way.

ZUCCHINI AND MUSHROOMS AU GRATIN

Wash zucchini and trim off ends (do not peel); cut in one-inch lengths. Cook, covered, in boiling salted water for about ten minutes, or *just* until barely tender. Drain and place in a greased shallow baking dish. Melt butter; add onion and cook gently for five minutes. Blend in flour; add milk and bouillon cube; cook, stirring until mixture boils and thickens and bouillon cube is completely dissolved. Add wine, mushrooms, parsley, Worcestershire sauce, salt, and pepper. Pour sauce over zucchini; sprinkle with cheese and paprika. Bake in a moderately hot oven (375° F) about 25 minutes, or until bubbly. Serves six.

2 pounds small zucchini
3 tablespoons butter
1 small onion, minced
3 tablespoons flour
1¼ cups rich milk
1 chicken bouillon cube (or 2 teaspoons chicken stock base)
¾ cup dry white table wine
1 (4 oz.) can sliced mushrooms, drained
2 tablespoons chopped parsley
½ teaspoon Worcestershire sauce
   Salt and pepper to taste
½ cup grated Cheddar cheese (or ⅓ cup grated Parmesan cheese)
   Paprika

P.S. Two pounds of scallop (pattypan) squash, diced, may be substituted for the zucchini.

Easy and very good is this herb-and-wine-flavored:

ZUCCHINI SAUTÉ

Wash zucchini and trim off ends (do not peel); slice crosswise paper-thin. Cook bacon slowly in a large skillet until crisp; drain on absorbent paper; crumble. Add zucchini and onion to bacon drippings; sauté gently, stirring often, until zucchini is lightly browned. Add remaining ingredients. Cover and cook for five to ten minutes, or just until zucchini is tender, stirring occasionally. Turn into a heated serving dish and sprinkle with crumbled bacon. Serves six.

2 pounds small zucchini
4 slices bacon
2 tablespoons finely chopped onion
¼ cup dry Vermouth
  Pinch each of thyme and rosemary
  Salt, garlic salt, and pepper to taste
2 tablespoons chopped parsley

BAKED STUFFED SWEET POTATOES

Scrub four large sweet potatoes or yams; bake in a hot oven (425° F) for 30 minutes, or until tender. Cut slice from top of each; scoop out contents with a spoon. Mash; add one-fourth cup *each* butter, brown sugar, medium Sherry, and chopped pecans; season with one-fourth teaspoon nutmeg and salt to taste. Beat until fluffy; pile lightly into shells. Bake in a hot oven (450° F) for ten minutes. Serves four.

A touch of orange is always welcome in a sweet potato dish.

SWEET POTATOES SEVILLE

Scrub sweet potatoes. Boil, covered, in their jackets for 20 to 30 minutes, or just until tender. When cool, peel and cut in quarters. Arrange in a single layer in a shallow baking dish 12 x 8 x 2 inches. Combine remaining ingredients in a small saucepan; heat to simmering; pour over sweet potatoes. Bake in a hot oven (400° F) for 20 to 25 minutes, basting and turning sweet potatoes frequently. Serves six to eight.

2½ pounds sweet potatoes or yams
1 cup (firmly packed) brown sugar
⅓ cup orange marmalade
¼ cup medium or sweet Sherry
1 tablespoon lemon juice
3 tablespoons butter
  Dash of salt

◦ XI ◦

Happy Endings

═══════════════════════════════════════

It's up to the dessert to "crown the feast," to add substance to a light repast or refresh the palate when everyone's saying, "I can't eat another bite!"

Wine flavors many desserts to perfection, especially when they feature fruit. One of the simplest (and best) ways to combine wine and fruit in a "happy ending" is to serve a bowl or basket of fresh fruits in season, a plate of one or more cheeses, and glasses of Port or red table wine. (Port harmonizes best with the milder cheeses; red table wine is good with either mild or "noisy" ones.) You can add crackers or melba toast to this flavorsome picture if you like, but try a slice of apple spread with creamy, mellow Blue cheese, or nibble some grapes along with a bit of sharp Cheddar, and maybe you'll agree with me that the fruit-cheese-wine trio is sufficient unto itself.

Fruit cups and compotes offer many possibilities for showing off wine as a flavoring. Here's one place in cookery where you can improvise to your heart's content and be almost certain of delicious results! The ingredients for success are simply a compatible group of fresh, canned, or frozen fruits (or a single fruit), a bottle of dessert or table wine, and perhaps a sprinkling of sugar or lemon juice to achieve the desired sweet-tart effect.

TIPS ON PREPARING FRUIT CUPS
AND COMPOTES

Peel, slice, or dice the fruits as necessary. Thaw frozen fruits; drain both frozen and canned fruits thoroughly. Mix the fruits with the wine of your choice, using just enough wine to flavor them properly. Don't drown them! Add sugar and/or lemon juice to taste, mix gently, and chill thoroughly. At serving time spoon the fruit and wine into Champagne glasses or dessert dishes, and there you are. Crisp cookies go well here, as do brownies or slices of your favorite cake. It depends on whether you want to "lighten or hearten" the meal.

Here are some good fruit combinations with suggestions for wines that go especially well with them:

1. Peach slices
   Pitted sweet cherries
   Pineapple chunks
   Sliced bananas (add at serving time)
   Wine: Port
2. Grapefruit sections
   Pineapple chunks
   Strawberries
   Wine: Rosé
3. Assorted melon balls, alone or with blueberries or red raspberries
   Wine: sweet Sauterne

4. Orange sections
   Sliced pears
   Red raspberries
   Wine: sweet Sherry
5. Seedless or halved seeded grapes
   Peach slices
   Diced pineapple
   Wine: Tokay
6. Canned salad fruits
   Wine: Muscatel
7. Grapefruit and orange sections
   Wine: sweet Sherry

You can use any of the above fruit combinations in the next two recipes. In these a wine-flavored syrup is poured over the fruit instead of wine alone.

GOLDEN FRUIT CUP

Combine wine, sugar, and orange peel in a saucepan; bring to a boil, stirring until sugar is dissolved; simmer five minutes. Remove from heat. Add apricot nectar, lemon juice, and salt. When completely cool, pour over fruit. Cover and chill several hours before serving. Serves six.

1 cup white table wine
½ cup sugar
1 tablespoon grated orange peel
½ cup canned apricot nectar
1 teaspoon lemon juice
Dash of salt
1 quart prepared fruit (see suggestions page 200)

FESTIVAL FRUIT CUP

Mix honey, water, cardamon, and salt in a saucepan; bring to a boil, then simmer five minutes. Remove from heat; add mint, wine, and lemon juice. Cool thoroughly; strain; pour over fruit. Cover and chill several hours before serving. Serves six. This is especially good over melon balls or grapefruit and orange sections.

½ cup strained honey
½ cup water
¼ teaspoon ground cardamon
Dash of salt
6 or 8 fresh mint leaves, cut fine, or the equivalent in dried mint
½ cup Port or sweet Sherry
1 tablespoon lemon juice
1 quart prepared fruit (see suggestions page 200)

When strawberries appear in the market it's time to enjoy

STRAWBERRIES IN ORANGE SAUCE

Mix cornstarch, sugar, and salt in a saucepan; gradually add wine and orange juice, stirring until mixture is perfectly smooth. Add orange peel and lemon peel. Stir over medium heat until mixture boils and becomes clear. Cool, then pour over berries. Cover and chill several hours to blend flavors. To serve, spoon berries and sauce into sherbet glasses or dessert dishes. If desired, top each serving with a spoonful of orange sherbet or a puff of whipped cream. Serves eight.

1 tablespoon cornstarch
½ cup sugar
Dash of salt
1 cup Rosé
½ cup orange juice
Grated peel of 1 orange
Grated peel of ½ lemon
1 quart hulled, washed strawberries
Orange sherbet or whipped cream (optional)

A good pear-and-wine dessert is

WINE-POACHED PEARS

Wash, halve, and core pears, leaving skins on. Combine sugar, corn syrup, wine, lemon juice, orange peel, and lemon peel in a saucepan; bring to a boil, stirring until sugar is dissolved. Add pears and simmer very gently for about 15 minutes, or until pears are tender. Turn pears occasionally during cooking. Remove pears to a serving bowl or dessert dishes; pour syrup over them. Serve warm or chilled. These are delicious plain or topped with whipped cream or vanilla ice cream. Serves four or more, depending on size of pears.

4 fresh pears
½ cup sugar
½ cup light corn syrup
½ cup sweet Sherry or Muscatel
1 tablespoon lemon juice
2 tablespoons grated orange peel
1 tablespoon grated lemon peel

When there's a nip in the air, one of these warm fruit desserts is a happy choice:

APPLE-MINCEMEAT CRUNCH

Arrange half the apples over bottom of a greased, shallow baking dish 10 x 6 x 2 inches; spread mincemeat over these; top with remaining apples; pour wine over all. Mix sugar, flour, spices, and salt; add butter; mix with your fingers or a pastry blender until crumbly. Sprinkle this mixture evenly over contents of baking dish, then pat down gently but firmly. Bake in a moderate oven (350° F) one hour, or longer, until apples are tender and crust is delicately browned. Serve warm with cream, *Sherry Hard Sauce* or ice cream. Serves six to eight. Rich and wonderful!

4 cups sliced, peeled apples
1 cup prepared mincemeat
⅓ cup sweet Sherry, Muscatel, or other dessert wine
1 cup sugar
¾ cup sifted all-purpose flour
½ teaspoon each: cinnamon and nutmeg
¼ teaspoon salt
½ cup softened butter

PEAR CRUMBLE

Pare, core, and slice pears; arrange in a greased baking dish 8 x 8 x 2 inches; sprinkle with wine and lemon juice. Mix flour, sugar, and spices; blend with the butter, using a pastry blender or your fingers; pat mixture firmly over pears. Bake in a moderately hot oven (375° F) for 30 to 40 minutes, or until pears are tender and crust is brown. Serve warm with cream or vanilla ice cream. Serves six to eight.

6 fresh pears
⅓ cup Port
1 tablespoon lemon juice
¾ cup flour
1 cup (firmly packed) brown sugar
½ teaspoon each: cinnamon and nutmeg
⅓ cup softened butter

Here's a group of truly ambrosial desserts and definitely not for calorie-counters!

MOLDED SHERRY PUDDING

Soften gelatin in the cold water for five minutes. Heat Sherry just to simmering; add softened gelatin, sugar, and salt; stir until dissolved. Let mixture cool thoroughly at room temperature. Beat egg yolks until thick and lemon-colored; gradually beat in cooled gelatin mixture. Fold in stiffly beaten egg whites and whipped cream, blending gently but thoroughly. Spoon into six individual molds or custard cups that have been rinsed with cold water, or use a one and one-half-quart ring mold; chill until firm. Unmold and serve with *Sherry Butter-Nut Sauce, Sherry-Caramel Sauce, Ruby Sauce,* or *Orange-Wine Sauce* Serves six.

1 envelope (1 tablespoon) unflavored gelatin
¼ cup cold water
½ cup sweet Sherry
½ cup sugar
Dash of salt
3 eggs, separated
1 cup heavy cream, whipped

P.S. For a delectable *Chocolate Refrigerator Pie:* Mix one and one-half cups chocolate wafer crumbs with four tablespoons melted butter; spread half over bottom of a 9 x 9 x 2-inch pan. Spoon the above *Sherry Pudding* mixture into pan; sprinkle remaining crumb mixture evenly over top; pat down gently with back of spoon. Chill until firm. Cut in nine squares of three inches each and serve plain or topped with whipped cream.

SHERRY CREAM RING

Soften gelatin in the cold water five minutes; dissolve in the scalded milk. Add sugar and salt; stir until dissolved. Let cool at room temperature, then add wine. Chill. When mixture begins to thicken (this won't take long!) fold in whipped cream. Pour into a one and one-fourth-quart ring mold that has been rinsed with cold water; chill until firm. Unmold and fill center with sliced strawberries, raspberries, peaches, or other desired fruit. Serve with *Currant Sauce*. Serves six to eight.

1½ envelopes (1½ tablespoons) unflavored gelatin
⅓ cup cold water
½ cup milk, scalded
½ cup sugar
Dash of salt
½ cup sweet Sherry
1 pint heavy cream, whipped

Bananas done this way are equally good as a dessert or as an accompaniment to baked ham, ham loaf, or broiled lamb chops:

BAKED BANANAS WITH SHERRY SAUCE

Peal bananas; cut lengthwise in halves; place, cut side up, in a shallow baking dish. Spread bananas thinly with jam. Mix remaining ingredients; spoon over bananas. Bake in a moderate oven (350° F) about 20 minutes, basting occasionally. Serve warm. Serves four.

4 ripe bananas
Apricot jam or orange marmalade
2 tablespoons sweet Sherry
1 tablespoon lemon juice
2 tablespoons melted butter
2 tablespoons brown sugar

I'm a great chocolate fan, and this simple but quite "dressy" dessert is one of my special pets.

CHOCOLATE VELVET

Melt chocolate bits in the top of a double boiler over hot water. Remove from heat; stir in Sherry and salt. Add unbeaten egg yolks, one at a time, beating well after each yolk is added. Beat egg whites until stiff but not dry; fold in chocolate mixture, blending gently until no trace of egg white remains. Pour into four sherbet glasses or dessert dishes and chill in the refrigerator for at least four hours before serving. (The dessert can be made a day ahead of time, if desired.) Serve with whipped cream. Serves four.

¾ cup semi-sweet chocolate bits
¼ cup sweet Sherry
Dash of salt
4 eggs, separated

JEWELED CREAM PUDDING

Dissolve gelatin in the hot water; add wine and salt; chill. When mixture begins to thicken, beat with a rotary or electric beater until frothy. Gradually beat in ice cream; fold in glacé fruit mix. (Mixture will thicken almost immediately.) Spread half the graham cracker crumbs over bottom of an eight-inch square pan; spoon pudding mixture evenly over crumbs; sprinkle remaining crumbs over pudding and pat down gently with the back of a spoon. Chill in the refrigerator for 24 hours. Cut in rectangles and serve plain or topped with whipped cream. Serves eight.

1 (3 oz.) package lemon-flavored gelatin
1¼ cups hot water
½ cup sweet Sherry
Dash of salt
1 pint vanilla ice cream
¾ cup prepared glacé fruit mix, chopped fairly fine
20 single graham crackers, crushed to fine crumbs

If you want to end a meal on a truly "heavenly" note, serve one of these.

PRALINE ANGEL PIE

Beat egg whites until foamy; sprinkle with cream of tartar; continue beating until stiff but not dry. Add sugar gradually, beating until meringue is smooth and glossy. Spread over bottom and sides of a well-greased nine-inch pie plate, making a depression in the center. (Do not spread meringue on rim of plate.) Bake in a slow oven (275° F) about one hour, or until delicately browned. Cool thoroughly.

MERINGUE SHELL

3 egg whites
¼ teaspoon cream of tartar
¾ cup sugar

Combine almonds and sugar in a heavy skillet; stir over medium heat until sugar forms a golden brown syrup. Pour immediately into a buttered plate. When cool and hard, put through food grinder. Beat egg yolks slightly in top of a double boiler; blend in flour; stir in milk and wine; add butter and salt. Cook over hot water for 10 minutes, stirring constantly until mixture thickens, then occasionally. Let stand at room temperature until cool, then stir in all but one-fourth cup of the ground almond-sugar mixture. Pour into cooled meringue shell. Chill in refrigerator for 24 hours. Just before serving, spread whipped cream over top of pie and sprinkle with the reserved one-fourth cup ground almond-sugar mixture. Serves 6 generously, 8 modestly. Elegant!

PRALINE FILLING

¼ pound unblanched almonds
¾ cup sugar
3 egg yolks
¼ cup flour
1 cup milk
⅓ cup sweet Sherry
1 tablespoon butter
   Dash of salt
1 cup heavy cream, whipped

CHOCOLATE ANGEL PIE

Prepare meringue shell as directed above in recipe for *Praline Angel Pie*. (For a "crunchy" touch, fold three-fourths cup finely chopped walnuts into the meringue before spreading it in the pie plate.) Place chocolate bits, Sherry, and salt in the top of a double boiler; stir over hot water until chocolate melts and ingredients are well blended. Remove from heat; cool slightly. Fold cooled chocolate mixture into whipped cream, blending gently but thoroughly. Spoon filling into cooled meringue shell; grate a little unsweetened chocolate over the top for garnish. Chill for several hours or overnight. Serves six generously, 8 modestly.

Meringue shell (see recipe for *Praline Angel Pie*, page 206)
¾ cup semi-sweet chocolate bits
¼ cup sweet Sherry
Dash of salt
1 cup heavy cream, whipped
Grated unsweetened chocolate for garnish

No doubt the most illustrious of all wine desserts is *Zabaglione,* or do you know it as *Sabayon* or *Zabaione?* However you spell it, this Italian creation of egg yolks, wine, and sugar is deliciously frothy, deliciously rich! No two recipes seem to agree as to how much of what goes into the pot, but here's the version I use and enjoy.

ZABAGLIONE

Combine egg yolks, sugar, and salt in the upper part of a cold double boiler; beat with a rotary beater until thick and lemon-colored; gradually beat in Sherry. Place over hot (not boiling) water; beat with a rotary beater until thick and fluffy like whipped cream. Remove from heat and spoon into Champagne or sherbet glasses. Serve warm or very, very cold. Serves four to six.

6 egg yolks
6 tablespoons granulated sugar
Few grains of salt
6 tablespoons sweet Sherry

In the realm of showy desserts, few can surpass this one. It's a last-minute, eat-it-now creation and definitely worth the effort.

VANILLA SOUFFLÉ, SABAYON

¼ cup butter
½ cup flour
1 cup milk
4 eggs, separated
½ cup confectioners' sugar
Dash of salt
1 teaspoon vanilla

Melt butter and stir in flour; add milk and cook, stirring constantly, until mixture thickens and leaves sides of pan. Remove from heat. Beat in unbeaten egg yolks, one at a time; add one-fourth cup of the sugar, the salt, and vanilla. Beat egg whites stiff; gradually beat in remaining one-fourth cup sugar. Fold egg whites into yolk mixture. Pour into a two-quart casserole that has been buttered and then sprinkled with granulated sugar. Bake in a moderately hot oven (375° F) for 45 to 50 minutes, or until puffed and golden brown. Serve *at once* with *Sabayon Sauce* (below). Serves six.

SABAYON SAUCE

Beat two egg yolks slightly in the top of a double boiler; stir in one-half cup white table wine, one-third cup sugar, one teaspoon *each* grated orange and lemon peel, and a dash of salt. Stir over hot (not boiling) water about ten minutes, until mixture is thick and creamy. Beat two egg whites stiff; fold in thickened yolk mixture. Serve at once.

SUNDAE SAUCES

A good sauce adds the finishing touch of flavor to many desserts. Gathered here are some traditional favorites and some new ideas. All are wine-flavored and recommended eating.

CURRANT SAUCE

Mix wine and cornstarch in a saucepan, stirring until perfectly smooth. Add jelly. Stir over medium heat until sauce boils and jelly is completely melted. Add orange peel and salt. Cool, then chill before serving. A good sauce for puddings or fresh fruit (especially strawberries or peaches). Makes about one and one-half cups.

½ cup sweet Sherry
2 teaspoons cornstarch
1 (12 oz.) glass red currant jelly (1 cup)
1 teaspoon grated orange peel
Dash of salt

CHERRY PORT SUNDAE SAUCE

Drain syrup from cherries; measure one cupful, adding water as needed to make that amount. Mix cornstarch and sugar in a saucepan; add Port and stir until smooth; add the one cup cherry syrup. Cook and stir over medium heat until mixture boils, thickens, and becomes clear. Remove from heat. Stir in remaining ingredients; add cherries. Chill. Serve over vanilla ice cream. Makes about two and one-half cups.

1 (1 lb.) can pitted dark, sweet cherries
1 tablespoon cornstarch
2 tablespoons sugar
⅓ cup Port
½ teaspoon each: grated orange peel and lemon peel
1 teaspoon lemon juice
Dash each of salt and cinnamon
1-2 tablespoons Brandy (if you like)

ORANGE-WINE SAUCE

Combine cornstarch, sugar, and salt in a saucepan; gradually add wine and orange juice, stirring until mixture is perfectly smooth. Add lemon peel. Cook, stirring over medium heat until mixture boils, thickens, and becomes clear. Remove from heat. Add lemon juice and orange sections. Cool, then chill before serving. Serve over orange or lemon sherbet, vanilla ice cream, or a combination of sherbet and ice cream. Also good with any pudding that requires an orange sauce. Makes almost two cups.

1 tablespoon cornstarch
½ cup sugar
Dash of salt
½ cup sweet Sherry, Muscatel, or other dessert wine
½ cup orange juice
2 teaspoons grated lemon peel
1 tablespoon lemon juice
1 cup diced fresh orange sections, or whole canned mandarin orange sections, well drained

VINEYARD MINCEMEAT SAUCE

In a saucepan mix cornstarch, sugar, and salt; gradually stir in wine and water, mixing until smooth. Stir over medium heat until mixture boils, thickens, and becomes clear. Add remaining ingredients. Heat thoroughly. Serve warm over any pudding that requires a "fruity" sauce, over squares of warm cake, or over vanilla ice cream. Makes about two cups. This sauce keeps well in the refrigerator, and is handy to have in reserve. It has a *wonderful* flavor!

1 tablespoon cornstarch
¼ cup (firmly packed) brown sugar
Dash of salt
½ cup Muscatel, sweet Sherry, or other dessert wine
½ cup water
1 cup prepared mincemeat
1 tablespoon lemon juice
1 teaspoon grated lemon peel
1 tablespoon butter

SHERRY-CARAMEL SAUCE

Melt caramels in a double boiler; gradually add wine and cream. Serve warm. A luscious sauce that is marvelous over vanilla ice cream and vanilla- or Sherry-flavored puddings. Makes about one cup.

½ pound packaged vanilla caramels
⅓ cup sweet Sherry
½ cup light cream

CHOCOLATE SUNDAE SAUCE

Combine all ingredients in a saucepan. Stir over *very* low heat until mixture boils, then continue cooking and stirring for 3 or 4 minutes, until thickened. Serve warm over vanilla or coffee ice cream. Makes about one and one-quarter cups sauce.

1 (6 oz.) package semi-sweet chocolate bits
¾ cup undiluted evaporated milk
⅓ cup sweet Sherry
1 tablespoon sugar
Dash of salt

Tarts are one of the very nicest party desserts. They're especially nice for buffet meals because they're so easy to serve. Of course, you can put any of the pie fillings in this chapter into tart shells instead of one large pastry shell, and here are some special tarts recipes I think you'll enjoy. If you want to end a meal on a delectably rich note, choose one of these:

CHESS TARTS

Cream butter and sugar together until light and fluffy. Add salt and spices. Add unbeaten egg yolks, one at a time, beating well after each addition. Add raisins, nuts, Sherry, and lemon juice; blend thoroughly. Spoon mixture into tart shells. Bake in a moderate oven (350° F) about 40 minutes, or until firm. Serve warm or cold with whipped cream or vanilla ice cream. Makes seven or eight tarts.

½ cup butter
1 cup sugar
Dash of salt
¼ teaspoon each: cinnamon and nutmeg
4 egg yolks
1 cup seedless raisins, rinsed with boiling water and drained
1 cup chopped walnuts or pecans
⅓ cup medium or sweet Sherry
1 tablespoon lemon juice
7 or 8 (4-inch) unbaked tart shells

CHOCOLATE CREAM TARTS

Prepare pudding and pie filling mix according to directions on carton for pudding, using the milk and Sherry as the liquid. Stir in instant coffee powder. Remove from heat and set pan in a bowl of ice water; cool thoroughly, stirring occasionally. Fold in whipped cream, blending gently but thoroughly. Pour mixture into tart shells; chill until firm. Decorate with additional whipped cream and a sprinkling of shaved chocolate before serving. Makes six tarts.

1 package chocolate pudding and pie filling mix
1 cup milk
¼ cup sweet Sherry
1 teaspoon instant coffee powder
½ cup heavy cream, whipped
6 (4-inch) baked tart shells
Additional whipped cream and shaved chocolate for garnishing

Wine is an ideal liquid for fruit cakes, which isn't surprising, since after all wine is fruit in another form. It combines beautifully with the fruits and spices, and the finished cake is mellow and rich-flavored.

Except for a few special cases, wine isn't particularly important as the liquid in "day-to-day" cakes. Its flavor just doesn't come through. Occasionally in a chocolate or spice or orange cake, wine makes a contribution, flavor-wise, but more often it's wiser to put it where it will really shine—as the flavoring for cake fillings, frostings, and toppings.

Here is one "everyday" cake in which I think wine really does make a delicious difference:

SHERRY SPICE CAKE

Mix raisins and nuts with enough of the flour so that pieces are well coated. Sift remaining flour with the baking powder, soda, salt, and spices. Cream shortening and sugar together until light and fluffy; beat in egg; add flour mixture alternately with Sherry, beating until smooth after each addition. Stir in raisins and nuts. Pour into a greased and floured square eight-inch pan. Bake in a moderate oven (350° F) for 40 to 45 minutes. Let cool in the pan. While cake is still slightly warm, spread with an icing made by combining:

½ cup seedless raisins
½ cup chopped walnuts
1½ cups sifted all-purpose flour
½ teaspoon baking powder
½ teaspoon baking soda
¼ teaspoon salt
½ teaspoon each: cinnamon, cloves, allspice, and nutmeg
½ cup shortening
1 cup (firmly packed) brown sugar
1 egg
½ cup sweet Sherry

When cake is cold, cut into squares. Makes an eight-inch cake.

1 cup sifted confectioners' sugar
1 tablespoon melted butter
3 tablespoons sweet Sherry

These two recipes are special pets of mine. They're easy to do, and the resulting cakes are handsome to behold:

CHOCOLATE DELIGHT CAKE

Prepare one (1 lb. 2 or 3 oz.) package devil's food or fudge cake mix according to directions on carton, substituting one-third cup sweet

Sherry for one-third cup of the required liquid. Bake in two (eight-inch) layer cake pans. Cool thoroughly, then proceed as follows:

Melt chocolate in a double boiler. Add sugar and wine; blend well, then cook, stirring constantly, for two or three minutes. Let mixture cool for about ten minutes, or just until luke-warm. Meantime, put cooled cake layers together with whipped cream between and spread remaining cream over top and sides of cake. Carefully swirl part of the lukewarm chocolate mixture over top of cake so that a little of the cream shows through here and there. Use remaining chocolate mixture to make vertical "ribbons" at intervals around the sides of the cake. (To make each "ribbon," take a little of the chocolate mixture on the end of a butter spreader or other dull-pointed knife and draw it up the side of the cake.) Chill cake until serving time. Makes a two-layer cake.

- **3** (1 oz.) squares unsweetened chocolate
- **6** tablespoons sugar
- **¼** cup sweet Sherry
- **1½** cups heavy cream, whipped

———————◆———————

"Funny Cake," a Pennsylvania Dutch dessert that looks more like a pie than a cake, is actually both. It's cake baked in a pastry shell. Before baking, a sauce is poured over the batter; when the dessert comes from the oven the sauce has disappeared underneath the cake. It's the sauce that determines the flavor of a "Funny Cake" and in this version Sherry does the trick delightfully.

SHERRY FUNNY CAKE

Line a nine- to ten-inch glass pie plate with pastry, making a high fluted rim. Prepare Sherry sauce, as follows:

Combine one-fourth cup wine and the brown sugar in a saucepan. Cook and stir over low heat until mixture comes to a boil. Boil one minute, stirring occasionally. Add remaining one-fourth cup wine and the butter. Cool while mixing this cake batter:

¼ cup sweet Sherry
¾ cup (firmly packed) brown sugar
2 tablespoons butter

Have ingredients at room temperature. Sift flour once before measuring. Measure into sifter: flour, baking powder, salt, and sugar. Place shortening in bowl. Sift in dry ingredients. Add milk and vanilla; mix until all flour is dampened. Beat two minutes at low speed of electric mixer, or 300 strokes by hand. Add egg and beat one minute on mixer, or 150 strokes by hand. Pour cake batter into pastry-lined pan; pour lukewarm sauce gently over batter. Sprinkle with nuts. Bake in moderate oven (350° F) 50 to 55 minutes. Serve warm. If desired, top with whipped cream or ice cream. This also makes a delicious coffee cake and is excellent for a brunch. Makes a nine- or 10-inch cake.

1¼ cups sifted cake flour
1   teaspoon double-acting baking powder
½   teaspoon salt
¾   cup sugar
¼   cup shortening
½   cup milk
1   teaspoon vanilla
1   egg, unbeaten
¼   cup chopped nuts (for topping)

CHOCOLATE AMBROSIA CAKE

Prepare one (1 lb. 2 or 3 oz.) package yellow or white cake mix according to directions on carton, substituting one-third cup sweet Sherry for one-third cup of the required liquid. Bake as directed in two (nine-inch) layer cake pans. Cool thoroughly. Put layers together with *Cocoa Whipped Cream Filling* (below). Frost sides and top of cake with *Sherry-Chocolate Frosting* (below). Sprinkle chopped walnuts over top of cake. Makes a two-layer cake.

Cocoa Whipped Cream Filling: Combine one-half cup heavy cream, two tablespoons cocoa, one-fourth cup confectioners' sugar and dash of salt in a bowl; chill several hours. Beat until stiff; gently fold in one-fourth teaspoon vanilla.

Sherry Chocolate Frosting: Melt three (1 oz.) squares unsweetened chocolate and five tablespoons butter over hot water. Remove pan from water. Stir in one-third cup sweet Sherry and dash of salt. Gradually add about three cups sifted confectioners' sugar (enough to give the frosting a nice spreadable consistency), beating until frosting is very smooth.

Good fruit cake recipes are legion. The ones that I'm giving you here are special favorites of mine. They're wonderful for gifts as well as for dessert and refreshment-time purposes.

WHITE CHRISTMAS CAKE

Mix and sift flour, baking powder, salt, and nutmeg; add fruits, coconut, and nuts; mix well. Cream shortening and sugar together until fluffy; add flour-fruit mixture alternately with wine, blending well. Fold in the beaten egg whites. Turn into two loaf pans (9 x 5 x 3 inches) that have been greased and lined with heavy wrapping paper. Bake in a slow oven (300° F) for two to two and one-half hours, or until a toothpick inserted in the center comes out clean. Remove from pans and cool on wire racks. When thoroughly cold, peel off wrapping paper and wrap cakes in waxed paper. Store in a tightly covered container. An orange or an apple may be stored with the cakes to keep them moist; it should be replaced from time to time. Makes about 4 pounds of cake.

2⅔ cups sifted all-purpose flour
1½ teaspoons baking powder
½ teaspoon salt
½ teaspoon nutmeg
½ pound golden bleached raisins, rinsed with boiling water and drained
½ pound prepared glacé fruit mix
½ pound glacé pineapple, diced
½ pound glacé cherries, halved
1 cup flaked coconut
1 cup coarsely chopped walnuts or pecans
⅔ cup shortening
1⅓ cups sugar
⅔ cup Muscatel or sweet Sherry
5 egg whites, beaten stiff but not dry

DOROTHY'S FRUIT CAKE

Pit and quarter dates. Rinse raisins and drain thoroughly. Chop nuts. In a large mixing bowl, combine all fruits and nuts with honey and wine. Cream butter and sugar together thoroughly; add eggs; pour over fruits and nuts. Sift together flour, salt, soda, and spices; add gradually to fruit mixture, mixing thoroughly. Turn into two greased loaf pans (8½ x 4½ x 2½ inches) lined with two thicknesses of greased waxed paper. Bake in a slow oven (300° F) about two to two and one-half hours, with a shallow pan of water on the bottom of the oven. Remove from pans to cool, but leave paper on cake until ready to use. Makes about five and one-half pounds of cake.

3 cups dates
3 cups light or dark raisins
2 cups pecans or filberts
1 pound prepared glacé fruit mix
¼ cup strained honey
¼ cup sweet Sherry
1 cup butter
1¼ cups (firmly packed) brown sugar
4 eggs, well beaten
2 cups sifted all-purpose flour
1 teaspoon salt
¼ teaspoon baking soda
1 teaspoon cinnamon
½ teaspoon each: cloves and mace

Here's an elegant cake to feature at a dessert party or to top off a "ladylike" luncheon:

PARTY CHIFFON CAKE

For this you will need a chiffon (or angel food) cake baked in a tube pan ten inches in diameter and four inches deep. If you make it yourself, invert until thoroughly cold, then remove from pan. Cut cake crosswise into two layers. Prepare filling as follows:

Soften gelatin in the cold water five minutes. Heat Sherry to simmering; add gelatin, sugar, and salt; stir until dissolved; add almond extract. Cool, then chill. When mixture begins to thicken, fold in whipped cream. Chill again just until thick enough to spread. Put cake layers together with some of the filling between; spread remaining filling over top and sides of cake. Chill for several hours. Sprinkle peanut brittle over top of cake about one hour before serving. Serves eight.

1 envelope (1 tablespoon) unflavored gelatin
⅓ cup cold water
½ cup sweet Sherry
¼ cup sugar
Dash of salt
⅛ teaspoon almond extract
1 pint heavy cream, whipped
1 cup crushed peanut brittle

What prettier sight than a handsome pie? It rewards the cook with a wonderful feeling of accomplishment and promises delicious things for all who partake of it.

I have yet to think that wine has a place in pastry making, but when it comes to pie fillings, wine plays an important role indeed. Take Pecan Pie, for example. The usual version, minus any wine, is very good eating, but please try this one. It's really delectable!

BEST PECAN PIE

Melt butter and stir in flour; add corn syrup, wine and sugar; cook, stirring constantly, until mixture boils. Gradually stir hot mixture into eggs; add pecans. Pour into pie shell. Bake in a moderately hot oven (375° F) about 45 minutes, or until firm. Serve warm or cold, topped with whipped cream or vanilla ice cream. Makes a nine-inch pie.

¼ cup butter
2 tablespoons flour
½ cup dark corn syrup
⅓ cup medium or sweet Sherry
1 cup sugar
3 eggs, well beaten
1 cup coarsely broken pecans
1 (9-inch) unbaked pastry shell

P.S. For an equally elegant *Walnut Pie*, substitute one cup coarsely broken walnuts for the pecans.

For *Mincemeat Pecan* or *Walnut Pie* (delightful and different), follow the recipe for *Best Pecan Pie* but make these changes: use three-fourths cup (firmly packed) brown sugar instead of the one cup sugar; reduce nuts to one-half cup and add to filling along with one cup prepared mincemeat. Serve warm or cold, plain or topped with whipped cream, vanilla ice cream, or Sherry-flavored hard sauce.

A package of vanilla pudding and pie filling mix is the starting point for this easy and flavorful

PEANUT CRUNCH PIE

Soften gelatin in the wine. Prepare pudding and pie filling mix according to directions on package for pudding, using the one and one-half cups milk as the liquid. Remove from heat; add softened gelatin and stir until dissolved. Add sugar. Cool thoroughly, then fold in whipped cream. Pour into pie shell. Sprinkle peanut brittle evenly over top of pie; pat down gently with the palm of the hand. Chill several hours or overnight. Makes a nine-inch pie.

1   envelope (1 tablespoon) un-
    flavored gelatin
¼   cup sweet Sherry
1   package vanilla pudding
    and pie filling mix
1½ cups milk
¼   cup confectioners' sugar
1   cup heavy cream, whipped
1   (9-inch) baked pastry shell
1   cup coarsely crushed peanut
    brittle

P.S. If preferred, the mixture can be spooned into eight sherbet glasses, lined with ladyfinger halves or not, as desired. Then the peanut brittle can be sprinkled over the top and the dessert refrigerated as directed.

This is a beautiful pie—beautiful to look at and beautiful to eat.

JELLIED APPLE BLUSH PIE

Soften gelatin in the cold water five minutes. Combine apple juice, wine, sugar, cinnamon, nutmeg, and lemon peel in a saucepan; bring to a boil, stirring until sugar is dissolved; simmer five minutes. Remove from heat; add lemon juice, butter, and softened gelatin; stir until gelatin is dissolved. Add enough red food coloring to give mixture a nice rosy hue. Cool, then chill until syrupy, stirring occasionally. Arrange half of the apple slices in bottom of pie shell; cover with half of the partially thickened gelatin mixture. Repeat with remaining apple slices and gelatin mixture. Chill until firm. Before serving, garnish top of pie with whipped cream. Makes one nine-inch pie.

1   envelope (1 tablespoon) un-
    flavored gelatin
¼   cup cold water
⅔   cup bottled apple juice
⅓   cup red table wine
1   cup sugar
½   teaspoon cinnamon
¼   teaspoon nutmeg
1   teaspoon grated lemon peel
1   teaspoon lemon juice
1   tablespoon butter
    Red food coloring
1   (1 lb. 3 oz.) can sliced pie
    apples, drained
1   (9-inch) baked pastry shell
    Whipped cream

Now for some light, airy, and very "party-fied" chiffon pies. These first two are refreshingly fruit-flavored.

AMBROSIA PIE

Soften gelatin in the wine. Combine orange juice, lemon juice, orange peel, lemon peel, one-half cup of the sugar, salt, and egg yolks in top of double boiler; cook, stirring, over boiling water for five to ten minutes, or until mixture thickens. Add softened gelatin; stir until dissolved. Remove from heat. Beat egg whites until stiff; gradually beat in remaining one-half cup sugar; fold into hot orange mixture; fold in one-half cup coconut. Pour into pie shell; chill until firm. Just before serving, whip cream and spread over pie; sprinkle with remaining coconut. Garnish with orange sections. Makes a nine-inch pie.

1 envelope (1 tablespoon) un-flavored gelatin
¼ cup Muscatel or sweet Sherry
½ cup orange juice
1 tablespoon lemon juice
1 teaspoon each: grated orange and lemon peel
1 cup sugar
Dash of salt
4 eggs, separated
1 cup flaked coconut
1 (9-inch) baked pastry shell
½ cup heavy cream, whipped
Orange sections for garnishing

LIME CHIFFON PIE

Soften gelatin in the wine. Beat egg yolks in the top of a double boiler; add one-half cup sugar, salt, and lime juice; cook, stirring, over boiling water until mixture thickens. Stir in softened gelatin, lime peel, and a few drops of green food coloring, blending thoroughly. Chill until mixture begins to thicken. Beat egg whites stiff; gradually beat in the remaining one-half cup sugar; fold into yolk mixture. Pour into pie shell; chill until firm. Just before serving, top with whipped cream. Makes a nine-inch pie. Pretty and refreshing!

1 envelope (1 tablespoon) un-flavored gelatin
½ cup Muscatel or sweet Sherry
4 eggs, separated
1 cup sugar
½ teaspoon salt
½ cup fresh lime juice
½ teaspoon grated lime peel
Green food coloring
1 (9-inch) baked pastry shell
Whipped cream

SHERRY-ALMOND CHIFFON PIE

Soften gelatin in the cold water. Beat egg yolks slightly in the top of a double boiler; stir in sugar, salt, and nutmeg, then slowly add wine. Place over hot water and cook, stirring constantly, for three or four minutes, or just until mixture thickens. Remove from hot water. Add softened gelatin and stir until dissolved; add almond extract. Let mixture cool, then chill. When it begins to thicken, fold in stiffly beaten egg whites and almonds. Pour into pie shell; chill until firm. Just before serving, top pie with whipped cream. Makes one nine-inch pie.

1 envelope (1 tablespoon) un-flavored gelatin
¼ cup cold water
4 eggs, separated
½ cup sugar
Dash of salt
⅛ teaspoon nutmeg
½ cup sweet Sherry
⅛ teaspoon almond extract
¾ cup chopped, blanched almonds
1 (9-inch) baked pastry shell (or 1 chilled (9-inch) graham cracker shell)
1 cup heavy cream, whipped

Here's
To You!

All festive gatherings—anniversary celebrations, engagement announcements, showers, wedding receptions, and just plain parties—call for special refreshments. A delightful libation for such occasions is a wine punch.

Food historians tell varying stories about the origin of the word "punch." Some say it is a contraction of "puncheon," one of the distinctive casks in which wine is aged. Others believe that the word has an Oriental derivation, that it comes from the Hindustani "panch," meaning five and indicating the number of ingredients involved. Whatever its heritage, a punch bowl suggests gracious hospitality.

There are no iron-clad rules for making a punch, but here are a few tips to follow:

1. If Champagne, ginger ale, sparkling water, or one of the fruit-flavored sodas is to be added, wait until the last minute before pouring it into the bowl. The whole object of a sparkling punch is to have it sparkle, so the later the sparkling ingredient is added, the longer the bubbles will last.

2. Use a fairly large block of ice, if possible. Ice cubes melt much more rapidly and dilute the punch with subsequent loss of flavor.

3. Chill all ingredients for an hour or so before putting into the bowl. This helps to prevent rapid melting of ice.

4. Most punch cups are of four-ounce capacity. Since cups should be filled only two-thirds full, one quart of punch will yield about a dozen servings. A good "rule-of-thumb" for estimating the amount necessary is to allow two and one-half servings per guest. However, you know your friends' capacities better than I do!

5. Flowers of the season garlanded about the bowl will dramatize the service. Or borrow an idea from the tropics and float a few posies in the punch.

ORANGE BLOSSOM CHAMPAGNE PUNCH

4 (4/5 qt.) bottles or 1 gallon white table wine, well chilled
8 cups orange juice (fresh or frozen)
1⅓ cups lemon juice
2 cups Cointreau
4 cups sugar
Several strips lemon peel
4 large bottles Champagne, well chilled

Combine white table wine, orange juice, lemon juice, Cointreau, and sugar in a punch bowl; stir to dissolve sugar. Give each strip of lemon peel a twist; drop into punch bowl. Add ice. Just before serving, pour in Champagne. Makes about 100 servings. Suggested garnish: Floating orange blossoms—real or artificial.

There's no trick at all to preparing this up-to-date version of the old-fashioned Country Champagne Punch. The original recipe called for a quart of water ice and one large bottle of Champagne, and the punch was served with the main course of a rather fancy dinner, much as sherbet is sometimes served as a refreshing meat accompaniment.

COUNTRY CHAMPAGNE PUNCH

2 quarts sherbet or water ice (pineapple, orange, lemon, or raspberry)
4 large bottles Champagne, well chilled

Place sherbet in a punch bowl. Add Champagne. Mix well, stirring until no lumps of sherbet remain. Serve in Champagne glasses or punch cups. Makes about 40 servings.

P.S. Other combinations that are good are raspberry sherbet and Rosé, or pineapple, lemon, or orange sherbet and Sauterne. Use the same proportions as given for sherbet and Champagne.

SPARKLING RECEPTION PUNCH

Combine frozen lemonade concentrate and pineapple juice in punch bowl. Add white table wine. Mix well. Add ice. Just before serving, pour in Champagne or sparkling water. Makes about 45 servings. Suggested garnish: Orange slices, maraschino cherries, or strawberries.

1 (6 oz.) can frozen lemonade concentrate
6 cups (1 large can) pineapple juice, well chilled
2 (4/5 qt.) bottles white table wine, well chilled
1 large bottle Champagne or sparkling water

STRAWBERRY-ROSE PUNCH

In a bowl combine strawberries, sugar, and one bottle of the Rosé. Cover and let stand at room temperature one hour. Strain mixture into a punch bowl. Add frozen lemonade concentrate; stir until completely thawed. Add remaining bottles of Rosé. Add ice. Just before serving, pour in Champagne or sparkling water. Serve at once. Makes about 60 servings. Suggested garnish: Floating gardenias.

4 (12 oz.) packages frozen sliced strawberries, thawed
1 cup sugar
4 (4/5) qt. bottles Rosé, well chilled
4 (6 oz.) cans frozen lemonade concentrate
2 large bottles Champagne or sparkling water, well chilled

For preprandial sipping perfect beverages are dry Sherry, dry Vermouth, or a dry Champagne. In case you want to vary the vinous preludes to luncheon or dinner, here are some popular wine cocktails.

WHITE WINE COCKTAIL

It's one dash of bitters in a cocktail glass, then three ounces of chilled dry white table wine. Add a twist of lemon peel and serve. Makes one cocktail.

THE BAMBOO

Add to one jigger (one and one-half ounces) of dry or medium Sherry an equal amount of dry or sweet Vermouth and a dash of bitters. Stir (don't shake) with cracked ice. Strain into cocktail glasses. Makes two cocktails.

P.S. When using medium Sherry and sweet Vermouth, add a maraschino cherry and a few drops of the cherry juice to each serving. With dry Sherry and dry Vermouth, add a cocktail onion or stuffed olive.

SHERRY SHRUB

Blend, shake, or beat all ingredients until thoroughly mixed. Store for three or four days in refrigerator to blend flavors. Makes eight servings. A popular luncheon-party cocktail. It looks pretty in a parfait or whiskey-sour glass with a maraschino cherry for extra flavor and color.

1 (4/5 qt.) bottle dry, medium, or sweet Sherry
1 (6 oz.) can frozen lemonade concentrate
Juice of 2 lemons

CHAMPAGNE COCKTAIL

For each cocktail, place one-half teaspoon sugar in a wide-brimmed Champagne glass. Add a dash of bitters. (Some like a twist of either orange or lemon peel, too.) Add well-chilled Champagne to fill, and stir lightly.

There is almost an endless variety of hot wine drinks, the majority of which have been known for generations. Basically, though, all of them are simply wine heated to just under the boiling point, sweetened with sugar, and flavored with spices. Recently, these hot spiced or mulled wines have become very popular in the winter sports areas.

Let's begin with the easiest recipe. From here, you may want to go on to further adventures with other spices, other wines, and with fruit juices to replace part of the water.

HOT MULLED WINE

In old recipes, directions say to heat the wine with a hot poker. Picturesque though the method may be, it's easier to do it this way:

Dissolve one cup sugar in four cups water in large saucepan. Add peel of one-half lemon and a dozen whole cloves. Boil 15 minutes. Strain. Add two (4/5 qt.) bottles dry red table wine; heat gently. *Do not boil.* Serve hot in preheated mugs or cups. If you like, garnish each serving with cinnamon stick, to use for stirring. Makes about 20 servings.

THE ARCHBISHOP

Stud two oranges and one lemon all over at one-inch intervals with whole cloves. Bake in a moderately hot oven (375° F) for one hour. Heat to simmering two (4/5 qt.) bottles dry red table wine with six whole allspice and two (three-inch) sticks cinnamon. Remove from heat. Add oranges and lemon; let stand one hour. Strain wine; reheat to simmering; add sugar to taste. Place oranges and lemon in heat-proof bowl; pour hot wine over fruit. Serve at once in hot mugs or cups. Makes about 12 servings.

P.S. To make this a *Bishop*, replace the red table wine with Port.

———◆———

A traditional Christmas beverage is *The Wassail Bowle*. In the original recipe the mixture was "frothed" with beaten eggs. This is an adaptation, and very good.

THE WASSAIL BOWLE

6 small cooking apples
1 tablespoon brown sugar
4 cups apple cider
¼ teaspoon nutmeg
½ teaspoon cinnamon
4 cups medium or sweet Sherry
¼ cup granulated sugar
4 thin lemon slices

Core apples. Arrange in shallow pan. Sprinkle with brown sugar. Bake in a moderate oven (350° F) for 20 to 25 minutes, or until tender. Set aside. At serving time, heat the cider to simmering and add nutmeg, cinnamon, Sherry, sugar, and lemon slices. Stir until sugar is dissolved. Cover tightly and let stand over low heat about three minutes (don't boil). Remove lemon slices. Pour into heat-proof punch bowl and garnish with halved, baked apples. Or pour over halved or quartered baked apples in mugs or cups. Makes 12 to 16 servings.

Martha Washington enjoyed this classic. It's really rich enough to be served for dessert.

SYLLABUB

Combine one quart cream (light or heavy—let your conscience be your guide) with one cup orange juice and the grated peels of an orange and a lemon. Add three cups of white table wine and one cup of sugar. Beat until well mixed and chill thoroughly. Serve in a large glass bowl. For decoration, whip one-half cup heavy cream and spoon islands of whipped cream on top of the Syllabub. Sprinkle a little grated orange peel on each island. Makes about 16 servings.

P.S. For another delicious touch, top each serving with a spoonful of vanilla ice cream instead of the whipped cream.

On a hot day, there's really nothing more refreshing than a tall, tinkling glass of wine and soda. This is the basic recipe. Try different wines with different sodas, dry and fruit-flavored.

WINE-AND-SODA

Simply pour half a glass (or more) of your favorite wine over ice cubes in a tall glass. Add sparkling water to fill, stir lightly, and serve. If you use a dry white table wine (traditionally a Rhine wine) and dry soda you'll have a *Spritzer,* a favorite in northern Europe for many years. If you use cracked ice instead of cubes, omit the soda, and add one tablespoon of lemon juice and a twist of lemon peel, you'll have a *Cobbler.* Garnish as you will, but a sprig of mint or a slice of cucumber adds to the cool look.

CLARET LEMONADE

Put two or three ice cubes in a tall glass. Fill about two-thirds full with lemonade. Now pour Claret or any dry red table wine (very carefully so that the wine remains on top) over the back of a spoon onto the lemonade. (It isn't really necessary to pour the Claret this way. It's just an interesting trick, and guests seem to enjoy watching the colors combine when they stir the lemonade and wine.)

A variation on the wine-lemonade theme is

PICNIC LEMONADE

Empty two trays of ice cubes into a large, wide-mouthed thermos jug. Add one (4/5 qt.) bottle dry red or white table wine, one (6 oz.) can frozen lemonade concentrate, and two (6 oz.) cans of water. Substitute frozen fruit punch, limeade, or orange juice concentrate for the lemonade concentrate, if you wish. In any case you'll have a most delicious cold punch ready to enjoy at picnic refreshment time. Makes about 12 servings.

———◆———

Symbolic of spring, good all summer, is this traditional bowl. Woodruff is a sweet-scented herb of European derivation. Some enthusiastic herb growers in this country raise it, and you may find the dried variety in pharmacies and herb stores. If you use the dried form, halve the amount.

MAY WINE
(Mai Bowle)

Place a small bunch (five or six sprigs) of woodruff (or one small bunch of mint and six crushed whole cloves) in a punch bowl. Add two well-chilled (4/5 qt.) bottles Rhine wine. Cover and steep 1 hour. Remove flavorings; pour in one more well-chilled bottle of the same wine, or one well-chilled large bottle of Champagne. Add two tablespoons simple syrup or sugar to taste. Stir well. Add two cups halved sugared strawberries, if you like. Just before serving, add ice. Float spring flowers (violets, anemones, etc.), a few sugared whole strawberries. and mint sprigs on top. Makes 25 to 30 servings.

WINING WITH DINING

In this country there are basically two kinds of wine names:

Generic: Such as Sherry, Burgundy, Rhine wine, and Champagne. Some of these are actually "place" names, indicating where the wines originated. However, all of them are practically "type" names today. To illustrate, "Burgundy" is universally recognized to be a rich, red, full-bodied dry wine.

Varietal: Such as Cabernet, Chardonnay, Riesling, and Pinot Noir. They are named for the variety of grape from which the wine in the bottle has been made. To bear a varietal name, a wine must derive at least 51 per cent of its volume from the grape whose name is used, and must have the flavor and aroma of that grape. Some varietal-named wines are made 100 per cent from the grapes named, others use many other grapes in their blends.

Here's a chart showing the five classes of wines and the wine types that belong in each class. The fourteen most popular distinct types appear in capital letters; wines of similar type characteristics are grouped underneath. Wines with generic names are marked (g), those with varietal names are marked (v).

TYPE NAMES MOST FREQUENTLY APPLIED TO WINES IN THE UNITED STATES

APPETIZER WINES

(g) SHERRY *(dry to sweet)*   (g) VERMOUTH *(dry to sweet)*

RED TABLE WINES

(g) BURGUNDY *(dry)*   (g) CLARET *(dry)*   (g) ROSE *(pink; dry to sweet)*
  (v) Barbera   (v) Cabernet
  (v) Charbono   (v) Grignolino
  (v) Gamay   (v) Zinfandel
  (v) Pinot Noir
  (v) Red Pinot
                            (g) VINO ROSSO *(semi-sweet)*

      OTHERS (g) Red Chianti *(dry);*   (v) Concord *(sweet)*
               (v) Ives   *(dry);*   (v) Norton *(dry)*

WHITE TABLE WINES

(g) CHABLIS *(dry)*   (g) RHINE WINE *(dry)*   (g) SAUTERNE *(dry to sweet)*
  (v) Chardonnay   (v) Riesling   (v) Sauvignon Blanc
  (v) Folle Blanche (v) Sylvaner   *(dry to sweet)*
  (v) Pinot Blanc   (v) Traminer   (v) Semillon
  (v) White Pinot   *(dry to sweet)*
                               (g) Haut or Chateau
                                    Sauterne *(sweet)*

OTHERS (g) White Chianti (*dry*); (v) Light
Muscat (*dry to sweet*);
(v) Catawba (*dry to semi-sweet*);
(v) Delaware (*dry*); (v) Elvira (*dry*);
(v) Scuppernong (*sweet*)

DESSERT WINES

(g) PORT   (v) MUSCATEL   (g) TOKAY
(*Red, White, or Tawny*)   (*Gold, Red, or Black*)
(v) Muscat Frontignan

OTHERS (g) Angelica, Madeira, Marsala, Sweet or Cream Sherry

SPARKLING WINES

(g) CHAMPAGNE (Gold or Pink)   (g) SPARKLING BURGUNDY
(The very dry Champagnes are   (*semi-sweet to sweet*)
sometimes labeled as "brut" or
extra-dry; the semi-dry as "sec"
or dry; the sweet as "doux.")

OTHERS (v) Sparkling Muscat (*sweet*)
(g) Sparkling Rosé (*dry to semi-sweet*)

P.S. *Specialty wines,* called "Special Natural Wines," have rather recently been developed. They are usually 20 per cent alcohol by volume and have natural (not synthetic) flavors added, such as herbs, spices, fruit juices. They bear unique brand names and are used for appetizer and refreshment purposes.

Vino Rosso wines, rightly listed under the red table wines, have, like Rosé, climbed rapidly in popularity in recent years. They are mellow red wines often labeled with Italian-type names and are good "family-dinner" wines. They are usually slightly sweet to semi-sweet, ruby red in color, and blander in flavor than the traditional dry red table wines.

After noting and trying the generally accepted wine-and-food combinations listed below, experiment and decide what *you* really like.

Appetizers	Dry or cocktail Sherry Dry Vermouth Dry Champagne

Soups
  First course
  Main dish
	
	Dry Sherry
	Dry red or white table wines

Seafoods, light meats (such as veal and pork)	Dry white table wines
Chicken, turkey, ham	Dry red or white table wines Dry Champagne Sparkling Burgundy
Red meats, wild game, duck, highly seasoned foods	Dry red table wines
Fruits, crisp cookies, nuts, fruit cake, pound cake	Dessert wines Sweet white table wines Sweet Champagne
Cheese for dessert	Port Dry red table wines

TIPS ON WINE STORAGE AND CARE

1. Store all wines in a cool, dry place, out of sunlight. A temperature between 50° and 60° is ideal.

2. Lay corked wines on their sides, so corks keep moist and air tight.

3. In case you are interested in building a wine cellar, there is a free booklet, titled, "Little Wine Cellar All Your Own," available from the Wine Advisory Board, 717 Market Street, San Francisco 3, California.

4. Recork opened table wines and keep in the refrigerator. These wines are very perishable and once opened, deteriorate rapidly. Some twosome families may find half-bottles a good idea.

A FEW WORDS ABOUT SERVING TEMPERATURES

1. If you like your appetizer and dessert wines chilled, refrigerate them for an hour or so before use.

2. White table wines and Rosés should be refrigerated for two or

three hours before serving. Remember, if they're *too* cold, you can't enjoy their flavor to the fullest.

3. Sparkling wines should be refrigerated for four to six hours before popping the corks. Or, they may be chilled more quickly in a wine or Champagne cooler, well filled with ice.

4. For best flavor, open red table wines an hour or so before pouring to allow them to "breathe." About the "correct" serving temperature for red table wines: It's pretty generally agreed that they are at their best at room temperature (60° to 70°). If your wine storage spot is below this (as it should be), bring the bottle to the desired warmth by letting it stand for a few hours in the room where it will be served. (If you live in a hot climate and don't have air-conditioning, you may have to put your wine in the refrigerator briefly.) If you definitely prefer red wines cool, go ahead and chill them. That's your prerogative!

SOME SUGGESTIONS ABOUT WINE SERVICE

1. If you don't have a really good corkscrew, buy one. It will add a lot to your pleasure in serving wine. Shop for one with these qualities: rounded worm edges, an open space down the center of the worm, and a point precisely lined up with the spirals of the worm. Confused? Here's an illustration of a leverage-type corkscrew with these specifications:

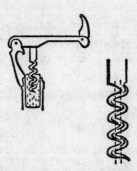

2. If you want to observe all the niceties of serving table wines, cut the foil or cellulose band about one-fourth inch below the lip of the bottle so the wine may be poured without touching the foil. Wipe

the mouth of the bottle carefully before putting in the corkscrew and again after you've pulled the cork.

3. The tradition of pouring a little wine into the host's glass first has its practical aspects. It gives him an opportunity to make certain that the wine is sound before serving it to his guests, and should there be any particles of cork in the neck of the bottle, they will fall into his glass.

4. To avoid dripping wine on the tablecloth, give the bottle a slight twist before raising its mouth from the pouring position. (If you have one of those dripless metal wine pourers, the problem is solved.)

5. So that the aroma and bouquet of the wine may be better appreciated, fill the glasses no more than half or two-thirds full.

6. Stemmed, uncolored glasses of simple design, slightly cupped in at the rim, are considered preferable to fancy colors and shapes. Wine is pretty enough in itself! Especially in the case of table wines, the glass should be large enough to hold an adequate portion when only about half full. Cost need not be a criterion for judging a wine glass. Some of the best designed ones are quite inexpensive. Furthermore your wine-glass wardrobe need not be extensive. You can buy a very good-looking six- to nine-ounce stemmed glass that will do nicely for appetizer and dessert wines as well as for the table wines. When using it for appetizer and dessert purposes, just don't pour as generously.

P.S. For the benefit of calorie counters, a table, *Average Values of Calories Per Fluid Ounce For Various California Wine Types*, recently prepared by Dr. A. D. Webb, Associate Professor of Enology, Department of Viticulture and Enology, University of California at Davis, gives these calories-per-ounce figures:

Dry red table wines .... 24 or 25 calories per oz.
                                     (according to type)
Dry white table wines .... 22 or 23 calories per oz.
                                     (according to type)
Dry Sherry .... 38 calories per oz.
Red Port .... 47 calories per oz.
Champagne (bottle-fermented) .... 25 calories per oz

How Many Servings in a Bottle?

The average serving of table wine or Champagne is about four fluid ounces; of appetizer or dessert wine, two to two and one-half ounces.

Size	Ounces	Table Wine— Champagne	Appetizer— Dessert Wine
FIFTH (4/5 qt.)	25.6	6+ servings	8-12 servings
TENTH (4/5 pt.)	12.8	3+ servings	4- 6 servings
SPLIT	6.4	about 2 servings	
QUART	32.	8 servings	10-14 servings
PINT	16.	4 servings	5- 7 servings
½ GALLON	64.	16 servings	20-30 servings
GALLON	128.	32 servings	40-60 servings

Index